Virginal Mothers, Groovy Chicks & Blokey Blokes:

Re-thinking Home Economics (and) Teaching Bodies

Dr Donna Pendergast

National Library of Australia
Cataloguing-in-Publication data:

Pendergast, Donna Lee.

Virginal mothers, groovy chicks & blokey blokes :
re-thinking home economics (and) teaching bodies.

Includes index.

ISBN 1 875378 39 1.

1. Domestic education. 2. Home economics - Study and teaching. I. Title.

640.71

Cover and text design by Ingrid Van Grysen of Australian Academic Press,
Brisbane.

Typeset in Melior by Australian Academic Press, Brisbane.

www.australianacademicpress.com.au

FOREWORD

The power of folklore is always so much greater than the power of rationality. It is for this reason that stereotypes matter, because they provide us with a way of locating ourselves in the social order in which we live our lives and do our daily work. Thus, regardless of how much we may resist stereotyping within our profession of teaching, we can all too easily find ourselves being flattered — or alternatively, discouraged — by remarks that place us in relation to a particular stereotype. Sandra Weber and Claudia Mitchell certainly seem to imply this in their title 'That's Funny, You Don't Look Like a Teacher' (1995). For better and worse, stereotypes are powerful ways of framing us all.

The two decades I spent working in high school certainly allowed me to see that teachers are no more immune from the effects of teacher stereotyping than any other section of the community. The idea that drama teachers are both excitable and alternative, or that physical education teachers are muscled and male, is as much a feature of staffroom talk as it is of student talk or media soapies. What I also learned in staffrooms is that teaching is very much an oral and anecdotal culture. Just as stereotypes matter to teachers, so too do the stories teachers tell about themselves and others. And so the re-telling of stories, the reporting of classroom incidents, the reworking of staffroom gossip, the reliving of victories and defeats — all these things do a particular kind of work on and for teachers. In this sense, they may be understood to be an important element in the social production of teachers' identities.

This is one of the reasons why this volume "Virginal mothers, groovy chicks and blokey blokes: Re-thinking home economics (and) teaching bodies" is an important one — not just for Home Economics teachers, but for all teachers. In it, Donna Pendergast explores productive possibilities of teaching 'in the margins' — that is, teaching in low status disciplines in which negative or bland stereotypes abound. The questions being posed here are tantalizing and troubling ones: Can self-identifying as a marginal teacher be a way out for an individual who finds themselves teaching in a marginal (negatively stereotyped) discipline? Is it a case of two negatives making a positive? As if so, what effects might this have on others within and outside the discipline?

The important work done in this book by way of response is to play with the geometry of margins and centres, to refuse a fixed location for any discipline area (including Home Economics), or for the teachers within any discipline, and this is a very important contribution indeed to the idea of teacher professionalism in an age of uncertainty.

Insisting on the shiftiness of power (that is, the power to name ourselves and others), the author focuses on a number of marginal individuals who seem pleasured in many respects by their very marginality. The 'non-typical' teachers whose practices she documents seem to have 'fun'. However, it is not the sort of fun that destabilizes Home Economics teaching in any profound way, even if it is fun that these teachers appear to have, in some respects at least, at the expense of their more 'mainstream' colleagues. Indeed, it seems that they needed the 'skilled and suffering' orthodoxy of Home Economics stereotyping to be firmly fixed in place in order to parody this orthodoxy and to be seen by their students to be 'a-typically' trendy. Their pleasure was made available because of, rather than despite, their marginality. This is in keeping with Judith Allen's (1992) reminder about the contradictions of what she calls the 'sleepout syndrome'. Being 'on the verandah' can mean being both excluded or cool. It is a place which can provide much needed relief from the heat of the kitchen, allowing the individuals who are located there to remain cool and fresh — if less secure and more exposed — than their counterparts inside the house. Perhaps unfortunately, the kitchen metaphor seems appropriate in the case of Home Economics teachers, whose folkloric attachment to the stove has disallowed so much by way of status within and outside schools. The important point is, however, that, while a self-identified 'non-typical' minority engage in moments of transgression, such moments do not work to subvert traditional schooling practice — they work to reinforce it.

There is more that is offering in this book, however, than an exploration of teacher identity. What it also provides is a very useful way out of the methodological cul-de-sacs in which traditional educational research so often finds itself. As a reader of educational research, I am frequently disappointed by research that, while claiming to be original, rarely surprises. Yet I understand that it is not an easy thing to design research that might really provide some surprises for the old hand as well as direction for the new. Donna Pendergast has managed to do just that. The author's determination to put under erasure more traditional methods of research seems a fitting way to interrogate apparent a-typicality in the teaching profession. In doing so, she shows us how traditional research methods can obliterate knowledge by collapsing difference into the familiar. She refuses the neat explanation and goes in search of the ironies, the doubleness and duplicity of teaching as professional work. Thus she allows us to glimpse beyond more orthodox 'findings' about teaching practices and identities to see a world of potential risks and pleasures, neither of which can be easily separated out from the other.

There is risk in anticipating pedagogical pleasure, there is pleasure in taking pedagogical risks. Pedagogical work has never been safe, but this book allows us to know more about the nature of the risks and the pleasures we take when we do the real work of teaching.

References

Allen, J. (1992). Feminist Critiques of Western Knowledges: Spatial Anxieties in a Provisional Phase? In K.K. Ruthven (ed.) *Beyond the Disciplines: The New Humanities*. (pp. 57–77), Canberra: Australian Academy of the Humanities.

Weber, S., & C. Mitchell, (1995). *That's funny, you don't look like a teacher.*London: The Falmer Press.

Erica McWilliam

Professor of Education
Queensland University of Technology

DEDICATION

My partner — Jeff

My parents – Edna & Ken

My family — Dianne, Greg, Bader, Ashley, Wendy, Bess,
Blyton, Zeke

My mentor — Erica

The exceptional home economics teachers
who are the body of this book

Contents

PREFACE

In Grade 4, I started keeping a recipe book, dictated by my mother, as she taught me to make what our family ate — scones, mock duck, tuna mornay, macaroni cheese, ginger fluff sponge. On the blue front cover of its stapled brown pages is my name and a lengthy address, written with flourishes in my developing handwriting:

Marie Brennan
6 Bell Street
Glen Iris
Melbourne
Victoria
Australia
The World
The Universe

This book helps me to re-read myself, beyond nostalgia for that little girl practising her skills of cooking, writing, mother's little helper. I can understand better with the resources offered through this book the individual way I was being positioned as a normal little girl, in a gendered body, taking up the particular point in time for Australia on the 'world stage' in the teaching of home economics and the aspirations for futures built into my suburban experience.

Donna Pendergast invites many kinds of readers with a broad range of interests to unpack the stereotypes of 'women's work', of teachers' work, and home economics' teachers' work in particular. Whether you read this as a prospective or experienced teacher, as a person with interest in Australia's global educational positioning, a feminist, a researcher or a curriculum theorist, there is plenty of food for thought here. She engages the reader with systematic opening up of the history of home economics and the way it has emerged as a subject in schools in Queensland, Australia. She puts this into a context, showing how the changing Australian approaches are related to the treatment of home economics elsewhere in the world. In doing this work with the literature, she provides us with an original way of understanding home economics curriculum and its teachers. This book fills a major gap in Australian curriculum theory.

Yet the book does not stop there. It goes on to 'reclaim' different, more challenging and provocative spaces and places for home economics. Using exciting concepts of carnival and the body, she invites us to move into unfamiliar territory. Those in the field of home economics will find both the familiar made strange and the strange becoming familiar as Pendergast encourages us to play with new opportunities to 'be' in home economics. The resources she provides for us to do so are clever devices for school, curriculum and teacher innovation. I expect you will enjoy reading the book as much as I did.

Marie Brennan

Professor of Education
University of Canberra

Introduction

Introduction

There is a teacher shortage crisis. The phenomenon is worldwide and it is expected to intensify. Some of the major factors leading to this situation include an insufficient supply of graduates; aging of the teaching workforce; increases in school student enrolments; and the loss of 'pools' of reserves of teachers seeking re-entry, some due to changing professions. Considerable research has revealed that along with this teacher shortage crisis there is a need to address the low status and desirability of the teaching profession, which appears to be a fundamental cause of the teacher shortage crisis.

One way the low status of teaching is evident is by considering teacher stereotypes, which typically produce teachers in an unappealing light, representing them as 'ordinary' and 'more negative' compared to those in other professions. For example, typical maths teachers have been described as "old, bald with glasses and wrinkles from thinking so hard, and very drab, with no friends"; and home economics teachers as having "bags under her eyes, dishpan hands and varicose veins". Such perceptions do little to enhance the job appeal and improve the status of the teaching profession.

But are these negative stereotypes typical? Do they represent teachers? That is, do teachers in their classrooms live out these negative images or is teaching misrepresented in the commonly accepted stereotypes of the field? This book challenges negative assumptions about teacher stereotypes, revealing teachers who actively resist dominant stereotypes. It achieves this by profiling home economics teachers who take 'pleasure' and have 'fun' in their teaching work, exploding the negative imagery of an ordinary teacher.

It is somewhat ironic that home economics teachers and their professional field is the means of challenging negative stereotypes of teachers in general, given that they are on the margins of the marginalised teaching profession. On this level, this book aims to encourage home economics teachers, students, academics, and practitioners, along with those interested in education, women's studies, sociology and postmodernism, to re-think the field of study known as home economics. The invitation to think and more precisely to re-think about home economics is premised on a simple principle. Systems and structures within modernist society have traditionally created groups who are favored or advantaged and those who are not. For example, the rich are advantaged over the poor, able-bodied over the disabled, white over black, male over female, public over private, paid over unpaid, and so on. The result of these dualities is that whilst one end of the dualism is privileged, the other is marginalised in and by society. Home economics is a classic example of a marginalised field of study when taken in a modernist framework. It is marginalised by society, and by and large, members of the profession have been compliant in this positioning in order to merely survive. The result of compliance, as this book uncovers, is that whilst typical home economics teachers ideally consider themselves to be 'skilled', in reality they also 'suffer' in the conduct of their work. This has a negative effect on the status of home economics teachers within the teaching fraternity, and more broadly beyond teaching into allied professions.

This book considers these 'typical', 'skilled' yet 'suffering' home economics teachers, and then, importantly, makes a shift to engage with home economics teachers who refuse the suffering stereotype. These home economics teachers engaged in a refusal to be 'normal' and 'typical' are having fun and taking pleasure from their teaching, thereby revealing a space for the counter-orthodox to be named and acted. Postmodernist thinking is the vehicle for this re-thinking of traditional ways of knowing which have unhelpfully dominated home economics as a field of study, curriculum area, research focus and professional endeavor. These home economics teachers may not be 'radical', but nor are they 'normal', 'traditional', nor 'moderate'. Indeed, as this book reveals, their failure to 'suffer' — like other teachers — is read by students as a pedagogical plus. The lesson learned from these home economics teachers is a valuable one that can be applied more generally to the teaching profession. From this thinking, insights can be gained from within the teaching profession itself to begin to address the status problems that beset it.

My views are the result of considerable research, analysis of the literature, coupled with a career as a home economics teacher and academic — some would say this is an oxymoron — much of which will be documented and explained within this work. I have used the Australian context and examples to support my work, but have drawn widely on international theorists, and this work is relevant to all home economics, students, teachers, educators, and professionals, no matter where their part of the world may be. Opportunities for further thinking are presented at the end of each chapter, and form the basis for guided scholarly activity.

Setting the Scene

The Ongoing Battle

It seems inconceivable to think that in the twenty-first
century, the curriculum subject known variously
as home economics, family and consumer studies, family and
consumer science, family management, human ecology and
many other amelioration's (henceforth referred to as home economics in this book) remains firmly in battle. This is not a recent
battle. This battle is with systems, such as school education
systems and university systems. These systemic battles are often
for the very existence of the field, with typically naive, ignorant
and predominantly economic rationalist arguments promoting
the demise of the field. Indeed, many systems have enforced their
preferred position, leading to the loss of departments, courses,
experts and ultimately the subject area itself. It is possible
to ensure the extinction of almost any subject area these days —
just remove funding and remove power. This strategy has been
successfully utilized around the world, and recently in particular,
in Australia.

There are also battles from within the field. It is the ultimate
irony that some members of their profession struggle to name
themselves as home economists. Some home economists
are embarrassed to identify with their field. Indeed, the many and
frequent name changes of the field is direct evidence of this very
'cringe', and of the apparently ceaseless need to seek societal
legitimation and credibility. These members of the profession are
apparently unwilling to acknowledge their place in their field, yet
typically fail to understand that the reason for their embarrass-
ment is their own unchallenged assumptions about power, which
are, ironically outdated in postmodern society.

These battles in and for the profession are not new. Indeed,
the history of home economics around the world documents
a series of ongoing battles. These battles inevitably return to the
origins of the field as problematic for home economics. As Apelt
(1989) explains:

> [F]or Home Economics there has always been one very profound influence,
> that being that our origins are primarily associated with what our society

has deemed to be women's work. It is vital we are aware of the legacies and social implications this has for the way the world views Home Economics (Apelt, 1989. p. 5).

It is the proposition of this book that home economists have been compliant in the very politics that ensures marginalization of their field of study. The pretence of some professionals not to be home economists is a typical example of compliant behavior — that is, behavior compliant with patriarchal assumptions about what is powerful in society. Further, that home economists acting creatively to scientize their field, or to legitimize it through such tactics as name changes which reflects the contemporary trends of society, actually acts as a negative force in the long term.

It is true that home economics is a curriculum core and/or elective in many secondary schools — and their equivalent — throughout the world. It is also true that it most often exists as a marginalized field of study classified as 'women's knowledge' and is devalued in the school curriculum. Home economics teachers frequently experience feelings of disempowerment and isolation, and are constantly asked to justify the existence of their field. Home economics teachers are often called on to provide morning teas and other inappropriate services in schools, reinforcing a lack of understanding about the subject and the role of home economics teachers by their colleagues. In this way, home economics is often seen for its product, rather than its intellectual processes. Nevertheless, whilst there has been considerable reform in the philosophies driving curricula around the world, and concomitant changes to the curriculum offered in schools, home economics has largely survived, though it has typically undergone chameleon-like transformations. Interestingly, through all of these changes, home economics has received limited attention by researchers, both from within and outside of the field. Of the scant research that does exist, it is the norm that modernist research techniques and philosophies are utilized; thereby producing normalized versions and 'truths' about the field. It is these very 'truths' that have led to the 'inevitable' marginalization and disempowerment of the field of study within modernist systems and structures.

The ideas presented in this book are new. They do not rely on tired research paradigms, nor assumptions about 'truths'. The need for this approach is championed by leading theorists in the field, who have called for non-essentialist approaches to research in order to re-think the thinking that has produced cul-de-sac positioning of home economics as a body of knowledge and a site of teacher practice. This book aims to highlight the need for a shift in the way of 'thinking' and researching about the field, and then proposes an alternative way of re-thinking that refuses modernist research traditions. The postmodernist framework takes up the challenge of working to locate a space outside the frame of modernist theory and methods, arguing that this epistemological shift is necessary to unsettle the idea that home economics is inevitably marginalised. The intention then is to reconfigure how we have come to think about home economics teachers and the profession of home economics as a site of cultural practice, in order to think it otherwise.

Shifting From Modern to Postmodern Thinking

Some of my earlier work (Pendergast, 1991) used a feminist post-structural approach to explore home economists within their field of study. At that time the field had been neglected as an arena of academic research. It still is. This may be explained in part by the marginal nature and purpose of home economics, or perhaps by a lack of real understanding of the field, or, as I have already suggested, by the traditional ways of thinking which have dominated inquiry into the field — or all three. This research revealed a pattern of constant remaking of the theory and practices of home economics that appeared to be an attempt to gain legitimation within a patriarchal hierarchy of knowledge. This legitimation imperative today remains at the forefront of the home economics profession. A recent example of this occurs in the 1997 Mission Statement of the Home Economics Institute of Australia (HEIA), namely the stated desire to "enhance the professionalism and legitimation of Australian Home Economists" (HEIA Council Minutes, April 1997).

There is no doubt that home economics is located in a gendered regime of power/knowledge that can and does have repressive effects. Because of this fact, it is the site of a constant legitimation struggle — hence the constant remaking of the field. The ideas presented in this book work out of the premise that mainstream speaking positions of home economists fail to challenge the taken-for-granted assumptions which produce dualisms of the sort that bedevil home economics. Home economics as a lived culture has failed to recognize the possibilities for reconstructing its own field of study beyond the confines of such dualisms. The result has been increasing marginalization because home economists have sought to gain legitimation within and through the very logic that ensures its marginal status. Even the very recent critical research that draws attention to this fact has been limited by the sort of theoretical approach taken (see for example, Brown, 1993; Henry, 1991, 1995). It tends to focus on problems (as ideology) — rather than possibilities.

This book presents an interrogation of home economics culture by reconceptualizing the field as being open to contestation and change, refusing an essential reading of cultural dualisms such as male/female, work/non-work, public/private — such as that implied in the very term home economics — home being the private space of the female housewife. It challenges such essential readings by interrogating the power relations in home economics that give shape to the culture as productive — both in repressive and positive ways. It works out of a theoretical perspective that rejects the idea that such power relations are necessarily oppressive, and this represents a departure from traditional critical research in the area. What is of interest then is how pedagogical power circulates as both positive and repressive for home economics as a site of pedagogy. It recognizes and names the difference that a non-essentialist reading of home economics might make possible.

In this book I present an exploration of home economics as a more than marginalised pedagogical culture in schools. I do so by focusing not on its orthodoxies or mainstream practice, but on some of the aberrations and discontinuities that indicate how the culture can and could be constituted otherwise. Thus it focuses on the spaces in which 'un-natural' meanings are produced in which counter-identities are formed, in which perverse practices are undertaken.

In keeping with poststructural approaches to educational research, I develop and apply a method that allows the examination of the field of home economics as a fluid category of pedagogical knowledge. The poststructuralist proposition at work here is that no culture is 'condemned' to marginality, but remains partial, open and contested. This work seeks to understand how the culture of home economics is being contested from within, in order to bring this to bear on totalizing perceptions of its marginality that are so widespread across educational and other contexts. In this way, the thinking will unsettle an understanding of home economics as inevitably marginalised within patriarchal relations in education and culture.

The book proceeds by presenting research about the construction of orthodox home economics teachers. This work uses modernist techniques, where home economics teachers were interrogated as docile bodies, self-governing according to versions of 'proper' professional practice in the culture of home economics teaching. Following this there is an exploration of how the culture of home economics is being contested from within by atypical home economics teachers. These teachers refuse to conform to 'proper', stereotypical versions of home economics professional practice. This postmodernist work uses a posthumanist approach that rejects the conception of the individual as a unitary and fixed entity, but instead as a subject in process, shaped by unconscious desires and language. This posthumanist project focuses attention on pedagogical body subjects as the 'unsaid' of home economics research. It refuses the simple margin/center geometry so characteristic of current perceptions of home economics itself. In this way, the inquiry interrogates the productive possibilities of teaching 'in the margins'. Finally, I present the implications of this work.

Significance of this Thinking

The thinking I present in this book is significant for many reasons. Principally, it responds to a call for quality, non-essentialist research and concomitant theory for the field of home economics (Brown, 1993; Grundy & Henry, 1995; Peterat & Khamasi, 1995). This call arises out of frustration with the present theoretical cul-de-sac.

My review of the literature in the field identifies two main directions for theorizing and research in the past. The first is that research and philosophizing in the area of theory, mission, focus, and purpose, has relied upon 'the masters tools' (Lorde, 1984) as theoretical and methodological frameworks. This has led to a 'replough(ing of) familiar academic fields' (Den Hartog & Alomes, 1991, p. 15) in home economics research. It is not that critical and feminist critiques have not performed an important function — it is rather that the research paradigms themselves in this area have become moribund. For an analysis of critical and feminist critiques and their contribution, refer to McWilliam (1997).

The second trend in research in the field has been a tendency to undertake narrow projects in specialized aspects of the field, typically working out of one sub-disciplinary base or subject matter. For example, recent Australian doctoral students tend to select a sub-discipline of the field as the focus of their work. This trend enables the researcher to focus on problems or issues of a manageable size, and these specializms or subdisciplines are typically characterized by orthodox research treatments

(Horn, 1993; Pendergast, 1996a). For example, the compartmentalized sciences of nutrition, textiles and food have a research base that typically reflect a positivist epistemology, given their use of quantitative methodologies and empirical science. On the other hand, the disciplines that deal with inter/intra-personal and family relationships, sociocultural and aesthetic environments, and psychosocial development historically have a research base that draws on phenomenology as an interpretive science (Bobbitt, 1993). The problem with this compartmentalization is that the sub-disciplines of home economics often neglect rhizomatic networks, overlaps, the surprises, leaps and discontinuities that could be — and ought to be made — among the various specializations of the field (Horn, 1993). A danger in the predictability of this research pattern is articulated by Becher (1990, p. 333) who warns:

> [W]hat are variously described as segments, sub-disciplines, specialisms, schools, sects and the like, form their own counter-cultures which may press against the overall culture of the discipline of which they form part, and thus may seem to threaten its unity.

This book goes further than Becher by insisting on the disunity as an important characteristic of the field, refusing the 'tidying imperative' that orthodox science of this sort can bring. In this study, the field is read as a 'play of surfaces' in acknowledgment of the diversity of the terrain of pedagogical practice that is named 'home economics'.

Postmodernist Theoretical Approach

The theoretical terrain I draw on is poststructuralist conceptualization of the body. The corporeal conceptualizations of interest here are located in feminist poststructural work informed by postmodern imperatives. The benefits of this approach are outlined by Maxine Greene (1994, p. 444), who notes the value of being "...skeptical of the structures and the systematic modes of thinking linked to structuralism ... point(ing) out what educators are loath to see" (Greene, 1994, p. 444). In the case of home economics, it means re-thinking the thinking that has positioned home economics as a field of marginal practice, and thereby been complicit in its marginal status.

My work takes as its starting point the idea that home economics teachers as professional knowledge workers have been limited in their ability to reconstruct the field of study beyond the confines of modernist dualisms. It works towards a practice of home economics in which essentialisms (including those of gender) can be re-thought. This involves applying a feminist poststructuralist analysis — specifically posthumanist body theory, in particular Mary Russo's (1994) analysis of the grotesque body (Mary Russo's (1994) analysis of the grotesque body is strongly influenced by the work of the theorist, Mikhail Bakhtin (1968), who theorises about carnival and the carnivalesque, and is considered to be extremely prominent and influential in this field) — to the work of a number of teachers who self-identify as practising on the 'margins' of home economics culture, to understand how such teachers accommodate and resist orthodoxies in the cultural practice of the teaching of home economics. In taking this approach, this work thus utilizes an embodied analysis of home economics and home economists.

Most studies ignore the material bodies of teacher and student unless in the frame of 'behaviors' (McWilliam, 1997b). In this study the material bodies of home economics teachers are read as inscribed by social and cultural meanings about the nature of the discipline itself. As a Bakhtinian interpretive lens is utilized, the theory of discourse and the carnivalesque offers a less-than-familiar reading of home economics teachers, and this is further refined to focus on Russo's (1994) theory of the grotesque body of the carnival. This approach enables analysis which offers other ways to think through problems of reproduction, resistance, and transformation (Grace, 1996). Home economics teaching as carnival and the ways these teachers have taken their pleasures and had their fun offers a disruption to the neatness of the modernist tidying imperative.

The following outline serves as an introduction to the themes that will be explored in the following chapters of this book.

Chapter Two: Negative History of Beliefs

Home economics like no other field has been influenced by its past, and if allowed, this history will continue to determine the future in decidedly negative ways. In this chapter, I recount the history of home economics in a particular context. The history of home economics in other parts of the world has been documented elsewhere. The history of home economics can be told in many different ways – each town, province, country in the world has a unique history of home economics. The importance of telling a history is to identify the factors that have constrained and determined that history.

Chapter Three: Home Economics – Marginal Subject/s

Chapter three has eight themes that serve as organizers for reporting the literature in the field of home economics. These themes are shown to have informed the development of home economics secondary education in the defined context. The themes also serve to indicate that the research in the field is embryonic and theoretically limited. Analysis of this research also shows that, despite the focus on the material body in the curriculum itself, home economics research has ignored the bodies of teachers and students, privileging the mind in line with most other educational research. This produces a pattern of accounts that is impoverished in terms of its ability to interrogate home economics as embodied and shifting as a cultural performance. An argument is made for a shift toward postmodernist epistemologies that includes a brief account of recent work in home economics and postmodernist research to date. The links between feminism and home economics are also documented.

Chapter Four: Body Subjects – From Modern to Postmodern Concepts of the Body

This chapter traces the need for a shift from modernist to postmodernist theorizing, focusing in particular on changing conceptions of the 'invisible' or 'unre-marked' body from the mind/body duality of the humanist subject to the posthumanist body subject as a culturally inscribed surface. It highlights the contrast between modernist and postmodernist traditions of research. The chapter argues a shift to postmodernist research in home economics in order to make a different sense of this site as a pedagogical field of performing bodies.

A rationale for the postmodern methods that have been selected for undertaking the work in this book is also outlined. An argument about the elements of posthumanist research that are useful for this home economics research is documented, noting that the particular discourse analysis attempted here is a conceptual tool for analysis that has been forged out of new body theory. It directs the analysis to cultural inscriptions on the individual and collective body of home economics knowledge workers and in the texts generated out of those material/textual bodies.

Chapter Five: Disciplining the Body of Home Economics Teachers

This chapter constructs home economics teachers as particular sorts of docile bodies, self-governing and disciplined according to versions of 'proper' professional practice that are made available in the culture of home economics teaching. This analysis is drawn from an orthodox, modernist analysis of two surveys of home economics teachers. This neat modernist analysis is followed by a re-thinking of what the data suggests about the body of home economics teachers, by casting a broad glance over the data. The dualistic production of the 'real' and 'ideal' home economics bodies is developed, and this is further worked into understanding the modernist duality as 'skilled' and 'suffering'.

Chapter Six: Four Odd Bodies – Home Economics as Carnival

This chapter looks at resistance to the 'normal' home economics body coming from within the Teaching body itself, in the form of four self-identifying 'atypical' teachers. The analysis aims to determine how their potentially transgressive bodies trouble the conventions of the profession, by refusing invitations to produce the skilled and suffering bodies of many of their counterparts.

Chapter Seven: Carnivalesque in the Home Economics Classroom

This chapter is a counter-orthodox reading of the home economics body. The interpretive tool in use is the grotesque body of the carnivalesque, drawing upon Bakhtin's (1968) theory of carnival and Russo's (1994) theory of the grotesque body of the carnival, both of which are elaborated in this chapter. This postmodernist work foregrounds the grotesque bodies which have been ignored and suppressed to date in home economics research through its rejection of the irrational and excessive in favor of rational experiences and explanations. The home economics body is re-described as a matter of desire and pleasure rather than as skilled and suffering. A strong theme that emerges is the complicity of home economics as the site and sight of heterosexual normativity. Using Foucault's (1985) construction of the ethical individual, analysis here reveals a home economics body that is 'immoderate', constantly struggling to remain 'continent', particularly with respect to the maintenance of heterosexual normativity.

Chapter Eight: A Shift from the Familiar to the unfamiliar – Re-thinking Home Economics

This final chapter of the book reflects on the transformative possibilities of undertaking postmodernist work for home economics. It considers the importance of this re-thinking to home economics teaching and status related issues and raises questions about the role of professional bodies representing home economics.

Further Thinking

This chapter explains the shift in thinking this book will demonstrate, that is, from modern to postmodern. Research the terms 'modern' and 'postmodern' with respect to research and theorizing and develop your understanding of these terms.

What is meant by the phrase, 'home economics is a more than marginalized culture'.

Negative History of Beliefs

Home economics is a classic example of a subject which has been bedeviled by perception of its relatively low status... It was a subject designed explicitly for girls, and taught almost exclusively by women. Its focus was on the private rather than the public sphere of activity, and unpaid rather than paid work. Its orientation was more towards the practical than the academic (Department of Employment, Education and Training, August 1990).

This statement from the Department of Employment, Education and Training, makes explicit a negative history of beliefs about home economics as a field of study. It acknowledges that home economics as a site of knowledge production is burdened by certain taken-for-granted assumptions about what constitutes valued and valuable knowledge in our society.

Home economics educators function within the context of these beliefs and assumptions, visualizing themselves as perpetually fighting against being 'othered' by an education system and broader society that relegates to the lesser preferred position of patriarchal formulations. It is a girl's subject (not boy's), taught by women (not men), focusing on the private domain (not public), and practical in orientation (not academic). When viewed from within this dualist framework, home economics will always be condemned to the margins, 'othered', 'disempowered' and 'marginalised', a positioning which inevitably leads to the disenfranchisement of home economists, their students and the field.

It could be argued, then, that home economics has simply been exposed for its shortcomings and that the field and all participants in it should accept there is nowhere to go but to the margins. Perhaps home economists should indeed accept the objectness of their aprons, settle for their sewing machines and concede to the dominant views and ways of understanding which places little value on their field of study. It is the intention of this book to posit an alternative. The alternative is to highlight the limited way in which the field has been explored and understood, and the relationship of this limitation to the reinforcement of certain narratives about the inevitability of the field being constituted in this way.

History of Home Economics

In the introduction to Marjorie Brown's book *Philosophical studies of home economics in the United States: Basic ideas by which home economists understand themselves*, she states the following:

> A critical analysis of the history of the profession and our understanding as professionals reveal that the past is a foundation upon which present and future advancement of knowledge rests (Miller cited in Brown, 1993, p. xi).

This is very accurate. Indeed, as already noted, home economics like no other field has been influenced by its past, and if we allow it, it will continue to determine our future in decidedly negative ways. For the purposes of this book, I will recount the history of home economics in the state of Queensland, in the country of Australia. The history of home economics in other parts of the world has been documented elsewhere. The history of home economics can be told in many different ways — each town, province, country in the world has a unique history of home economics. The importance of telling a history is to identify the factors that have constrained and determined that history. It is surprising how similar these are across the various domains.

Home Economics in Queensland, Australia

In order to fully appreciate the current position of Home Economics in the Queensland education system, it is necessary to be reasonably conversant with its historical origins. This chapter — whilst not intending to present a comprehensive historical coverage of the field of study (which is thoroughly documented and accessible in other places, for example Logan [1981]) — provides the reader with the historical context of the field.

Home Economics is understood, translated and practiced differently from state-to-state in Australia and country-to-country in the world (Smit, 1991, p. 43). Because of the variations in the nature of Home Economics according to its location, it is necessary to trace the historical origins of Home Economics that are characteristic of Queensland. In so doing, it is possible to understand the impact of the historical origins on the current position of the field. It is necessary to point out that many similarities do appear in various states of Australia and other countries, and that Home Economics in Queensland is a product of pre-existing forms of the subject, being informed by other localities throughout its history.

Modern Home Economics in Queensland has been cultivated from two major influences. The first is the British — a natural enough influence since Australian education was initially based on the British system, as a colonial settlement. This British influence focused on the need to train women in the scientific theory and practice of skills for homemaking in a young, pioneering country. The second influence was inspired by the American approach which reformed the focus of Home Economics to management and the family. This American influence was not realized in Australia until the mid-twentieth century.

Historic Legacy: Apology or Applause?

History is often used as an apology for the present predicament of Home Economics. However, this summary will reveal that perhaps applause is more appropriate — since Home Economics and its predecessors were an early tool of feminism in the fight for equality.

Although it is possible to identify the formal beginnings of Home Economics in Queensland as recently as the late nineteenth century — and I would contend the mid-twentieth century — writers have traced the historical origins of the subject back to the days of the philosopher Aristotle. Jehne, as cited by Henry (1987a, p. 1), claims that Home Economics' origins were evident when Aristotle wrote a chapter entitled *The Theory of Household Management* in his first book of politics several hundred years B.C. Henry (1989, p. 18) supports this notion with an explanation of the name home Economics as being derived from the Greek words 'oikos' and 'nomos' meaning 'house' and 'law' respectively. Thus 'oikonomike' (economic) is a combined study of the law of the house — a management approach to households.

Jehne asserts that evidence exists to support the concept of the economy being based around the household, with a male in the chief managerial position. This concept prevailed until the seventeenth and eighteenth centuries, when the Industrial Revolution caused economic hardship with subsequent social changes to the domestic unit. Reiger (1985, p. 17) explains the changes with the man:

... as the breadwinner on a wage, the provider, and the woman and child as dependents were fundamentally new concepts that grew out of the social arrangements associated with industrial, capitalist society.

The changes were largely consequential to the necessary development of 'specialist' skills in order to locate a role in the capitalist economy. In such an economy, it occurred that women could not retain full time employment and also undertake the biological function of reproduction, as well as domestic management. In this way, gender separation into the areas of paid employ and unpaid household work evolved as discrete areas of specialisation (Wolpe, 1988, p. 270). As a result, there was strong support for the notion of education to train girls for their future roles in this society in the field of household work, whilst boys were prepared for paid work (Eyre, 1989, p. 25). Mander (1987, p. 1) explains the attitude, which became well established by the eighteenth century:

> [G]reat interest was shown in the education of girls, replicating an emerging recognition of changes taking place in the structure and function of the family as an institution. With the expansion of the agricultural and industrial revolutions, the nuclear family was becoming more independent of the social milieu than it had been in feudal times, and male and female roles within it were becoming more defined and separated. Now work was separated from the home and to participate men had to journey to it, while women stayed home to care, now increasingly alone, for the family.

The British Influence: Scientizing 'Women's Knowledge'

In the British colony of Australia, this accepted social configuration combined with a pioneering spirit to create a uniquely emerging society. Mander describes why, in Australia, the notion of family became an important focus:

> [A]ustralia had never experienced traditional family life, and there developed here an even stronger ideology in support of an ideal family where there were separate spheres of influence for men and women (Mander, 1987, p. 1).

Queensland had a permanent European settlement from 1824 and by 1850 the first State School was opened (Henry, 1987, p. 14). The British education system provided the basic, initial formula for Australian education structures. Colonial governments became involved in education for the good of citizens, enabling the spread of a common system of education for all (Angus, 1986, pp. 3–4). The aim of the uniform, public system was to "...erode the divisive barriers of class and religious differences by promoting a common code of citizenship and public standards" (Angus, 1986, pp. 3–4).

This democratic approach to education was complemented by a belief that a common education system would be an appropriate avenue to develop social harmony by creating a 'literate and domesticated public' (Angus, 1986). Schools were established to perpetuate the societal status quo by educating in conformity and self-restraint, within an existing social order. The system legitimated inequality by exercising control over the recipients of knowledge through differential access and by awarding success according to performance in subjects that were seen to count as 'knowledge'. This traditional notion and educational environment prepared students for their station in life, equipping them for their various functions in the economic and social order. As Angus (1986) explains:

> ... themes of social control and social mobility ...are inextricably interrelated in the history of mass education in Australia. Social mobility was offered within an existing social order which was not itself to be examined as part of the educational enterprise...On the one hand, the education system was to entrench a social hierarchy which preserved disadvantage and legitimated inequality, and which could be climbed by children of the lower classes only if they became like their better (Angus, 1986, p. 6).

It was this educational environment that perpetuated the concept of educating one 'for their station in life'. Angus (1986) explains this notion of social control to be a traditional approach to mass schooling in Australia, which is regarded as a 'means to fit people for their various functions in the stable economic and social order'. It is into this conventional climate that the antecedents of Home Economics, extracted from the British education system in the form of needlework and cooking, were introduced to prepare women in the lower socio-economic sector to be effective domestic workers and thrifty household managers in the young, pioneering country of Australia (Mander, 1987, p. 1). This in essence was social control of women. Thorne (1980) explains that an:

> ... examination of the role of ideology in education generally and Home Economics specifically showed that the subject had been both the victim and vehicle of social ideologies to a degree experienced by no other subject. It had therefore been determined by social and economic concerns rather than educational ones (Thorne, 1980, p. 15).

As early as 1860 under Queensland's first Education Regulations, some state schools were teaching needlework to 'young ladies' (Mander, 1987). Logan (1981, p. 3) records that "...needlework was to be taught for at least one hour every school day". In New South Wales, a review by a Directoress of Needlework praised the value of the subject for girls, suggesting it had:

> ...moral benefits for the public schoolgirl...By its means the individuality of schoolgirls is brought out and developed; it teaches them to embellish their homes; it inculcates habits of neatness and industry; it adds to the

comfort of domestic life; and therefore proves itself a boon to the community at large (Kyle, 1986, p. 47).

Needlework was without dispute a dominant and central theme in the schoolgirls program. It gained new status and merit when in 1875 minimum achievement levels for progression to higher grades of needlework were formulated under Standards of Proficiency (Logan, 1981).

Bolstered by the success of needlework for girls, School Inspectors who had seen a recently devised subject Domestic Economy in Britain speculated on its value for women in Australia. The British subject of domestic economy evolved during the eighteenth century, where application of pure scientific advances were affecting all facets of society — with application to areas such as agriculture, technology and inevitably the home. British Home Economists trace their origins to this period (Mander, 1987).

The British tradition emphasized practical skills and the application of scientific principles to the home. This scientific approach brought with it the benefit of a type of respectability and legitimacy amongst other subjects, and offered no threat to the socially constructed norms of masculinity since women were only borrowing science from the traditionally male domain to apply it to the unpaid realm of the home. Women did not compete in men's knowledge fields, and subsequently there was no threat to the power structures in the then modernist society. As Attar (1990, p. 102) points out "[T]here were benefits for male scientists in supporting a separate science for women, which would avert the prospect of female competition". As such, Home Economics was founded on what some have described as a contradiction — science and the home (Reiger, 1990). Domestic economy succeeded in scientizing women's knowledge.

Buoyed by the success of domestic economy in Britain, Australian inspectors of education promoted the need for a similar program, considering it to be an essential component of girls' education. There were several reasons for the promotion of domestic economy for girls in Australia. The foremost reason for advocacy of the subject was a shortage of employees as "good industrious domestic servants" (Kyle, 1986, p. 46). There was difficulty in filling vacancies due to the low status perceptions of the job. By providing a subject that prepared girls for what was deemed as their appropriate employment, reformers believed the introduction of a specific subject with training methods for domestic workers would ensure a rise in status. The subsequent effect would be to fill the vacancies.

Although this mission of supplying domestic servants was paramount, the low status of housework and domestic activity underscored the role of women in society. This led to the second reason to push for the introduction of domestic economy — the route of legitimizing women's knowledge through recognition in education. Kyle (1986, p. 46) explains that:

> ... the more radical women of the 1880's and 1890's sought a greater share for women in formal education, employment and political life, and these women included the suffragists, they saw women's maternal and domestic role as being central to their life. Therefore, they pressed strongly for female education that would fit women for that revered and special duty. But they did not want female education to be viewed as unimportant if domestic. Rather, the task was to upgrade women's domestic vocation to a level whereby society would view it with more respect and perhaps working class girls would be encouraged to embrace that domestic role more readily, more industriously and with greater efficiency.

With the adoption of this mentality, the state clearly had a major part in the education of women for their motherhood role in the future. The impact of this approach is analyzed in the work of David (1984, 1987), who explores the mechanisms by which policy ensures the regulation of 'motherhood' through social control. In fact, David argues that:

> [R]aising the question of the nature and characteristics of motherhood as either unpaid work or paid 'caring' work is important for understanding the relations between women today. ... It is not only their lives as children that are mapped by the ideological assumptions, but their opportunities, activities and 'work' as adults. Without close attention to the ways notions of motherhood are deeply embedded in not only social and economic relations generally, but the practice of schools and other child care agencies, policy changes can only build upon the inequality between the sexes (David, 1984, p. 5).

In 1881 in Queensland, domestic economy became a component of the education schedule for girls, strongly supported by both male and female educators. This subject is generally accepted as the forerunner to home economics' in Queensland. This was home economics first exposure to feminism — and it was firmly supported by feminists as it was seen to be a positive, vital force for legitimizing women's knowledge. It is from here that the history of Queensland home economics is generally documented. This is supported by the Home Economics Association of Queensland, which celebrated a century of Home Economics education in Queensland in 1981.

The focus of domestic economy in Australia and Queensland was:

> ... on the provision of food and clothing and the creation of the Home Environment in the early settlement of Australia. Students were taught

how to restore and maintain the household through laundry work, mending and house cleaning. As a school subject, this study was justified by the belief that such training was appropriate for girls' future roles as domestic servants and for homemakers (Home Economics Association of Australia Position Paper, 1984, p. 1).

Without doubt, in its earliest forms, home economics was determined by social and economic concerns rather than educational ones (Thorne 1980; Eyre 1989; Brown 1988b). It was introduced specifically as women's knowledge, as an 'education' and preparation for women's role in society, as deemed appropriate by men and other women in male-defined institutions. Women were prepared for menial domestic labor until they married and established their own families, after which their skills would benefit them in carrying out the duties inherent in their biologically determined destiny. There is no doubt, with the wisdom of hindsight and according to modern-day definitions, that the antecedents of Home Economics were established to reinforce the gender specific division of labor typical of a patriarchal society — a mechanism for oppression, and an agent of socialization in a patriarchal society which led to the construction of conventional feminine identities. Yet, at the time, it was also a vehicle for supporting the value of women's unpaid work through formulation as a school subject. In this way, it aimed to value women's work.

In Britain the growth of domestic economy was "phenomenal" (Carver, 1979, p. 3). However, in the various states of Australia there was considerable resistance to it (Cooper-Cameron, 1987; Mander, 1987; Logan, 1981). Mander identified some of the reasons for the lack of appeal:

> [I]t is clear that while the rhetoric was meant to inspire women for their finest and natural duty — motherhood — the domestic arts was designed to meet the needs of low status individuals — women — and especially the dull and the working class, and the field was expected to fulfill its tasks in the poorest of facilities (Mander, 1987, pp. 2–3).

Australian women generally did not aspire in parallel with the predominantly male conceived notions of education for women, though there were few challenges — a reflection of the powerlessness experienced by women in a traditional, patriarchal society (Mander 1987; Kyle 1986; David 1984,1987). Regardless of this reluctance to study domestic economy, girls were left no option but to conform. As Kyle (1986, p. 217) explains:

> ...female students rejected much of the domestic curriculum permeating state schools by the 1900's...State schooling has played a key part in keeping women in their perceived traditional place. Like every other major organization in this industrialized nation, it carries with it and perpetuates

old inequities from the past. New recruits are shaped and prodded into the old conforming ways.

The British influence set a precedent for the subject in Australia and subsequently at state levels. This was the first major influence that contributed to home economics in Queensland, the second was a Canadian/American influence.

The United States and Canadian Influence: Reform

With minor amendments, the domestic economy approach to home economics was maintained in Queensland well into the twentieth century, despite radical reforms in the field at the turn of the century in America. The reforms in America were the result of two factors: a recognition of the failure of the earlier forms of Home Economics to liberate women from biologically determined conventional positions of femininity (Carver, 1979) and a concern that the institution of home and family was deteriorating, and "if the family failed, society would also fail" (Jax, 1985, p. 23). The first factor was a political one. Carver (1979, p. 9) explains that "[T]he late nineteenth and early twentieth century was a period in which women sought to win political equality. Advocates of women's rights revolted against the restrictions that were placed upon women in education, professions and politics".

The second factor was concern for the institution of home and family. This concern stemmed from the impact of industrialization that manifested itself in increased divorce, perceived irresponsible social behavior and other undesirable changes (Jax 1985). These two factors, combined with the realization that certain educational initiatives were underway which seemed to address either/or and sometimes both of the issues, but that there was no uniform, integrated approach. Carver explains:

> [A]ll over the country people had been working individually and in groups for the betterment of home living, but at this time there existed no uniformity in the nomenclature or content of courses offered in this area. What was evident ... was the need for someone to co-ordinate these fragmented efforts in a combined force. (Carver, 1979, p. 9)

In 1899, as a response to this a group of "like-minded women" (Mander, 1987, p. 3) led by Ellen Richards, met to discuss "the need and purpose for a new field of study in education that could help the home and family" (Jax, 1985, p. 23). The group strongly supported the need for such a field, and over the course of ten consecutive annual conferences held at Lake Placid — named *The Lake Placid Conferences 1899–1908* — the convictions of the group were crystallized into a field of study. This is heralded as the most important decade in the history of the field of Home Economics (Burgess, 1983).

'Home Economics' — the name — was born of the American reforms during the Lake Placid conference of 1901. The title was to represent a field of study and its purpose was to "...unify the divergent home oriented courses aiming to give a girl a sense of her responsibilities necessary to place the house on a scientific basis" (Mander, 1987, p. 3).

Ellen Richards, considered the founder of home economics (Burgess, 1983, p. 11), said of the name:

> [H]ome Economics: home meaning the place of shelter and nurture for the children and for the personal qualities of self sacrifice for others, for the gaining of strength to meet the world; economics meaning the management of the home or economic lines as to time and energy as well as mere money (Richards cited in Mortvedt, 1984, p. 49).

This alludes to the definition of the field of Home Economics as recorded by the reform group during the Lake Placid Conferences:

> [H]ome Economics in its most comprehensive sense is the study of laws, conditions, principles and ideals which are concerned on the one hand with man's (sic) environment and on the other hand with his (sic) nature as a social being and is the study of the relation between those two factors (Mander, 1987, p. 3).

The definitions carry some interesting sociological messages. The former sets the boundaries very clearly as the 'home' — a word which under scrutiny appears to be not only a physical structure but to be synonymous with family — and encourages self-sacrifice for others, both highly feminized notions. The 'family' as a social structure is recognized by many critics as a chief institution of patriarchy, reinforcing the oppression of women (Curthoys, 1988). The definitions also introduce the notion of management of the home. The latter definition of the field interestingly is framed in masculine terminology, which constitutes an overt attempt at patriarchal approval. Both definitions lie starkly controversial in modern sociological critique, by reinforcing the oppression of women in the domestic sphere. Even at its initiation, the founders of Home Economics had difficulty in narrowing the field to one focus, they could not unanimously agree to focus on management or the family instead opting for a dual focus coupled with a scientific base.

Added to this lack of clarity was the realization that the field lacked exclusive knowledge, but rather drew upon other disciplines for knowledge that was then applied. The implications of this scenario are far-reaching and are exemplary of the ongoing attempts over the generations to make Home Economics knowledge valuable. Badir explains the implications:

> [T]he outline of a discipline was laid out, a comprehensive mission statement had been defined, but the content of the discipline was seen as being what others already knew. Unlike chemistry or physics where the relationships of ideas defined the content of the discipline and made it possible to move beyond the parent discipline — philosophy — in the case of Home Economics the parameters of the discipline became established before research had been conducted or the subject matter developed. A line was drawn around household, with all its implications. The knowledge believed to be needed for the practice of the discipline had already been developed in other disciplines. Persons trained in Home Economics were to become interpreters of knowledge already available (Badir, 1990, p. 22).

However, considering the constraints of ideology of the time, it seems that these ameliorations were highly regarded by male and female alike. To men, home economics offered no threat to valued knowledge; to women, it gained a few points towards liberalizing their perceived functions, by incorporating management and interpersonal relationships studies, and adding to valuable knowledge within the acceptable parameters of the traditional feminine preserve.

It is interesting to note that Ellen Richards, generally accepted as the founder of home economics, was selected by an Australian, nation-wide popular newspaper as one of one hundred exceptional international women for making a lasting impression on the world in our previous millennium. The one hundred millennium women were, to quote the text, "neither exhaustive nor a ranking of the most important or the most influential. It is meant to be inspiring, to remind everyone that women have not always been as invisible as society has tried to make them" (Cosic, 1999, p. 19). Her brief summary read:

Ellen Richards (1842–1911)

> Richards invented the science of ecology and was the first woman admitted to the prestigious Massachusetts Institute of Technology, the first to graduate in chemistry, its first female faculty member and first science consultant to industry. Yet she was refused a doctorate in 1873 on the grounds that she was female; at one stage, to remain in the scientific realm, she was forced to accept an unpaid role as assistant professor in charge of the women's laboratory. Her analysis of pollution in air and water inspired the US Public Health movement and her Food Materials and Their Adulteration influenced the passage of the Pure Food and Drug Acts (Cosic, 1999, p. 23).

The founder of home economics had been acknowledged as one of the past milleniums exceptional international women who have made a lasting impression, but 'home economics' was not made visible and explicit with her. When Richards was fighting to be recognised, that is during the late nineteenth and early twentieth century, was a period in which women sought to win political equality with men in many arenas. Advocates of women's rights revolted against the restrictions that were placed upon women in education, professions and politics. This era is known as the First Wave of Feminism. Ellen Richards had been a victim of discrimination based solely on gender.

What we see then is that the emergence of home economics is the culmination of Ellen Richards struggles to be valued in a masculinized sphere of study — she defined a new field of knowledge, that is, she scientized what was traditionally seen to be 'women's work'. In doing so, she used a masculinized framework for legitimising women's knowledge. In postmodern terms, she is said to have relied on 'the masters tools' (Lorde, 1984). That is not the type of re-thinking that I will be advocating. Indeed, as I have already made clear, this approach can never succeed, but for the First Wave of Feminism at the end of the nineteenth century this strategy was considered to be extremely revolutionary. It followed the philosophy of conforming to and thereby privileging masculine traditions by agreeing to play by the rules set by males — in this case — the academy of the university. One hundred years of experience later we know that using 'the master's tools' reinforces their legitimacy and their value, making them increasingly powerful and forcing the others into the margins. To understand this concept is to have a powerful understanding of the social construction of patriarchy, which is the foundation of modernist thinking.

The Abyss: From Domestic Economy to Reform

This American reformation, progressive though it was for its era, did not influence home economics education in Queensland until 1972. It was at this time that home economics as defined and named by the American reformers was largely adopted. Until then, the intention and practice of home economics subjects in Queensland were still bound by a commitment to the traditional British model — with a philosophical and conceptual foundation favoring the predominantly scientific approach to practical domestic skills, rather than the predominantly management approach of the American reforms.

The period between the introduction of domestic economy in the late nineteenth century and the adoption of the turn-of-the-century American reforms in the late twentieth century, was char-

acterized by minor changes in the content, name and other superficial aspects of the subject. The prevailing focus remained on scientific applications for domestic skills. For example, a name
change from Domestic Economy to Domestic Science in 1913
reflected increasing emphasis on Science education generally,
and a rejection of the values of thriftiness, which are implied
in the word economy (Henry, 1989).

The area where significant change did occur was with its introduction at higher levels of education. In 1913 home economics
became an examinable subject at Junior and in 1939 was awarded
matriculation status (Logan, 1981). With the introduction of the
senior course in 1939 there was continuity from grade 7 to matriculation. Tertiary studies in home economics focused on the preparation of home economics teachers, and prior to 1938 all home
economics teachers were first trained as primary school teachers
and then selected and studied specialist subjects related to the
field in their own time. Having completed the subjects, students
were awarded a Diploma of Domestic Science (Logan, 1981).
In 1938 a specific three year long preparation for home economics teachers was introduced.

Throughout this time — under its various titles — home economics retained a significant place in the education of girls
in Queensland. It was a mandatory subject for girls in their compulsory years of schooling. As an elective subject — at the senior
level — it went through phases of popularity that reflected societal events of the time. For example, during the World War Two
period, it enjoyed popularity, and this can be attributed to the
political environment that encouraged the notion of family and
strengthening Australia with the family as its core unit (Logan,
1981). Home economists were admired for their efforts. Society
in the 1950's saw the model middle-class standards of family life
— with the male as head of the nuclear family household
and females generally being economically dependent and responsible for the nurturing of their family (Reiger, 1990). Home economics knowledge sat well in this picture, with females being
channeled into selecting the subject in order to replicate the ideal
family life.

However, society began to change, due to factors such as economic strife, massive consumerism and increasing divorce rates
(Reiger, 1989). These changes ultimately manifested themselves
in the family, and growing disquiet among females was stirred.
Reiger explains that it became:

... apparent that those economically dependent on men were very vulnerable in times of increasing divorce rates. Other contradictions included the way in which the focus on mothers as being responsible for meeting children's every need soured in view of the consumerist pressures. Out of many of the pressures, and old resentments about sexual and domestic violence, the second wave of the women's movement was born (Reiger, 1990, p. 6).

The second-wave feminist movement of the sixties and seventies was not unified, with three major approaches: the radical, socialist and liberal feminists. These varied because of their historical origins, with the most visible form of feminism being the radical feminist. From the onset, it was apparent that radical feminists and home economics did not meld, with radical feminists strongly condemning the field for perpetuating and modeling damning traditional stereotypes of females in the home. Home economics was seen to be oppressing females. Reiger (1990, p. 6) describes the response of home economists to radical feminism as "tend[ing] to keep their distance, sympathizing with those who argued that the new radical feminists wanted to devalue the homemaking tasks with which they identified".

But it was only the radical feminists who held this view, while the liberal and socialist feminists were far less discriminatory — some applauded the field for making women's knowledge an acknowledged — if devalued — educational endeavor. At the school level, home economics as a subject responded defensively by 'grabbing' more of the pure and social science knowledge that became available in the knowledge boom. They saw this as a prop, and a way to further validate the field against criticism.

As a response to emerging social, economic and political demands of the 1960's, the Queensland State Education Act of 1964 abolished the scholarship examination and increased the age of compulsory school attendance to the age of fifteen (Logan, 1981). Along with this change, a new awareness of alternative educational approaches was encouraged. In 1965 there was an international residential summer school for home economics at Cornell University, to which a Victorian — Jean Pollock — made Australian representation. She met with the international leaders of the field. Pollock found a subject which was described as being "more theoretical than practical, with a different content" and as Mander explains this had an impact in Australia, with "[M]any subsequent changes in the methods and directions of the subject ... traced to the ideas of Jean Pollock brought back from the United States" (Mander, 1987, p. 3).

The model Pollock found had been derived from the Lake Placid Conferences – initiated and developed more than half a century before her exposure to them! The model saw home economics as the application of science to the family and home, with a strong decision-making and social science component. It did not focus on domestic skills. This led to the modification of syllabus documents that reflected a commitment to the process of change.

In 1972 in Queensland the Amended Education Act allowed the recommendations of the Radford Report to be implemented, amongst which it recommended the abolition of external examinations at both junior and senior levels. Home economists grasped the opportunity to implement major reforms to the field based on the American model, with changes to the name, content and approach.

This is the birth of Home Economics in Queensland. It was at this historical point, particularly with the overt adoption of the name home economics and changes at philosophical levels which were evident in changes to the focus and content, that home economics as defined by the American Lake Placid Conferences, 1899–1908 truly came into fruition (Home Economics Association of Australia Position Paper, 1984, p. 1).

Adoption of the 'Old' New Reforms

Henry (1989) identifies the theme of the 1973 Draft Syllabus in Home Economics that emerged as a result of these changes as "learning to live effectively". The Draft Syllabus spelled this out:

> [H]ome Economics rests on a broad interdisciplinary basis which includes such disciplines as sociology, biological and physical sciences, psychology, education, economics, management and architecture. Home Economics integrates these disciplines around a central concern — the well-being of the individual within his (sic) environment (Board of Secondary School Studies, 1973, p. 2).

Seven key content areas of the field were distinguished, these being: Food and Nutrition; Clothing and Textiles; Housing; Management; Human Development; Design; and Consumer Studies. Badir explains that adoption of American reforms may have been too late — that perceptions of the field were well and truly constituted and practices firmly entrenched — under the preconceived notions of the British approach:

> [M]any of the problems which beset home economics today can be related to the failure to pick up that early approach (American influence) to examine it, to twist and to turn it until all the many relationships (concepts) were seen and documented. The basis could then have truly been laid for the development of a truly interdisciplinary approach to the formation of some new theoretical constructions using borrowed theory from other dis-

ciplines; to the development of a body of knowledge which came out of research based on those concepts (Badir, 1990, p. 23).

But even with the adoption of the somewhat old new reforms, home economics was not keeping up with social change. The challenge by feminists in the 1970's regarding the intention of home economics continued, with radical feminists strongly condemning the field for perpetuating and modeling damning traditional stereotypes. Home economists responded defensively, grabbing even more pure and social science knowledge produced in the knowledge boom as a way of legitimizing and bolstering their field, all the while cringing at the extremists who devalued homemaking tasks with which the home economists identified (Reiger, 1990).

The critics impacted on home economics successfully, and this is evident in minor changes that occurred. For example, in 1980 with a major change in the Queensland Education sector from Radford to Review of School Based Assessment (ROSBA) based on recommendations from the Scott Report, there was opportunity for a shift in the focus of the home economics syllabus whilst the document underwent changes to conform to the requirement of the newly instituted state educational reform. This fortuity was not overlooked, with a subsequent shift in focus from the well-being of individuals and families to management — previously included in the field in the more limited form of decision-making. This permutation attempted to counter criticism leveled at home economics, as previously described. The usage of terminology that seemingly removed the focus from the domain of the home and 'women's work' to broader notions of 'management' that, it was hoped, implied a higher status, represented an attempt at achieving endorsement from critics. In a more recent review of the syllabus in 1987, the field continued to emphasize the management focus. A further review of the syllabus in 1991 adopted a wellbeing of individuals and families focus. A major rewrite of the senior syllabus in 2000/2001 has further developed the focus on individuals and families and the optimization of their wellbeing. This occurs at a time when the government initiative to converge vocational and general education in schools is at its pinnacle. Hence, home economics teachers are encouraged to teach in vocationally oriented fields including hospitality, early childhood and fashion, along with their traditional field of home economics. The impact of this has been profound, with many home economics teachers opting to redirect their entire or significant energies into one or more of the vocational fields, at the expense of home economics.

In the tertiary sector, until 1980, there were no tertiary qualifications in Queensland — in the field of home economics that were not directly linked to teacher preparation. In 1980 the Bachelor of Applied Science (Home Economics) course commenced, which aimed at producing graduate Home Economists for industry (Logan, 1981). In 1990, with the amalgamation of the then Queensland Institute of Technology and Brisbane College of Advanced Education (where home economics courses were located) home economics was first seen in the pages of a University handbook in Queensland — at the Queensland University of Technology. Since then, the home economics degree was renamed to Family and Consumer Studies, before it was dropped from the University curriculum. Again home economics can only be studied in Queensland Universities as a teaching qualification. However, there are concerns about the adequacy of the teaching courses available, along with the quality and diminishing number of graduates produced.

A recent national study by Pendergast, Reynolds and Crane (2000) that was prompted by a Council of Deans (Preston, 1998) investigation into the supply and demand of teachers in a range of fields across Australia, coupled with anecdotal evidence of a shortage of home economics teachers in at least some states and territories of Australia; and the employment of unsuitably qualified teachers teaching home economics subjects due to a shortage of home economics qualified teachers, found that:

- there is a growing shortage of home economics trained teachers to meet a continuous demand;
- the major reason for the growing shortage of home economics teachers is a lack of appropriate tertiary teacher preparation courses;
- in recent years there has been a reduction in home economics teacher preparation courses;
- teacher preparation institutions have not addressed the broad range of home economics related subjects that home economics teachers are expected to teach; and
- in their experience, home economics teachers are more likely to witness home economics teacher shortages in their school situation, as compared to oversupply.

In many parts of Australia, including Queensland, home economics teachers believe that the main reasons for a shortage of home economics teachers is the lack of, or poor quality tertiary preparation courses (Pendergast, Reynolds & Crane, 2000). This has created a circular loop, which has led to students not choosing to study home economics, with the effect of a further reduction in resource allocation to these programs, culminating in a loss of specialist home economics staff from programs. This in turn leads to students not selecting the program, and so on.

There is no doubt that current Home Economics in Queensland is a product of the major events documented in this chapter, and as such is diffuse in its intent and extensive in its diversity. It is able to be translated in numerous ways. The subtle changes that have occurred in home economics are not always reflected in the classroom in ways that are recognizably consistent. There are advocates for each 'version' of home economics, and practitioners in the field are aware that these are practiced despite reforms to governing syllabus documents. This is the historical legacy of home economics in Queensland.

Further Thinking

Investigate the history of home economics or another field of study in the context in which you are currently studying or working. Document the major turning points in curriculum development and account for these changes. Whose interests were/are being served by these changes? Whose interests are not served by these changes?

The history of home economics education is littered with attempts by the profession to legitimize itself within the power regime that was considered to be powerful at the time. Identify where the driving force for the power regime was based, and what it was attempting to achieve.

Gender issues are extremely relevant to home economics. Explain how modernist society, in the creation of the dualist society where male/female are accepted as a given, has affected the status of home economics. Is this true for other subjects?

One of the strengths, but also a problem for home economics, is that it is understood, translated and practiced differently from region-to-region, and country-to-country throughout the world. In what ways is this a strength for home economics? In what ways is this a weakness?

This chapter acknowledges that Ellen Richards is generally accepted as the founder of home economics. It notes that she was selected by an Australian popular newspaper as one of one hundred exceptional international women for making a lasting impression on the world in our previous millennium. Yet, in the brief summary of her achievements, there is no mention of her role in founding the field. Explain the reasons for this omission.

Home Economics –
Marginal Subject/s

Home economics today is in turmoil. There seems to be among us in the field a frantic search for identity and status, a general confusion about what we are doing and what we ought to be doing, an embarrassing sense of guilt about our "image", and, among the dedicated professionals, a deep questioning of the meaning of home economics and its reason for being in today's world (Creekmore, 1968).

This comment could well be argued to typify the position of home economists and their field of study for the entire post war period. There has been continual discussion about the mission, the focus, the purpose, the definition, the name, the content. This discussion happens in local, state, national and international settings. The fact that this comment is not taken from the latest journal of home economics theory — though it may well have been (see for example American Home Economics Association, 1993; Peterat & Khamasi, 1995; Derkley, 1997) — but was published thirty years ago indicates that the dilemmas of today are not new. In fact, Brown and Baldwin (1995) trace the roots of such questions back to 1902, in the years when home economics was struggling to be identified as a field of study and there was a lack of theory through which to legitimate the field.

Throughout this struggle, 'home economics' has been on the timetable of many generations of school students in many countries of the world. During this time there have been major changes to the content, processes, skills, outcomes and value of the subject, but there is a paucity of research which goes beyond merely presenting chronological histories of the field during these re-workings. Currently, home economics is offered in many educational settings, across a range of years. This begs the question: why is it that after more than one hundred years of home economics education and a demonstrable commitment by students to study it, the field remains in turmoil? Why with decades of addressing the same issues and concerns does the profession of home economics teaching appear to be no closer to resolving its dilemmas? Why is it that home economists continually remake the field of home economics, transforming it through scientific, management, consumer, family and other discourses, by changing the name, the focus, the mission — and yet the field has continued to be stigmatised as 'condemned' to the margins in the culture of schooling? To explore these questions it is necessary to look at the themes and assumptions which have informed a large number of curriculum shifts and which underpin research in the field. In particular, it demands consideration of the epistemological terrain of the research itself. The review that is undertaken here focuses on the Queensland and Australian context as a particular site of home economics pedagogy, and when appropriate, draws upon international trends and influences where they have impacted on this unique context, as part of a 'cargo cult' mentality. It is noteworthy that all too often we have relied on the intellectualism of our international scholars to lead the way, and perhaps this is part of some of the local issues to be addressed.

This chapter sets out the thematics and underlying assumptions of the research base of home economics made evident through the literature, arguing that the epistemological limits reflected have disallowed certain identities and practical possibilities. The chapter culminates in recognition of the need to depart from humanist accounts reflected in the literature, whether they are psychological/curriculum or critical feminist accounts that proceed using the logic of ideology critique in favor of a more risky but potentially more fruitful means of inquiry.

There are eight (8) themes or underlying assumptions that emerge out my reading of the 'body' of the research of home economics. These, listed below, form the structure for the remainder of the chapter, with each theme being elaborated in turn through the literature. The themes/assumptions evident in home economics research literature in Queensland and Australia are:

- home economics research as a small and piecemeal body of work;
- the historical pattern of the uncritical adoption of off-shore developments;
- struggling for legitimation;
- problematising of home economics re-form;
- what is to be learned;
- social justice agendas and home economics;
- initial and tentative 'experimentations' with post theorizing; and
- the difficult relationship of feminism and home economics.

It is interesting to note the extent to which these are in keeping with what Marjorie Brown (1993) has described as the current dissatisfactions and misunderstandings of the profession of home economics. Marjorie Brown is considered to be the leading international scholar in the field of home economics amongst her contemporaries (Vincent, 1994). She suggests the following concerns are felt world wide as grievances among home economists, though they all may not be felt by all members of the profession:

- the splintering of specializations and of knowledge in the profession;

- the loss of common professional purpose;

- an anti-intellectualism which thwarts the use of reason and a depth of understanding;

- reluctance on the part of many professionals to be publicly self-reflective about their own concepts and beliefs together with an assumption that any self-interpretation of home economics is final;

- lack of respect in the academic world and in public opinion;

- the questionable legitimacy of authority in home economics; and

- an apolitical orientation of members of the profession (Brown, 1993, p. 417).

The text that follows will juxtapose Brown's concerns and grievances with the themes or trends emerging from the Australian literature to determine if and how they parallel and inform each other. In doing so, it insists that the very 'naming' of home economics as 'grieving' is part of the cultural predicament of home economics itself, more than mere documentation. Along with other practices, it constantly brings marginality into being by constantly re-naming the condition as 'normal'.

Themes in the 'Body' of the Research of Home Economics

Home Economics Research as a Small and Piecemeal Body of Work

What research exists? What thinking has taken place? Is there any theory of home economics? What does the body of home economics research look like? In answering these questions, patterns in home economics research emerge.

Research in home economics does exist and is characterized by three main trends. The first trend is a general lack of research theorizing the field compared with other professional fields of study, both in international and local settings. Brown and Baldwin (1995, p. 7) lament this trend stating:

> ...it seems that, historically, home economists have paid scant attention to theory for we find only scattered reference to the need for theory development and even less to critical examination of the content of theories in home economics journals throughout much of this century.

In her list of concerns felt by home economists, Brown (1993) points out that this trend in research towards an anti-intellectualism thwarts the use of reason and depth of understanding, and thus leads to a misunderstanding of the profession of home economics.

In perhaps their most significant contribution to home economics theory, Brown and Baldwin (1995) joined forces to prepare a paper entitled *The Concept of Theory in Home Economics*. This is a culmination of their work over the years, with various prevailing concepts of theory described and critiqued, and with examples in home economics literature cited. They document and critique the limitations and assumptions of theoretical approaches including eclecticism, the formal model, positivism, anti- theoretical bias, theories of meaning including phenomenology, linguistic analysis, and hermeneutics. What emerges from this comprehensive collation is firstly a need for theorizing of the field and secondly, the need for an alternative conceptualization of theory beyond the dialectical, which they argue overcomes the shortcomings of other approaches presented. They also note a growing interest, over the last decade, in theory within the field. It is not the intention of this book to revisit the work that has been done by Baldwin and Brown (1995), but rather to focus on the Queensland and Australian context as a particular cultural site of home economics pedagogy.

This leads to the second trend in home economics research, the unquestioning use of positivist epistemologies, with little evidence of approaches that work across the grain of essentialist thinking (Baldwin, 1995; Jones, 1995). By way of example, the following studies and their brief summaries represent the type of essentialist approaches that have dominated home economics research. Callahan (1993) found that responses from 574 of 827 students in introductory home economics classes identified positive influences in selecting home economics as a major: friends, high school home economics teachers, and home economics faculty. Negative influences were family, other high school teachers, radio advertisements, and campus recruitment. Moe (1991) used the Bem Sex Role Inventory three times by 84 female home economists to describe themselves, to describe home economists, and to describe home economists as an outsider would. They described themselves as masculine and a home economist as undifferentiated or mixed; they thought non-home economists would describe home economists as feminine.

Cunningham's (1992) study collected descriptive information about 152 Nebraska home economics teachers and their curriculum orientation(s). The questionnaire was adapted from the Curriculum Orientation Profile designed by Babin (1979) and revised by Carlson (1991). Teachers responded to 45 statements on a Likert-type scale. Nine statements reflected each of five curriculum orientations; technology, critical consciousness of social reconstruction, personal relevance, cognitive process, and academic rationalism. Miller's (1991) research involved sending Indiana vocational home economics teachers a 58-item questionnaire designed to determine reasons for their dissatisfaction with their jobs. These teachers had been identified in an earlier study as being dissatisfied with their jobs. Respondents numbered 367 (80 percent); 56 added notes explaining their feelings. Computer forms were electronically read and analysed statistically using chi square for determining differences and Pearson Product Moment for relationships. Significant correlations were found for 27 test items, most on factors relating to administration. Differences were found for 10 factors with most in the administration category. Teachers with occupational assignments seemed to be least dissatisfied; teachers with assignments for both vocational and non-vocational classes seemed most dissatisfied. Dissatisfaction prevailed for both assignment and category. Results implied that home economics teacher educators need to emphasise teachers' multiple roles and opportunities to create a more positive attitude.

Brown (1993) also notes that the 'empiricist position' is the prevailing view of knowledge and action, of theory, and of the role of the philosophy in home economics. By way of example see Banes (1992) whose research findings are that a female dominated profession such as home economics should focus on developing realistic attitudes toward careers, awareness of socio-cultural conditioning, and management skills. A leadership development model has four competencies: favourable attitudes, psychological and social preparedness, technical/administrative skills, and political astuteness; Dykman (1993) who suggests the "new" home economics focuses on combating sex stereotypes, living skills that include balancing work and family, outcomes-based education that integrates academic and vocational skills, encouragement of male enrolment, and helping students deal with serious social problems; and Smith (1993) who presents constructivist global education as the morally and ethically defensible position to hold, and illustrates the need for continued research of a philosophical nature in home economics and home economics education.

As already noted, it is not that this work does not perform an important function in theorising the field, but rather, that new, unpredictable readings of home economics do not become available, a shortcoming also recognised by Brown (1993).

The third trend is the undertaking of specialised but narrow projects in specific aspects of the field, typically by disciplinary base or subject matter. Newell and Green (1982) explain that disciplines are variously characterised by their subject matter, their method, their perspective, and/or the questions they ask. They go on to define interdisciplinary studies as "inquiries which critically draw upon two or more disciplines and which lead to an integration of disciplinary insights" (p. 24). This is supported by Vaideanu (1987, p. 494) who explains the meaning of interdisciplinarity as:

> ...[an] encounter and cooperation of two or more disciplines, each of which brings with it, at the level of theory or of empirical research, its own conceptual approaches, ways of defining problems, and research methods.

If we accept that home economics is interdisciplinary in nature, then it brings with it the characteristics of individual disciplines, including particular conventions in research and theory. The emphasis on research in recent years in home economics has been towards specialization by disciplinary base or subject matter area in order to focus on problems of manageable size and these are typically characterized by the dominant positivist research tradition. For example, the sciences of nutrition, textiles and food have a research base that historically reflects positivist analyses, quantitative methodologies, and the empirical sciences. On the other hand, the disciplines that deal with inter/intra-personal and family relationships, socio-cultural and aesthetic environments, and psychosocial development historically have a research base that is characterized by phenomenological work associated with qualitative methodologies and the interpretive sciences (Bobbitt, 1993).

This is problematic for home economics in that interdisciplinary research implies interdisciplinary fields of study and a variety of research methodologies utilized collaboratively. Most of the research named as 'interdisciplinary' by home economists, is a cooperative effort with one or more scientists in the core disciplines (Horn, 1993). Moreover, it is an effort that neglects the connections and overlaps that could be made among the various specializations of the field. This is a serious limitation in a field which typically deals with issues that, as Horn (1993) explains, do not fit conveniently into narrow categories or disciplines.

A key reason why interdisciplinary approaches to learning, and interdisciplinary research have not gained more attention in home economics is a trend towards more 'scientific' research (Vincenti, 1990). Its prescribed methodologies tend to atomize knowledge into components in order to control variables, isolate phenomena from their context, and develop generalizations.

Hence, given that home economics is interdisciplinary in nature, and given that the disciplines upon which it is constructed privilege research traditions, it is important to understand the differing characteristics and features of these research methodologies and to appreciate the potential contribution of *both* qualitative and quantitative research, and hence the benefits of interdisciplinary research using both sets of methodological tools become apparent. It is important that home economics, as an interdisciplinary field, recognizes the benefits of interdisciplinary research. Indeed, as Vaideanu (1987, p. 489) has suggested "...interdisciplinarity has been regarded as an idea with a great future, [and] a refuge for superficial researchers...".

This concern is also reflected in Brown's (1993) dissatisfactions with the profession of home economics. She described it as the 'splintering' of specializations and of knowledge of the profession. The problem with this piecemeal approach is that the sub-disciplines of home economics often neglect the connections and overlaps that ought to be made among the various specializations of the field (Horn, 1993) and put at risk the unity of the field of study. Of course, all these people calling for 'more unity' do not see 'blowing things apart' as relevant, unfortunately.

As a result of the theoretical and methodological impoverishment of home economics research, "home economists worldwide have worked under incredible pressure to maintain their discipline. This is not a local but an international phenomenon" (Thompson, 1995b, p. 53). McCullers (1988) has urged that sound theory must be an integral part of research and has sought to encourage home economists to take research and scholarly activity seriously.

Uncritical Adoption of Off-shore Developments: The Australian Pattern

In Australia, research, theorizing and scholarship in the field of home economics is in its infancy (Pendergast, 1996a) and is constituted principally by empirical work (Jones, 1995), as noted in the previous section. In the international environment, recent research in and about home economics theory and philosophy is limited to a small band of researchers, and has generally been carried out by those within the field but off the shores of Australia — see for example Baldwin (1990, 1991, 1995) and Brown (1980, 1981, 1984, 1988a, 1988b, 1993). Furthermore, Australian home economists have typically simply adopted the theorizing of international writers (who base their research in other contexts, such as Marjorie Brown in the American context) for the Australian cultural setting with little adjustment or argument. This pattern is not unique to the field of home economics. For example, Richard Johnson (1997) has explored the adoption of trends in the area of early childhood education, where there has been a similar unequivocal adoption of overseas approaches to the field with what amounts to little intellectual debate. He terms this trend a type of 'cargo cult' mentality where 'primitive' cultures unquestioningly accept 'advanced' cultural perspectives, ultimately leading to the colonization of the field. In this way, a 'flattening-out of local cultures' occurs (Johnson, 1997, p. 22) and dominant discourses prevail. The cargo cult concept emerges from anthropological literature that in essence describes the reaction of primitive societies to advanced societies. As described by Lindstrom (cited by Johnson, 1977, p. 20):

> [C]argo cults develop when primitive societies are exposed to the overpowering material wealth of the outside industrialized world. Not knowing where the foreigners' plentiful supplies come from, the natives believe they were sent from the spirit world. They build makeshift piers and airstrips and perform magical rites to summon well-stocked foreign ships and planes…the faithful still expect the Americans to arrive soon, bringing with them lots of chocolates, radios and motorcycles.

This cargo cult mentality can be applied to the theorizing and research of home economics in Australia — the 'primitive culture' — that has unerringly adopted the perspectives of the 'advanced' British and American scholars in this field.

Brown (1993) has also identified a trend of unquestionable acceptance of conventional authority in home economics. She argues that power to shape and reshape home economics as a field of study has been confined to a select group of individuals and they have changed the course of home economics to an extent beyond that of a reasonable influence (Brown, 1993, pp. 482–483). This becomes more important for home economics in the Australian context in terms of a cargo cult mentality, and is further reinforced by the ongoing and continuous struggle for legitimacy by those in authority outside the field.

The uncritical adoption of off-shore developments in the field of home economics is perhaps most strongly recognized when tracing the history of the field in Australia, and will be addressed within the framework of the third theme — the ongoing and continuous struggle for legitimation.

Struggling for Legitimation

One way of understanding the history of home economics is as a struggle for legitimation. Home economics has a history of attempting to conform to norms imposed by others, seeking validity and recognition for itself as a valued and valuable field of knowledge. Critics accuse home economics researchers and teachers of having a 'survivalist mindset' in their struggle to legitimize their field (Maidment, 1990), and that this has led to a lack of substantive theory development and a tendency to change at the slightest criticism of the field of study, criticisms which are usually based on perceptions, rather than the 'reality' of the practices of the field. Home economics is not alone in this trend. As Maidment (1990) explains, we are all caught up in such struggles because we are all seeking legitimacy, and that "all institutions in society, no matter how powerful, obtain their legitimacy from the perceptions of people" (p. 47). Again, Brown (1993) has identified this struggle for legitimation as a grievance held by many home economists at an international level.

Dominant perceptions about the nature of home economics, and therefore its legitimacy, are generated out of a range of practices, not least of which are the historical origins of the field. For home economics, these origins have been very much about women's work and the roles of women in society, as I have described previously, and home economics is very much a collage of influences, developed over time, and reactant to international changes in the field, including ongoing desire for recognition as a high status curriculum choice.

For example, contemporary home economics as a school curriculum offering in Queensland has been cultivated from two major influences — British and American. The British influence has been strong because of the tendency to adopt British customs and systems into colonial Australia. The first subject linked to 'home economics' is domestic economy and this was based on the British equivalent and introduced into the Queensland curriculum in 1881 (Logan, 1981). The British influence focused on the need to train women in the scientific theory and practice of skills, which were modified for homemaking in the young, pioneering country of Australia. These early home economics subjects were known by such names as domestic economy (1881), domestic science (1920), home science (1934), home craft (1964) and home management (1964). These were unashamedly designed to prepare women for life roles through the construction of desirable feminine identities in the home and workplace (Eyre, 1989; Brown, 1988a; Badir, 1990; Logan, 1981; Pendergast, 1991). Such conventional stereotyping was achieved by educating women in knowledge that was selected — generally by males in powerful positions in the education sector — as appropriate for these roles. Several critics have acknowledged the strong role of home economics teachers in perpetuating social norms (Thorne, 1980).

The context within which 'home economics' emerged as a field of study as influenced by America is described in the following text, presented in the *From Parlor to Politics and Beyond* exhibition at the Smithsonian National Museum of American History in Washington D.C. The permanent exhibition documents the emergence and importance of home economics in America, making visible the social justice agendas that have been foundational and persistent in the field of study since its inception. The statement reproduced here at length also identifies the political shift and limitations that have resulted from attempts to legitimate home economics through modernist approaches:

> [B]etween 1890 and 1925, women developed a powerful political language and imagery, applying the values of home and family to public life. While women's political culture empowered them at this period and served as a bridge from the private to the public sphere, it also set patterns and boundaries for women's political participation that have continued to the present.

> Many problems faced by these women have re-emerged in our own time with a new and demanding urgency: waves of new immigration, homelessness, racial divisions, threats to the environment, substance abuse and addiction, affordable health care, the well-being of our homes and families, questions about women's roles, and world peace.

Can the political language and imagery developed by women at the turn of the 20th century be adapted to today's politics and empower women once more with a new immediacy? Or will women create a powerful new political culture — one that incorporates values of home and family but transcends old boundaries to reach full political partnership and equity with men? (Smithsonian National Museum of American History, 1997).

Badir (1990) argues that it is the failure of the Australian education sector to adopt the American reforms earlier which has led to the current problems of the field, the lingering perceptions of 'cooking and sewing' from the British model being the Achilles heel of home economics as a set of Australian educational practices. The struggle to push beyond this folkloric perception and so achieve legitimation has been ongoing and continues today, both as a struggle over content to be delivered to the minds of students, and as a struggle for better positioning near the centre of the politics of school knowledge.

Home economics struggle for legitimation is not unique. As Madeleine Grumet (1988) explains, the struggle for legitimation is to be expected in all Western models of schooling given that education is dominated by male experience, ignoring women's lived experience as trivial. She argues that education has been distilled into an economic system that purposely ignores "experiences of family life, of bearing, delivering and nurturing children" (1988, p. xv) as they have no economic value. Where the struggle for legitimation is caught within this mode of rationality, home economics will always be relegated to the margins of what is considered to be valued and valuable knowledge and process. In order to refuse closure of this sort, Grumet (1988) urges the shift to a 'middle way' that challenges the rationale of such a construction, and so reinforces the very dichotomies and categorizations that invariably produce marginalities.

In seeking legitimation within the existing structures — for example the ongoing change in focus, terminology, purpose, content and so on — home economists have failed to understand the complicity of home economics re-form with the very rationality that they have struggled against.

Problematizing of Home Economics Re/form

The literature reveals that much of the re/form which home economics has been continuously involved in has been framed within the very politics from which it is seeking to escape. One of the ways this has been made possible is through the practice of 'naming' as a language game. The use of terminology, and in particular, changes to the name of the field reflect what is currently fashionable in language as established by the order of power/knowledge which prevails as a 'regime of truth' at any one time. In his book, *The Archaeology of Knowledge*, Michel Foucault (1972) presents a methodological inquiry into knowledge, history and discourse and self-criticism. In particular, he articulates knowledge as "an area between opinion and scientific knowledge, and it was embodied not only in theoretical texts or experimental instruments, but in a whole body of practices and institutions". From this emerged 'truths' relevant to the time. Home economics in Queensland, for example, has been known variously as domestic economy, domestic science, home management, home economics, human ecology and now, family and consumer studies, but none of these names are 'solutions' to the 'problem' of home economics — they all come with new problems of legitimation attached. Brown and Baldwin (1995, p. 29) acknowledge this implicitly, arguing that such change reflects a lack of rational professional clarity, which results in:

> limited understanding, distorted communication within the profession, and inability to help others examine their ideas. Persuasion is not rational but irrational: it takes on qualities of force, manipulation, contempt for others, and dogmatism. Theories of meaning would go beyond intelligibility of language to understand different forms of validity claims and how each is validated.

Midgley (1989) also argues that the name change/language issue in home economics demonstrates a lack of serious learning about society. However, both writers possibly miss the importance of such constant name changes as well. Language games are serious and have real effects on the work of those who must teach and learn out of the reconstituted disciplinary area.

A study into how professionals in the field perceive the function of the profession's name and the name 'Home Economics' was undertaken by Shipley (1989). The study reveals some interesting findings, and demonstrates the confusion that exists about language and naming in the field. Shipley's extensive survey (there were 561 respondents in the survey) of American university students and academics revealed that the functions of name identified by respondents were to: 'readily identify what professionals do'; 'represent the areas of study in the Department'; and to 'describe the uniqueness and diversity of our field'. The name home economics was most frequently chosen as the preferred name, however, the majority of the respondents chose one of the other twelve names incorporated in the study as the most preferred. The twelve names listed in their order of preference are:

1. Home Economics;
2. Human Resources and Family Studies;
3. Human Resources and Consumer Services;
4. Family and Consumer Resources;
5. Family Resources and Consumer Services;
6. Family Studies and Consumer Services;
7. Human Resources;
8. Consumer and Family Resources Education;
9. Human Ecology and Resources;
10. Family Resources, Consumer Services, Nutrition and Education;
11. Family Resources, Human Services and Education;
12. Human Ecology;
13. Child and Family, Food and Nutrition, and Home Economics Studies (Shipley, 1989, p. 23).

As concluded in the study, the result indicates a "lack on consensus among those within the field of home economics about their professional name" (Shipley, 1989, p. 23). This can be read as both a strength and a weakness — as an indication that fixity does not exist — that room exists for movement, play, fluidity, as well as a sign of 'unresolvedness' (weakness) and loss of common purpose (Brown, 1993).

More recently, international home economists have changed their name to 'Family and Consumer Science' or 'Family and Consumer Studies', privileging the 'family' component, and so insisting on the wellbeing of individuals and families as the core. This change is in direct response to the positive change in acceptability of the term 'family' which emerged from the International Year of the Family in 1994. This is an example of the way home economists perform language games, seeking to legitimate the field by the use of socially fashionable terminology. Of course home economists are not the only profession to use such tactics. Yet, it could be argued that other fields such as mathematics and science have not been compelled to play such games so often with so much at stake.

The historical origins of the subject, with concomitant language issues, serve as just one example of how home economics remains 'unfinished' — with all the possibilities and problems this entails, including its complicity with the politics it struggles against. Yet home economics has been described as problematic for more reasons than this. Henry (1989), for example, identified seven factors which encompass the problematic nature of home economics: historical context; various interpretations; low status; practical nature; gender bias; values position; and relevance. Building on this, I added (Pendergast, 1991, 1992, 1995a, 1995b) several other factors: theory-versus-practice dichotomies; research void; name and terminology perceptions; and political non-involvement, along with the argument that these are symptoms rather than problems. Siedle (1993) also identified many of these 'problems' in developing a strategic plan for the advocacy of home economics on behalf of the national professional association for home economics in Australia. However, it is not these factors that are the problems of the field per se. Rather, these are the manifestations of a more encompassing, all-consuming problem — the location of home economics and home economists within a broader field of education, health, business, industry and consumer-related knowledge. While home economics is neither static nor 'condemned' to a reactive role within this order of power/knowledge, it experiences more repression than invitations to lead in such an order. Thus home economics continues to be depicted, and to depict itself, as a marginal site of knowledge production.

What is to be Learned?

What is to be learned in home economics? Certainly, much research criticizes the knowledge of home economics. Perhaps the most vociferous critic with regard to the educational value of home economics for students and what is to be learned is Dena Attar (1990). Attar's publication *Wasting girls' time: The history and politics of home economics* contains a scathing commentary on the contribution of home economics education within the British education system. She argues that home economics fails to offer a legitimate field of study and reinforces the marginalization of women in society through the subject matter selected. The book sent shock waves around home economics professionals' world wide, and these were felt particularly strongly in Australia, due to the origins of the field being closely aligned to the British model. Local researchers took up the comments and have used many of the criticisms to consider what is to be learned in the subject.

Within the Queensland context, Patricia Eiby (1989) undertook research to determine the potential value to students from the study of home economics. She compared differences between students who had studied home economics and those who had not, in terms of students' perceptions of their competencies in life skills. Through the use of statistical analysis, Eiby argued that home economics students have enhanced perceptions of their abilities related to life skills, compared with students with no home economics education. Of course, this is a classic example of the circular logic of escaping marginalization through research that uses as its referent another marginal area — that is — life skills.

A further study of home economics education in Queensland was commissioned and undertaken by the Board of Senior Secondary School Studies in readiness for a revision of the Senior Syllabus in Home Economics (BSSSS, 1989). The survey was administered to all senior high schools in Queensland (285) with a 61.8% (176) response rate. This research included data from many of the stakeholders of home economics education, including male home economics students, female home economics students, home economics teachers, principals and guidance officers. The research provided a comprehensive and often contradictory version of the vocational and other benefits of the subject, including the reasons for choosing it, how the subject has measured up to expectations, strengths and weaknesses, and so on. The findings of the survey, as documented by Pendergast (1991), revealed that the main reason students selected home economics was for the practical skills component, which are perceived to be an important contribution to their future life roles. For girls, it was indicated that this was in readiness for unpaid work, while for boys, paid work was emphasized (for example becoming a chef). However, after participating in the subject, students considered there was inadequate time to develop the skills they desired and thus the common recommendation for improving the subject was the removal of some of the 'theoretical' components to be replaced with more 'practical' skills. This suggestion was also supported by home economics teachers. However, it was noted that such a shift would strongly reinforce the stereotypical images of the subject as 'cooking and sewing', which in the context of the feminization of the subject reinforced its negative image and low status. Here again is manifested another problem of circularity where the solution gives birth to the problem.

When compared with other subjects, it was suggested in this same study that home economics was perceived by non-home economists to have very low status and value. Recommendations for addressing this concern included emphasizing career opportunities and encouraging a greater number of males to become home economics teachers in order to act as positive role models for male students. The flow on from this was seen to be that boys be encouraged to study the subject, and this would lead to an enhancement of the image and the status of the subject. This is an example of what can be referred to as a 'circular' legitimisation strategy.

Further, the image of 'cooking and sewing' and the concern over the name of the subject and the use of other terminology uniquely defined for use in home economics, led respondents to the conclusion that there were unresolved gender bias issues in the field. Comments across the spectrum of respondents revealed a range of opinions on the suitability of the subject for males and females, as well as the practicality of encouraging males into the field. For example, concerns were raised about the lack of male teachers and male-oriented teaching resources. There were comments by male students that suggested they saw themselves as pioneer-like, challenged into engaging in a subject where females are preparing for their future domestic roles. Recommendations included the de-feminizing and masculinizing of the subject to make it inclusive of both male and female students. Moreover, strong recommendations were made by some to remove it from the school curriculum. The predominant theme throughout the discussions seemed to be that home economics remained too gender-specific, catering too exclusively for females.

A similar study by Jones (1994) attempted to provide an account of what was happening in home economics in the secondary curriculum across Australia. Over one thousand respondents — home economics teachers, students, parents, principals and representatives of school curriculum committees — were surveyed about the value, roles, purpose, curriculum and contribution of home economics. Of two hundred and fifty three (253) parent respondents, the key terms essential, necessary, important, fundamental, vital, invaluable, emerged to describe the knowledge and skills parents see home economics providing. From students' points of view, the most frequently cited reasons given for valuing study in home economics were that it was enjoyable, interesting, exciting, challenging, relevant, and useful. Furthermore, students said they found it less stressful than other subjects because of the way it was being conducted, while not being a bludge (Jones, 1995). Some reasons students gave for not choosing to study home economics included that: it did not fit their study program; it had already taught them enough in previous years; it did not fit into their career path; it was common sense; and that it was stereotyped by boys as 'girl's stuff' (Jones, 1994).

Home economics teachers were asked to comment on the future directions for home economics. A summary of the directions most frequently advocated included: the maintenance of a survival/life skills approach; to ensure the practical does not become subservient to the theory; to become vocationally oriented, particularly in hospitality, tourism and child care work; and to move the focus of study from the home to the wider world of industry and commerce (Jones, 1994, p. 46). As an outcome of this extensive project, Jones (1994, p. 54) proposed three possibilities for the future directions of home economics in Australia. These are:

- possibilities lie in recalling that home economics has its roots in concern for the vulnerable in society, including the young and the elderly, the poor and the dispossessed, the neglected, and — above all — women;

- possibilities lie in recalling home economics has a history of interest in the education of women; and

- possibilities lie in recalling the reconceptualization of home economics in terms of critical social science.

These possibilities begin to make the shift to the sixth theme evident across the research literature, that is, the emergence of social justice agendas for home economics.

Social Justice Agendas and Home Economics

Social justice issues have increasingly found their way on to the education agendas of the 1980s and 1990s. In particular, girls increasingly became the focus of educational equity policies and initiatives with various projects conducted, for example the *Project of National Significance in the Education of Girls*, funded by the Department of Employment, Education and Training. In this project, Smit (1991) examined the potential of the home economics curriculum for broadening girls' post-school options. Home economics was selected for investigation because of the existence of gender issues associated with the curriculum area that had not previously been the focus of gender work. The most significant finding of the project was that home economics can improve girls' post-school options. Drawing on this data, Kenway (1993) explored the notion of home economics as an inclusive curriculum, focusing on the possible contribution of home economics to the education of males and females, in addition to its role in enhancing girls' futures. Kenway emphasised a need for demythologising patriarchally approved structures of society, and suggested there was a need to undertake this challenge through the development of strategies to revalue traditionally undervalued outcomes (Kenway, 1993).

Further research into a reconstituted home economics inclusive of a social justice agenda was undertaken by Margaret Henry (1989, 1991, 1995), who investigated the many interpretations of home economics by applying as a conceptual foundation Habermas's Theory of Cognitive Interests. This critical framework was utilized in order to determine how home economics could be interpreted from a technical, practical or an emancipatory orientation, and how particular approaches to the field could transfer it to the more desirable 'emancipatory' approach, reflecting a shift to social justice agendas. Henry's (1995) doctoral dissertation proposes a possible definition of 'well-being' — which is a descriptor commonly used in relation to home economics. In this work, two theoretical positions about well-being were merged — that of critical theorists (and particularly Jurgen Habermas) and that of feminists. The two theoretical positions were conflated in an attempt to "establish a definition for well-being that might provide a way forward for the latter part of the twentieth century" (Henry, 1995, p. 2). This led Henry to argue that home economics as a field of study can facilitate emancipatory education and thereby fulfill social justice agendas.

Similarly, social justice imperatives are evident in research by Burke and Pendergast (1996). We report on current thinking and attitudes of home economics tertiary students, secondary home economics teachers and graduate home economists in industry towards the home economics profession and the professional bodies that represent it. Findings of this research, based on focus group methods, indicated several major themes regarding the nature, purpose and direction of home economics in terms of relevance and application, diversity, and the need for greater professionalism. With regard to relevance and application, it was found that home economics has a high degree of relevance for all due to its focus on daily living and well being. The study of home economics was seen to develop knowledge, skills and processes that are transferable from paid to unpaid work settings. With regard to the significance of the diversity of the field, it was found that the strengths and weaknesses of the field of home economics are its diversity, which provides both difficulties and opportunities. Home economics graduates are seen as superior because of their diversity of knowledge and skills, communicative confidence and skills, scientific knowledge, process and literacy. In the final theme, that of the need for greater professionalism, four major issues were mapped by Burke and Pendergast. These are:

⌐' Economists need to address areas of inequity in the social order, as well as within the field itself. It was seen as a powerful yet under utilized tool with which to address social justice issues.

⌐' The professionalism of home economics was open to serious questioning, due to the lack of a common philosophical basis for education, and the need for greater commitment to research and higher education.

⌐' There was a need to establish stronger links between home economics education and employment options, and to promote this knowledge.

⌐' The professional bodies representing home economics need a clear, unambiguous and uncluttered goal. They should focus on enhancing the profile, encouraging higher education and professional development, lobbying and maintaining the quality and integrity of home economists (Adapted from Burke & Pendergast, 1996, pp. 19–20).

Again, this research highlights the greater significance, in recent times, of social justice agendas and their relevance to home economics in-as-much as it reads home economics as a site for social production and reproduction of identity, advocating a more overt political role for home economics.

Initial and Tentative 'Experimentations' with Post Theorizing

There is a slow emergence of theorizing and research in and about home economics which steps beyond the confines of positivist and critical conceptual frameworks. This theorizing offers new perspectives and directions for the field. To date, little of this work has occurred in Australia. However, its impact is beginning to be felt at the local level.

There is some research that has attempted to step beyond the essentialist approaches. My own work (Pendergast, 1991, 1992, 1995a,b) investigated the relationship between language, social institutions and individual consciousness, and how this was reflected in subject positions adopted by home economics educators in secondary and tertiary education sectors. This deconstruction of home economics utilized poststructural theory presented from a feminist perspective (e.g. Weedon, 1987). The research integrated a number of separate studies. The major study drew upon over one thousand pages of transcript from a conference of over one hundred home economics educators debating the future of the subject in secondary schools. It also analyzed three of the most commonly used textbooks in Queensland schools, along with transcripts from a number of audio taped home economics classes, a survey to all undergraduate students studying tertiary home economics in Queensland, and focus group discussions with undergraduate students, to provide a reading of home economics as a cultural site. This study searched for specific forms of discourse that framed pedagogy, and these were broadly categorized as subject positions — with three distinct positions being located. These were characterized by the descriptors: traditional; validator; and gender magnanimous. This project argued both a critical point (that home economics was overly dependent on appropriating masculinity) and at the same time celebrated home economics as a women's field of knowledge. These views reflect the first two in the three-tier approach to feminist struggle as conceptualised by Davies (1989). This approach employs the principles of Kristeva and Moi, and Davies (1989) has argued the importance of a three-tiered approach to understanding the usefulness and potential of feminist theory. In a sense, this three-tiered approach can also be used to represent the historical evolution of feminism in three overlapping generations:

- the fight for equal access to the male symbolic order;
- the rejection of the male symbolic order and the celebration of femininity;
- the rejection of the male/female duality.

The first tier aims at providing females with equal access to the male symbolic order that is characteristic of patriarchal society. It does not question the existence of male female duality, but assumes the legitimacy of its existence. In this way, women are expected to become empowered through the adoption of masculine identities. The second tier offers a route whereby women celebrate femaleness and reject maleness. As in the first tier, this option assumes the existence of patriarchal society that maintains the social order of gender, reinforcing the male/female dichotomy of essential difference. The third tier presents a strategy that does not have the patriarchal principle of male female duality central to its formulation. It rejects the assumption that there is an essential difference between men and women that cannot be accounted for through discursive and textual practices through which the constructs 'male' and 'female' are established and maintained as fundamental structures of society.

After locating the subjectivities argued as emergent in the discourses, the impact of such discourses on the marginalised position of home economics within patriarchal society were considered. This research highlighted the need for a comprehensive deconstruction and subsequent reconstruction of the subject — in order to retain a place in the education of students. According to this approach, it is only through rejection of male/female duality, or in Davies (1989) terms, a shift to the third tier of feminist thought, that advocacy strategies become genuinely enabling.

Two Canadian researchers who have challenged the confines of essentialist thinking in home economics are Peterat and Khamasi (1995). Working together, they have utilized what they describe as 'postmodern sensibilities' (1995, p. 5) in order to critically read philosophically divergent home economics curricula in Canadian provinces. The purpose of their work is to raise questions about the ways home economists think of home economics curriculum in postmodern times, and questions the form and place of curriculum documents. The outcome of their work is summarized in the following statement, where they urge a change to the way home economists develop their curriculum:

> [W]e identify greater urgencies in strengthening home economics curricula than a unified conceptualization, and suggest re-readings of perennial problems which have paralyzed home economics practices in recent years. Thus, we propose that disarray of curricula may hold many positives in the postmodern time (Peterat & Khamasi, 1995, p. 4).

This perspective insists on the values of postmodernism as a mode of thought, one that reinforces the notions of global plurality of competing subcultures where no one ideology or episteme dominates (Slattery, 1995). As Doll (1993) describes this imperative to postmodernism, it is mobilized by a desire to promote the notion of a multifaceted matrix to be explored, rather than a linear trajectory nor as a course to be run. Brown (1993) has alluded to this in her understanding of one of home economics' grievances, noting reluctance on the part of many professionals to be publicly self-reflective about their own concepts and beliefs together with the assumption that any self-interpretation of home economics is final.

Eyre (1991) has also called attention to the absences, the silences, the hegemonic values contained in the curriculum in Canada, describing home economics curricula as "sexist, classist, racist and heterosexist" (p. 103). In response to this, Peterat (1993) and Smith (1993, 1995) have advocated a 'global perspective' for home economics education, and have undertaken some action research projects that document the effectiveness of such an approach. Smith (1993, p. 1) explains that global education acknowledges the increasingly interconnected, interrelated, global nature of the world we live in and encourages learners to:

> ...know the relationship between knowledge and power, know the interdependent, interconnected and interrelated nature of the world and their place in it, know their histories and experiences matter and that the world is not reducible to knowledge, and know what they say and do can change the world. They see themselves in the global interdependent world, in relation with the world, where harmony and stewardship are essential for survival.

From the action research project, Peterat (1993) noted that the most frequently recommended student activity for achieving a global education learning was research. She argued that home economics global education could be distinguished from other discipline global studies by its focus on "families and individuals in understanding implications and consequences of larger realities and policies; and in viewing families as a locus for action within families and in the larger society" (Peterat, 1993, p. 6). The approach taken by this research to developing this global curriculum was described as collaborative. The major issues argued potentially to threaten its effectiveness were the political effects of dominant ideologies such as patriarchy, individualism and capitalism that were held to work against the key values of global education such as equity, food security and fair resource distribution (Smith, 1995). Interestingly, this reflects another of Brown's (1993) 'grievances', namely the apolitical orientation of members of the profession. Brown argues that home economists should become politically informed and active, both involved actively in politics and utilizing informed politics in the classroom (1993, pp. 483–484).

The Difficult Relationship of Feminism and Home Economics

As constantly highlighted in this chapter, the ongoing concerns of home economics are embedded in the historical origins of the field. The origins of this field link it initially with the preparation of women as domestic servants and later as homemakers. However, the woman considered to be the founder of home economics, Ellen Richards, was a critic of the early feminist movement, and expounded an antipathy to feminism (Ehrenreich & English, 1978). Regardless of this perspective, almost all home economics practitioners are female, with a significantly higher ratio of females choosing to study in the area beyond compulsory years. As a result, the field of home economics is gendered in a way that appears fundamental and foundational, and in ways that militate against achieving high status as a site of Western knowledge production.

The importance of adopting a feminist stance for interrogating the field seems undeniable, and increasingly theorists in home economics are adopting such a perspective (Peterat, 1990). Support for this is easily found in the wider academic community. For example, Greene suggests that:

> [W]omen's lives have far too seldom been used as starting points for research; and to use them as a basis for criticism of certain dominant knowledge claims usually oriented to the lives of men might well correct a number of distortions and partialities of focus (Greene, 1994, p. 453).

Grumet (1995, p. 36) has explored the relationship of education and reproduction to build "discursive bridges between home, where we were children and raise our own children, and school, where we work with other people's children". The rationale for this, as previously outlined in this chapter, is that education is structured around men's experience, ignoring women's experience as a legitimate base (Grumet, 1988). Grumet explores the maternal role of teaching and looks to the contradictions between reproduction and patterns of gender identity as a space for exploration and transformation.

However, the relationship between home economics theory and research and feminist theory and research is not an easy one with the relation between the two "during the past two decades at times angry and antagonistic" (Peterat, 1990, p. 33). In an address to the Fourth Women and Labour Conference held in Brisbane, Pixley (1984) argued that through the study of home economics, traditional stereotypes will be reinforced. She stated that "the old message will be reinforced, woman's place is in the home, ensuring that their families are 'eating right' whilst they 'put a smile in their voices', under the tutelage of a home economist" (Pixley, 1984, p. 427). For Pixley, clearly an undesirable positioning of woman against woman! On the other hand, there are some who argue that home economics has always been feminist in its conceptions, but that mainstream feminists have been reluctant to ally themselves with the field because of their naiveté about it, based upon stereotypical perceptions. For example, Thompson (1997, p. 10) argues that:

> ...feminists might find it hard to accept that home economics poses a frontal challenge to the hegemony of patriarchal thought, social organisation, and control mechanisms from a family perspective. Yet it does.

There have been few attempts by (non-home economist) feminist historians and philosophers to explore this idea more fully. Thompson (1997, p. 11) explains that it 'has fallen outside' their interests because home economics "stands in its own historical space as a coherent epistemological and ethical system that emphasises praxis". However, there are several internationally prominent home economists who have contributed to a growing feminist critique of home economics including Badir, Thompson, Peterat, Pendergast and more recently Henry. In particular Thompson (1995b), through what she describes as bringing home economics and feminism into dialogical relation, has the following view:

> [A]s a feminist and a home economist, I find feminist theory helpful in explaining our present position. Our devalued, privatised, invisible world, the "oikos" became a private sphere. The very thing that has happened to women in general has happened to home economists particularly, and even to home economics as a profession (Thompson, 1988, p. 11).

This view arises out of her work (Thompson, 1986, 1988, 1990, 1991, 1992a, 1992b, 1993a, 1993b, 1995a, 1995b) developed and articulated, since 1985, in which she explains the devaluing of home economics in society. She identifies two spheres in society known as the Hestian and the Hermian paradigms. This theory emerges from Greek mythology, and has as an assumption the ordering of society as Hestian — the center of the home or the private sphere linked to women; and Hermian — the work or center of public life linked to men. Thompson argues that because home economics is associated with the Hestian sphere it is devalued in society — the hermian public sphere is the world while the hestian private world is something else, the 'other'. The model therefore proposes a duality of systems within which, inscribed by patriarchy, males and females have been differentially valued and empowered (1995a).

Thompson has come in for some strong criticism for reinforcing dualities, and for oversimplification of contemporary society (Brown & Baldwin, 1995) by insisting on the comparison with ancient Greek society that is acknowledged as being comprised of more distinct public and private spheres than contemporary societies. By way of addressing such criticism, Thompson has recently reconceptualized her theoretical model (see Thompson, 1995a, 1995b), suggesting it be utilized as a perspective that "goes beyond gender to make activity in both domains equally respected and recognized as equally valuable for society" (Thompson, 1995b, p. 55). The problem with such an approach remains that any binary formulation such as private/public or hestian/hermian, must privilege one sphere or domain, whatever the intention to 'balance' them. Nevertheless, Thompsons's work goes further than any other in highlighting some ways in which feminism offers an empathic reading of home economics.

Latterly, Thompson has urged that a way forward for home economics research is through reflexivity, defined for Thompson's purpose by Wilkinson (1988, p. 493) as "disciplined self-reflection". Lather goes further in unpacking reflexivity explaining it is "thinking about the things we think we can't think without" (McWilliam, Lather & Morgan, 1997: video segment). This 'reflexive home economist' position is necessary because "Home economics must be reconciled in some way with women's history, feminist history, the history of science, and the history of education" (Thompson, 1997, p. 11).

Badir (1990, p. 98) was one of the first internationally recognized home economists to challenge home economics to consider the links between home economics and feminism. She lists five issues of feminist relevance which she believes home economists must deal with. They are that:

- home economics is female intensive;
- home economics is embedded in the context of the family;
- home economics is seen as a suitable "science" for women;
- home economics is losing ground;
- home economics has been accused, by feminists, of holding women back.

Each of these issues presents a challenge to home economics as a subject, and home economists as practitioners, but there are few willing to deal with the enormity of the challenges this raises. One of the disincentives is a lack of understanding of the many possible interpretations and approaches to feminism. Given that the breadth of feminist work is unknown to many, feminism is seen as an essential position, and a threatening one. Particularly threatening is the perception that adopting feminist values means the individual is regarded as being a lesbian, with lesbian in turn incorporating dysfunctional 'non-feminine' values and characterizations.

Contrary to this media-inspired perception of 'essentialized' feminism, there are many different forms of feminist politics based on the various possible perceptions of relations between men and women. These range from socialist to separatist and to Marxist, to liberal and humanist, and to poststructural and eco-feminist. Each form of feminism subscribes to differing views of the nature of power and social relationships existing between the sexes, and consequently has different goals, methodologies, values and theories, so that, while the purpose or goal of feminism, as explained by Weedon (1987, p. 1) is "...a politics directed at changing existing power relations between women and men in society", this does not collapse into a 'one size fits all' position.

It is important that the links between home economics, feminism, and also the family, are not regarded as trivial (Peterat, 1990), particularly if home economists accept the idea that "(t)he central focus of home economics education is the wellbeing of families and individuals in their everyday activities" (Curriculum Corporation, 1996, p. 3). Given the historical origins of the field of study and its legacy about the 'appropriate' preparation of women for their future life roles within patriarchal society (Apelt, 1989; Badir, 1990; Bielski, 1987; Logan, 1981; Meighan, 1981; Pendergast, 1991; Reiger, 1990) as well as its focus on optimizing the wellbeing of individuals and families, home economics remains ripe for criticism from feminists. Indeed, as Smit argues:

> [W]ithout doubt, one of the greatest challenges to home economists is that being raised by the women's movement ...At the centre of the antagonism between both feminists and home economists appears to be the issue of the "family" (Smit, 1991, p. 11).

'Family' is an issue for feminists given that it can be used to 'depoliticise' broad social movements and to stereotype 'appropriate' ways of conducting social life. For example, one of the points of discussion that is often raised is that of women and work, both paid and unpaid. Some feminists have argued that:

> ...women today are still largely socialised in a manner that sees housework and associated family responsibilities as principally a female area. Accordingly, the majority of Australian women conform to a lifestyle that involves prolonged periods at home (Draper, 1989, p. 85).

For this and other reasons feminists have been critical of 'family' as a discursively organized site of social production. For many feminists the family may represent the most oppressive force of patriarchy, designed by men to keep women powerless. For some, the family represents the power difference between men and women, with sometimes physical, social and economic dependence of women on men. For some critics, the family develops learned helplessness and a dependency in otherwise independent, functional individuals (Pendergast, 1996b).

The links between the purpose of home economics (i.e. to optimise the wellbeing of individuals and families) and the questions feminism raises about families, opens many challenges for home economics theorists. It can be seen through the emerging research that feminist awareness of issues around gender and social justice and the social construction of knowledge has been a catalyst for more reflective and critical research into home economics (Apelt, 1989; Badir, 1990; Thompson, 1988). In recent work, Thompson (1997, p. 10) proposes that the work of Offen (1988) may "hold the key to reconciling home economics and feminism". Thompson explains how she believes the approach suggested by Offen (1988) may be useful, linking this with home economics:

> [Offen] believes we must take the initiative to reshape the world to our own purposes by 're-thinking' the male dominated family and its politics in a way that incorporates, rather than excludes, the sociopolitical aspects of women's experience. She challenges feminists to reappropriate the relational path of our intellectual heritage. When they do, they must sooner or later refer to the work of home economists, past and present...In reclaiming power of difference, they will see home economics in a new light and weave its history — without dissembling, distorting or redefining it — into the total tapestry of women's history to disclose its emancipatory, liberatory feminist potential (Thompson, 1997, p. 10).

However, to date, the epistemologies that feminists have brought to bear in home economics research have relied upon a particular sort of dialectical reading that inevitably locates home economics as symptomatic of 'the problem of patriarchy'. This approach reinforces those binary formulations that see the private world as 'home' and the domain of women, with family the responsibility of women. In this way, home economics has nowhere to shift to, but remains trivialized, condemned forever to rail against the rationality of patriarchy. The theoretical tools for reconstituting home economics as pedagogy of possibility have proved to be inadequate to push beyond this conundrum.

The Need for a Shift in the 'Body' of Home Economics Research

Almost all of the home economics research works within the parameters of essentialism with a modernist philosophy at their core, and this view is supported by other writers in the field as indeed being the trend. The need to shift beyond this restrictive lens to avoid the trap of conspiracy theories of patriarchy that is evident in the work of others underpins the rationale for the epistemological shift made in this book.

As is evident from this chapter, many of the trends, grievances, concerns — whatever one chooses to call these — about home economics, emerge from its origins and purpose as a field for the study of the private domain with a focus on 'women's work' in the unpaid sphere of the home. It is located in the least desirable of the dualities presented within modernist frameworks and understandings. Feminist attempts at addressing the concerns have been unable to step beyond these limitations because the sort of feminist theorizing being brought to bear on research in home economics to date utilizes conceptual tools which provide essential readings of 'woman' as other. Such theorizing tends to 'fix' knowledge and bodies by using the essentialist categories of gender (male/female) and of the materiality of gender. Humanist accounts of pedagogy in the classroom fail to speak sufficiently about the sexed body of the teacher and learner and how notions of what is 'normal' are performed out of these bodies in ways that are not simply 'outside' the curriculum but ARE the curriculum. Thus it ignores almost entirely the embodied nature of the pedagogical work itself. 'Body' is rendered the excess baggage.

It is imperative that home economics research work on behalf of women, for all of the reasons that have been previously documented. However, it is my argument that a shift in the epistemological terrain of the research itself is well overdue, given that feminist research as a modernist project offers nothing new for home economics as a site of knowledge production.

In this chapter I have recounted the key theoretical positions in the field of home economics in Queensland through the identification of eight major trends. In addition, the 'grievances' that Brown (1993) has identified as experienced by home economists, either in their comprehensive sense or part thereof, have been seen to be integral across the trends. Brown's suggestion that these are international grievances certainly appears to be borne out in the home economics literature in Queensland, Australia.

Further Thinking

There are eight themes presented in this chapter as being evident in home economics research:

- home economics research as a small and piecemeal body of work;
- the historical pattern of the uncritical adoption of off-shore developments;
- struggling for legitimation;
- problematising of home economics re-form;
- what is to be learned;
- social justice agendas and home economics;
- initial and tentative 'experimentations' with post theorizing; and
- the difficult relationship of feminism and home economics.

From your own experience with home economics, list examples fitting these categories. Are there any gaps in these themes? Make suggestions for areas that have been neglected, and provide examples to support your views.

The idea of cargo cult is one that has affected Australian home economics significantly. For the context in which you are located, is cargo cult a significant effect? Is your community the producer or recipient of the cargo cult? In what ways has this affected the development of home economics in your region?

One of the problematics of home economics has been the focus on striving to legitimize the field within patriarchal structures. Explain how you understand this to be a problem for the field. How can the profession use the tool of legitimization without being caught by its effects? Provide examples.

The relationship between feminism and home economics has been explored at length in the work of Patricia Thompson. Thompson uses the private/public rephrased as the hestian/hermian duality as the rationale for much of her early thinking. In what way can the profession use this understanding as a starting point, rather than a final point for thought? Does this apply to other subject areas?

Body Subjects — From Modern to Post-modern Concepts of the body

> There is no one truth, says the postmodernist voice. There is no single monological description of physical or human phenomenon. To recognize this is to become awake to the processes of our own sense making in a radically different way: to question technical and specialized authorities, to engage with intensified awareness in acts of becoming different, acts of redescribing and redefining ourselves and our contacts with the world (Greene, 1994, p. 440).

The need for reconfiguring an approach to studying home economics is championed by Marjorie Brown who is viewed by her contemporaries as the philosophical voice of the profession of home economics. Brown (1993) argues that this field of study and the research and theorizing associated with it has unquestioningly adopted the traditions of modernity, with individualism and empiricism as foundational assumptions and that, as a consequence, the subject has become 'clouded', but not in ways that might be helpful to the pedagogical processes of home economics. Brown (1993) along with Grundy and Henry (1995), urges home economists to step beyond modernist conceptions and to re-think thinking about home economics. In support of this plea, McWilliam (1993, pp. 203–204) insists that it is important for educationalists more broadly that "potentially transformative education research be forthcoming to challenge traditional research practices" as they are applied to pedagogical analysis and this includes "more methodological 'risks', more eclectic research models". The theoretical terrain mapped here responds to such a challenge.

In this chapter I develop an understanding of the thinking about human 'being' which is used to inform the non-traditional approach taken in this book. I trace the shift from modernist to post-modernist thinking in terms of changing conceptions of the body from 'humanist' to 'posthumanist'. This shift signals the exhaustion of Enlightenment epistemologies and their theorizing of pedagogical phenomena. It is not that such approaches have not built up a useful share of knowledge about pedagogical processes; it is simply that 'new sense' needs to be made of such processes, and this is only made possible through new ways of thinking about the nature of phenomena under study. It is how a posthumanist conception of 'body' can be used to interrogate the home economics teacher as a 'body of knowledge' which is of interest. This allows 'materiality' of teaching of pedagogy itself to be brought forward for scrutiny as something integral to, not separate from, home economics curriculum.

The Disappearing Body — A Humanist Perspective

Modernity is recognised historically as emerging in the aftermath of the revolutions from about the seventeenth century onwards (Heller, 1990). It is a period of Enlightenment with a "vision of a peaceful world governed by scientifically oriented sweet reasonableness" (Agassi, 1992, p. 214). According to Sztompka (1993, pp. 71–3), there are some general features which typify modernity. These are: individualism — the belief in emancipated individuals who are self-determining and responsible for their success and failures; differentiation — the advent of a growing number of specialised, narrowly defined features in for example, employment; rationality — the notion of the bureaucracy as central to organisation, with science in a privileged location; economizm — the domination of social life by the economy; and expansion — the notion of progress and a world view. As such, modernity is the era of essentialist thought typified by a grand or metanarrative. Further, the Latin origin of the word 'modern' is 'modo' which means 'just now' (Appignanesi & Garratt, 1995). Modernity is characterised by research as a secular humanist engagement with the world in which philosophers develop objective science and universal morality and law through a fundamental belief in human rationality. Here, the individual is 'knowable' by applying universal 'truths' (Hatcher, 1993). This 'truth' is formulated in a discourse of binary oppositions such as male/female; mind/body; science/nature; objective/subjective, which inevitably privileges one binary element over the other. In the mind/body duality, 'mind' is the privileged binary, making the 'body' disappear and become the 'Other' to the mind (Vick, 1996) in the same way that critical analyses have made home economics Other to valued school knowledge.

Jenks (1996) explains that modernity has a strong foundation in Enlightenment and emancipation that emerged from a sense of 'progress' underlying the modernist conception. In this way modernist thought:

> ... gave rise to a confident cultural attitude of 'being in control' This was a control based on: the possibility of objective knowledge through rational process; the primacy of centered, communicating selves; and the conviction that difference was reconcilable through analysis and discourse. Such bases ensured that the ensuing attitude was both sustaining and comfortable. This attitude was deeply rooted in the necessity, the viability, and the moral certainty of 'progress' (Jenks, 1996, p. 16).

This notion of 'progress' in modernist thought presumes the inevitability of improvement in the human condition (Gastil, 1993; Lyotard, 1993). In this sense, progress acts as the unifying thread of modernity (Pillow, 1996) through which "...a whole set of cultural configurations, [are] established under modernity's motif of 'progress'" (Jenks, 1996, p. 18).

One of the major forms of intellectualising of the modernist era is structuralism. This is described as "the idea of a system: a complete, self-regulatory entity that adapts to new conditions by transforming its features whilst retaining its systematic structure" (Gibson, 1984, p. 12). The theory of structuralism evolved from the apriori assumption that structures exist in society. According to Gibson (1984) structuralism is a theory and a method which is characterised by six basic idiosyncrasies. The first of these is a sense of 'wholeness' — the notion that it is the large collective, not the smaller parts which is determinate. The second is that 'relationships', not things, are the focus of structuralism. The third is 'decentring the subject', that the subcomponents are products and players of the larger system. The fourth characteristic is 'self-regulation', the notion that the system maintains itself and perpetuates its own survival. The fifth dimension is the 'snapshot' method. This is where a piece of evidence at one time is used to build a picture, in preference to developing a picture over time. The final aspect is 'transformation', the possibility for change. Acclaimed structuralists include Saussure, Piaget, Althusser and Levi-Strauss. The education system and policy making in general have been interrogated as 'rational structures' in modernist, patriarchal society. This theory looks for models which are there and constructs the world through these existing configurations. This approach typifies the way the 'Other' becomes located and understood as 'Othered', and hence dominant paradigms become the hegemonic norm.

In more recent times, structuralists have been censured because they accept common sense assumptions about 'society structure', that is, the approach constructs its object of study by abstracting from the social practice and social context. For example, scientific knowledge constructs the world through structures — lists, equations, formulas, theorems. These structures are given the status of truth and they are considered to be scientifically upheld notions of the truth. Truth regimes work through power and knowledge thereby identifying scientific knowledge as valuable knowledge and expectedly, scientific knowledge is valued as high status wisdom. This in turn reinforces the "structural" approach to knowledge because it can be defined and structured, it is considered to be valuable knowledge. The structuralist approach therefore becomes its own greatest validator and reinforcer (Pendergast, 1996a). The existence of male/female duality is an example of an assumption of difference that works as an underlying principle in defining a structural version of society as 'patriarchal'. This structural naming acts as a regulator for determining appropriate practices for males and females.

A number of feminist writers have argued that this structuralist model is "of doubtful utility" for feminist politics (Fraser, 1992, p. 55) — that there is a need to shift beyond such traditions of modernity. One of the issues for such feminists is that structuralism, when translated into policy, fails to engage with the materiality of its subjects. Pillow (1996) explains, for example, that the field of policy theory, development and analysis can be viewed as the vehicle for achieving the political project of modernism, and thereby leading to 'progress'. This is possible because of faith in modernist claims of a highly rational, conscious mind of a knowing subject who aims to achieve a better world for themselves and others. Pillow suggests that "the political project of modernism is carried out through the construct of the rational, caring, benevolent subject (or state) which situates an 'other' in need of help" (1996, p. 5) She argues this is true of policy, including educational policy, where theorizing through a rationalist perspective entrenched in modernist discourses and practices is the norm. Such practice ignores the bodies for which they are intended. Rather, such policy is concerned with the control, shaping and surveillance of disembodied individuals at a macro level — there is an accepted lack of agency — a disembodied approach — in policy theory. Pillow (1996, p. 8) terms such policy formulation a modernist approach to policy theory, development and analysis using "naturally enlightened norms without bodies".

Humanist Theory and the Mind/body Duality

As outlined in the previous section, the modern era has at the core of its social scientific research a humanist project that holds that human nature has certain essential and stable characteristics. The humanist conception of human 'being' is that of an autonomous individual potentially fully conscious and capable of agency. This is true of 'critical' structuralist conceptual frameworks as well as 'a-political' analyses that work out of personality theories or psychological learning theory of one sort or another. This human condition is evident in everyday life and is guided by the objectivation of the self (Heller, 1990; Eckermann, 1997) and the internalization of social norms that are habitually reflected in social order (Mestrovic, 1993).

Within this humanist framework, the modernist humanist 'personality' is typified by the following 'progressive' traits. They:

- are ready for new experiences, change and innovation;
- are ready to form and hold views on a wide range of issues;
- are oriented towards the present and the future, not the past;
- have efficacy, in particular mastery over the natural environment and control over social problems;
- trust the regularity and predictability of social life;
- have a sense of distributive justice;
- are interested and place value in formal education and schooling; and
- have respect for the dignity of others, including those of inferior status or power (Adapted from Sztompka, 1993, pp. 77, 78).

The resultant metanarrative is one of an autonomous, free-floating (disembodied) individualism to which the researcher can apply universal ethical, social, and rational principles that are intended to be for the good of society and individuals. This conception of the human individual enables social order to be maintained through the acquisition and living out of social norms. In its logic, all social phenomena are available to be analyzed in terms of individuals and their non-human environments (Agassi, 1992).

The failure of this logic to take account of the bodies of human beings has been noted by a range of authors (Brodribb, 1992; Shilling, 1993; Butler, 1993; Grosz, 1994; Pillow, 1996). Pillow (1996, p. 13) explains that such logic frames human beings as 'disembodied' individuals who are:

... unreflexive about their assumptions, disclusive of subjects, and removed from bodies in the sense of ignoring critical considerations of gender, race, sexuality and class issues while at the same time objectifying and subjecting bodies to simplistic discussions of gender, race, sexuality and class.

Further, the humanist perspective reinforces the marginalization of certain groups with respect to other groups, women for example being subordinated to men; blacks beings subordinated to whites; and the reinforcement of dualities which ensure power of one over another.

This humanist understanding informs much of the rationality that underpins the way our society is constructed, including institutional education. Greene (1994, p. 423) for example, suggests that there is more or less "untroubled reliance on the paradigms of mainstream science and the benign consequences that should follow from their use" in the schooling system. Cleo Cherryholmes (1988) too points to some of the common uses of metanarratives in the field of schooling including Bloom's taxonomy (from 1964), and Schwab's paradigm of the practical (from 1972), arguing that such normalizing metanarratives currently form the foundation of major systems and structures within schooling, including assessment systems.

The way the truth about teaching gets 'fixed' by such metanarratives is evidenced in a book edited by Turney (1981) entitled, ironically, *Anatomy of Teaching*. It boasts that it is a comprehensive, up-to-date review of research about teaching and education, incorporating and evaluating Australian and international studies, and drawing upon major educational theories. And so it is, as a modernist picture of teachers and teaching formulated within the modernist epistemologies. As expected, it provides frameworks and structures, flow charts, maps and tables for understanding the vast range of factors relevant to teachers including the contexts, concepts and models, planning, skills, strategies, resources etc of teaching. Working out of process/product research underpinned by personality theory, the book has humanist accounts of teachers at its core. And this is typical of much contemporary educational writing that builds on psychological theories and models of personality, behaviorist or cognitivist theory. The fleshy 'anatomy' of the teacher, however, as the embodied subject of research, is omitted. Nowhere is it made clear that a teacher has been and continues to be 'some body who teaches some body' (Ungar, 1982, p. 82).

The metanarrative teaching-and-learning of educational psychology has functioned to legitimate educational theorising, acting as regulators of educational discourse, maintaining the teaching/

learning binary, and controlling educational objectives (McWilliam, 1996b), thereby acting as an institution of normative coercion (Turner, 1997). Greene (1994, p. 450) argues that it is only recently that such forms of legitimation and control have begun to be challenged by new notions of 'performativity' or views of knowledge conceived as power. This change in epistemological orientation provides an opportunity for new reflectiveness in educational research and theorising.

Home Economics as a Modernist Construct

Literature relevant to home economics research has relied heavily on modernist tools that continue to shape home economics culture as a humanist enterprise. What is of interest for this book is what it is that the humanist project has been *unable* to say about home economics as a pedagogical site, and this focuses attention on pedagogical body subjects as the 'unsaid' of home economics research.

The most recent research in home economics indicates that a shift is being called for, but not enacted. Brown (1993) for example, advocates a shift in research beyond modernist parameters, but fails to do so in her own work, which draws upon Jurgen Habermas' structuralist framework of communicative rationality. Building upon Brown's work, Grundy and Henry (1995) also utilize ideology critique (in particular, Habermas's Theory of Cognitive Interests) as a conceptual framework for the development of a 'critical' theory of home economics. In this work, the three knowledge-constitutive interests of technical, practical and emancipatory interests are applied to various approaches to home economics to "explore grounds on which claims for legitimacy of the subject can be made" (p. 283). However, gaining legitimacy depends on working within the constraints of binary oppositions, a dialectic tradition that moves to fix identities and outcomes. Indeed, Habermas "explicitly divorces" himself from postmodernism, retaining his concern for "rationality, universality, and the likelihood of rational consensus" (Greene, 1994, p. 440; Mestrovic, 1993).

Grundy and Henry (1995) argue that the variety of definitions of home economics represent varying epistemologies which, in turn, represent fundamental orientations towards being human. They go on to urge a move towards the 'higher ground' of emancipatory interests, which is:

> ... concerned with confronting issues of power and domination, and with empowering individuals and groups to act with autonomy and emancipation.

Emancipatory knowledge seeks to break through the hitherto taken-for-grant-ed view of the world and moves towards a freedom which neither the technical nor the practical interest allows (Grundy & Henry, 1995, p. 282).

This approach is supported by Baldwin (1989) who suggests there are three ways in which home economics can become emancipatory: to promote enlightenment; seek to empower students; and have an overall goal of emancipation of those whom it serves. Although this is the most innovative work to date in theoretical research in home economics, this research remains caught within the humanist metanarrative which position the researcher as hero, ideology critique as theoretical savior, and the teacher as actual savior — a redemptive enterprise (Popkewitz, 1997). In the light of what has been argued as a 'humanist' project, this work is very clearly embedded in a vision of a new pedagogical order that is not characterized by an epistemological break with modernist rationality.

In response to the call from Brown (1993) to re-look through postmodernist lenses (and for the reasons indicated as the limitations of the modernist project), the thinking in this book works to locate a space outside the frame of modernist research theory and methods in undertaking educational research in home economics. The research recognizes the need for a shift in epistemology by focusing on the body as privileged in home economics as a pedagogical culture. This is an interesting shift in that the field of home economics is already concerned with the body — in quite explicit ways. The nutrition, dress, management, health and so on of the body — as well as the 'mind' — are recognized as essential areas of attention in order to achieve the accepted purpose of home economics, that is, to optimize the well-being of individuals and families. This demands transcending the modernist dualism of mind/body.

Home economics is not the only area of study seeking to re/member itself (Shapiro, 1994). The general shift towards postmodernist research has, according to Sztompka (1993), resulted from an increasing disenchantment with modernity over recent decades. He suggests there are six (6) key grounds on which modernity has been challenged, all with direct applications to the mind/body duality and the notion of individualism. These are:

- alienation of individuals from work, politics, culture, family etc;

- recognition of humans as individualistic if not controlled by cultural norms;

⌣• decay of community through the loss of individuality;

⌣• birth of ecological consciousness to challenge economic rationalist positions;

⌣• recognition of modernity's production of global inequality and imbalance and forming of dependencies; and

⌣• threat of war and of total destruction of humanity (Adapted from Sztompka, 1993, pp. 79–81).

Other scholars focus their criticisms more particularly on the conduct of research itself. Patti Lather (1991b, p. 21) states that "the essence of the postmodern argument is that dualisms which continue to dominate Western thought are inadequate". Grand narratives and totalizing approaches towards social categorization "(will) always leak" (Hamilton & McWilliam, in press).

For research in the education field, this inadequacy can be represented by the 'disappearing teacher'. So much current research inquires into the learning needs of students and related social justice agendas that the teacher is at risk of becoming a 'no-body' of educational discourse (McWilliam, 1996b; 1997). For instance, McWilliam argues that teachers have been "disembodied by educational jargon" such as that associated with social justice agendas, to the extent where the "quality of the entire 'performance' [of teaching] is assessed by ignoring the utterances and actions of the teacher altogether" (1996b, p. 16). As a consequence, teachers have become 'no/bodies' in the discursive construction of educational practice. In the light of such criticism, the rest of this chapter moves to lay the foundations for an understanding of educational subjects as 'body subjects' — both textual and natural entities engaged in pedagogical events.

The Teacher's Body — A Postmodern Perspective

What makes any theorizing 'post' modern? Jenks (1996) suggests that it was Bell in 1973, and later Touraine in 1984 and 1989, who drew theorists' attention to the change in the "traditional fabric of relations that made up modernity" (p. 16), and that such writers can be argued to have initiated the era of the 'post' modern. The use of the 'post' prefix suggests therefore that postmodernism follows on from modernism, and that there is a direct relationship between each. However, as Bordo (1992) notes, 'post' is a "slippery notion" which cannot be constrained to the linear category of time, but is more a reflection of modernity's "endless infatuation with innovation" (p. 160), as postmodernism both troubles and engages with modernism (Gastil, 1993). In fact, as Henry (1996) makes clear, postmodernism is not anti-modern in its thinking, but is an extension of modernist thought condemned always to engage with the projects of modernity. Jenks (1996) follows this view using the term 'late-modernity' to characterize the shift from the purpose of modernity as being progress and the notion of utopias and grand narratives to a condition of "avoidance, or minimization, of dystopias" (p. 18), a process of "de-traditionalization" (p. 19). This view is supported by Lyotard (1984) who speaks of the death of the metanarrative as representing a decline in collective aspiration and progress and hence a shift from modernity. For him, modernity always contains post-modern moments.

Thus, to define postmodernism is clearly no easy task. Each discipline typically has its own preferred position (Bordo, 1992), a characteristic which contributes to the controversial nature of postmodernist inquiry (Henry, 1996). Further, there is in educational circles, some derision of the term which often inspires controversy. Indeed, Popkewitz (1997b, p. 18) warns that "the word postmodern conjures up strong emotions and images ... as do the names of competing teams in a sports match ...". Richard Rorty (1989) speaks of the 'special resentment' such writers inspire in more orthodox others. For Lyotard, who introduced the concept of postmodernism (Fraser & Nicholson, 1990), it is a condition by which the grand narratives of legitimation are no longer credible. In support of this view, Squier (1995, p. 119) suggests that the dominant feature of postmodernism is its:

> ... challenge to the master narratives of Western metaphysics and philosophy, with their bases in binary oppositions: mind/body; male/female; self/other; first world/third world; human/non-human.

Through such a challenge, postmodernists seek "to develop conceptions of social criticism which do not rely on traditional philosophical underpinnings" (Fraser & Nicholson, 1990, p. 21), and so reject positivist foundations of the meaning of knowledge and truth, and totalising narratives which govern power relations (Connor, 1989). This explanation is supported by Jencks (cited in Bordo, 1992, p. 160) who suggests that "anything resisting or deconstructing common assumptions of culture" is post-modernist. As such, postmodernism serves as a broad category which is characterized by a general critique of contemporary society, and is acknowledged as a fundamental turning point in social thought (Flax, 1990; Hatcher, 1993).

That post-modernist thought exists is not contentious, and the many aspects and versions of its existence have been debated on the philosophical front for some years now. It is not intended to revisit such debates in this text, but to acknowledge, through its usage, the potential value post-modernist thought offers educational research of this kind, where dialectical critiques have led to "counsels of despair" (Simon, 1988, p. 1). Perhaps the greatest value of postmodernism is that it offers the opportunity for dialogue across difference (Henry, 1996), where difference resists collapse into familiar categories, by staying in play.

Postmodernism and Feminism

Given postmodernism's interest in playing with difference, it is perhaps understandable that feminism and postmodernism, acknowledged as "two of the most important political-cultural currents of the last decade", for some time "kept an easy distance from one another ... there have been remarkably few extended discussions of the relations between them" (Fraser & Nicholson, 1990, p. 19). But as Hatcher (1993) contends, feminism and postmodernist thought are conceptually aligned. She explains (p .7) that:

> ... the general movement of feminism sits within the postmodern because it challenges notions of self, knowledge, and Truth so powerfully in the questions raised by feminists in their examination of the analytic category of gender and Otherness.

Fraser (1992, p. 68) is in accord with this view, suggesting that a pragmatic theory of discourse allows for the critique of essentialism and patriarchy "without becoming post-feminists". Davis uses the text "(post)feminist" to represent this theoretical perspective (Davis, 1997, p. 13). It is important to note the parallels between feminism and postmodernism in that both have sought to develop new paradigms for social criticism that are not reliant on the metanarratives of traditional philosophical underpinnings.

Postmodernism, Poststructuralism, and Feminism

Poststructural theory emerged in France out of a disillusionment with scientific and macro-political theory, which is patriarchal in nature (Weiner, 1993). Theories of poststructuralism evolved to contest the assumption that structures do and must exist outside language. "Post" very definitely, refers to "after" structuralism, but it is engaged with structuralism also. Poststructuralism is the theoretical position which is evident in the works of Derrida,

Lacan, Deleuze, Foucault and others. It engages with but also makes problematic both Neo-Marxism and instrumentalism as research approaches. Moreover, it blurs distinctions such as quantitative-versus-qualitative, noting the epistemological assumptions that underpin such logic. Postmodernism and post-structuralism are terms which are used interchangeably by some (Lather, 1991; Weiler, 1991). Others differentiate them by using postmodernism to represent an era of thought which includes a range of theoretical approaches including poststructuralism (Waugh, 1992). Weiner (1993, p. 3) suggests that "the strength of poststructuralism lies in its claim to create new analytic frameworks for defining and exploring social relations". As a 'postmodern' approach, poststructuralist theory challenges many of the assumptions about truth and knowledge that have been taken for granted in our society (Petersen & Lupton, 1996). Poststructural analyses differ from structuralist analyses fundamentally in that they recognize the importance of 'agency' as well as structures in the production of social practices (Weiner, 1993, p. 3). Poststructuralism contends that people are not passive recipients of socialization but are active in taking up discourses through which they are shaped. In this way, discursive spaces are opened up where individuals are able to resist 'essential' subject positioning.

According to Weiner (1993), poststructuralism relies on a number of central ideas. The first is the role of language in defining social meaning, social organization and individual consciousness. Language is considered to be the major system through which and by which meaning is constructed, cultural practices are organized, and individuals understand their world (Scott, 1990). Moreover, poststructuralism uses the principle of discourse to show how power relationships and subjectivity are constituted. It is through language systems as discourse that a socially produced sense of ourselves — our subjectivity — is constructed (Kress & Hodge, 1979; Weiner, 1993; Pendergast, 1996). Fraser (1992, p. 61) explains discourses as:

> ... historically specific, socially situated, signifying practices. They are the communicative frames in which speakers interact by exchanging speech acts ... set within social institutions and action ... the concept of a discourse links the study of language to the study of society.

Subjectivity then refers to the conscious and unconscious thoughts and emotions of the human 'being', their sense of self and their ways of understanding their relation to the world (Weedon, 1987). Furthermore, subjectivity is thus never a fixed or essential entity, but is multiple and shifting, given that we are 'subject to' and 'the subject of' meanings constructed in and through discursive systems.

In understanding truth claims as constructed through discourses, poststructuralists reject the notion that knowledge can be objectively TRUE, arguing that it is linked to the system of power which reaffirms it as the truth and therefore reinforces its power. Thus poststructuralists "take universals and truths to be problematic and open to scrutiny" (Weiner, 1993, p. 5), rejecting the grand narratives and binary dualities which typify modernist thought. Weiner (1993) outlines the final central concept of poststructuralism as a challenge to the liberal humanist approach to the individual, with its claims of rationality, fixity and consciousness.

Emerging from these debates is a feminist 'take' on poststructuralist theory, which rejects taken-for-granted assumptions and established meanings of gender and sex difference, which collapse the 'Other' into the familiar. Such theory seeks to illuminate the construction of subject positions or subjectivities as open, partial, fluid, rather than 'fixed' by Enlightenment logic. Feminist poststructuralist theory identifies discursive practices and demonstrates: where they come from; whose interests they support; how they maintain sovereignty and where they are susceptible to change (Weedon, 1987). Clearly then poststructural feminism has an important role to play in educational politics (Weiner, 1993). Weiner urges that poststructuralism be linked with feminist action in education in order to challenge the universalities of predominant curriculum epistemologies, to adopt a feminist praxis and feminist pedagogical approaches which allow for possibilities of the expansion of feminist counter-discourses in education, and to consciously position feminist educators within educational practices.

Posthumanism

Posthumanism can be conceptualized as a theoretical position within a poststructuralist conceptualization. Its relevance is particularly important for generating fresh understandings of the *positioning* of educators in pedagogical settings. McWilliam, Lather and Morgan (1997, p. 5) explain that:

> [P]oststructuralist 'posthumanism' casts doubt on the adequacy of that optimistic view of human beings as fully conscious and rational, arguing instead that we are shaped by our unconscious desires and by our language, and that our history and society give us our 'personal' selves or 'subjectivity'. This poststructuralist reconceptualizing of the 'self' marks

a centrally important shift from modern thinking and is crucial to poststructuralist feminism.

This shift in conceptualizing the self refuses the Cartesian notion of the separation of the knower and known by means of a foundational mind/body dualism.

Halberstam & Livingston (1995, p. vii) assert that we are now in the posthuman era, where the notion of a humanist philosophy has been surpassed, though it remains engaged with, and that posthumanism emerged out of a "disenchantment that is both anti-aesthetic and anti-scientific" (Halberstam & Livingston, 1995, p. 1). Posthumanism casts doubt on the adequacy of the humanist view that humans are fully conscious and rational. Instead the argument is that we are shaped from factors including language and unconscious desires (Gastil, 1993). In this way, we have personal selves or subjectivity. Jenks (1996, p. 17) contends that postmodernity "… calls forth a constant, reflexive, representation of self" (p .17) and the conception of the individual is that of the post-human, de-centered subject which is culturally inscribed or constructed and at the same time self-shapes in ways that are not always predictable or linear. Posthumanism rejects the conception of the individual as a unitary and fixed entity, but instead a subject that is always in the process of becoming.

The emergence of posthumanism and in particular the notion of a 'posthuman' body can, according to Halberstam & Livingston (1995, p. 3), be attributed to "the causes and effects of post-modern relations of power and pleasure, virtuality and reality, sex and its consequences". However, the posthuman does not necessitate the abolition of the human nor a linear understanding of human for it is not an evolution; but rather "participates in re-distributions of difference and identity" (Halberstam & Livingston, 1995, p. 10) away from the modernist tendency to categorize difference and thereby absorb it into the familiar. This imperative is born of a broad cultural shift which is characteristic of postmodernity — an insistence on the 'otherness of the Other' (Hamilton & McWilliam, in press), and a refusal to collapse difference into the familiar — a refusal to favor the mind over the body as occurs in the mind/body dichotomy of modernity.

Posthumanist Theories of the Body

'Body theory' is relatively recent, emerging within the last decade or so and receiving considerable attention since this time. According to Shilling (1993, p. 15), the development and popularity of body theory can be attributed to four main factors:

the second wave of feminism; the ageing of Western populations; a shift in the structure of advanced capitalist social systems; and increased knowledge about what bodies are. It is a distinct area of study within the field of philosophy and sociology, and has emerged along with a rise in what Shilling describes as "popular interest" in the body in general in our high modern society (1993, p. 1). In support of this view, McWilliam (1996a) and Davis (1997) argue that bodies are now a fashionable topic across a broad range of disciplines, including academia and popular culture such as media and cultural studies, with Davis (1997, p. 1) going so far as to suggest there is a 'body craze'. Importantly, most body work has tended to focus on women's bodies (Cranny-Francis, 1995), though bodies of all kinds are increasingly gaining attention. So profound is the recent contribution of body theory that Eagleton (1990) suggests it is one of the most precious developments of radical thought in the last decade. However, as Brunner (1996, p. 9) notes, "there is still a relatively small corpus of critical work devoted to the signifying body". Further, there is a fear that 'body work' may somehow disregard, trivialise or condone concerns of sexual harassment, and even sex panic, where 'bodies' are central.

Prior to and despite this shift, there has been a long-standing tradition that the body has to be interrogated not as the site of capability, but as a distraction from (mental) effort. It has been characterised as the shell within which the mind functions — promoting the notion of a mind/body duality (Bordo, 1992). Until recently, this duality went unchallenged. It was considered that the mind defined humans as social beings. Body theory moves beyond this perspective and that of thinkers such as Erving Goffman and Michel Foucault, who Davis (1997) suggests has "probably done more than any other contemporary social theorist to direct attention to the body" (p. 3) and who made early attempts to undo this dual approach to mind and body, which was typical of sociological theory (Shilling, 1993). Cranny-Francis (1995) identifies this critique of the mind/body modernist dualism as the "most fundamental move in the reassessment of the body". McWilliam (1996a, p. 16) also argues that new body theories offer innovative approaches to theorising which can transcend the traditional "mind/body dichotomy (which) has privileged the mind as that which defines human 'being', while the body has been interrogated as the excess baggage of human agency".

New theories of corporeality recognise the body as far more than a shell which is formed of essential, stable characteristics which are universal — that it is a "subject of discourse as well as an object of external gaze" (McWilliam, 1996a, p. 17). This view is supported by Bordo (1992, p. 166), who suggests that we now have the theoretical tools to see the body "both as a living cultural form and as a subject of scholarly theorizing — as a significant carrier and register of culture". In support of this, Shilling (1993) has coined the phrase "absent presence" to encapsulate the historical lack of treatment of the body in sociology. She argues the need to recognize that mind and body are "inextricably linked as a result of the mind's location within the body", as a concept central to body theory (p. 13). Shilling (1993, p. 5) uses the concept of the "body project" to describe the body as an "entity which is in the process of becoming". In so doing, the body is acknowledged as open to reconstruction and remaking. The body is significant as a personal resource and as a social symbol representing the self — an identity. In this way, bodies are framed as ongoing projects of self-making, always in process, as "malleable entities which can be shaped and honed by the vigilance and hard work of their owners" (Greene, 1994, p. 5). McWilliam (1996a, p. 17) emphasizes the particular value of body theory as "its recognition that the body must be interrogated as unfinished or incomplete as a cultural production, always in the process of becoming, lacking finality but yet amenable to completion". This provides those with an interest in body theory with the opportunity to explore continually evolving bodies and the problem of analyzing something so shifty. However, the notion of an unfinished work is seen as a strength of the theory, as Shilling (1993, p. 12) explains:

> ... the body is most profitably conceptualized as an unfinished biological and social phenomenon which is transformed, within certain limits, as a result of entry into, and participation in, society.

The foundations of this perspective are that:

- The human body at birth is itself the product of evolutionary processes that are affected by social as well as biological processes.
- As the body develops it is taken up and transformed, within limits, by social factors.
- The body is not only affected by social relations but forms a basis for and enters into the construction of social relations. (Shilling, 1993, p. 199)

Shilling (1993) suggests that the body as a project in postmodernity involves two propositions: the knowledge and ability to intervene and alter the body; and a growing awareness of the recognition of the body as an unfinished entity that can be transformed. The transformation is unlikely however, to be a 'certain drama', as modernist notions of 'empowerment' can too often suggest.

The Materiality of Bodies

Butler utilizes the concept of material — the body and its contours; and materiality of the body — the effect of power, as a way of conceptualizing body theory (Butler, 1993, p. 2). She uses the notion of matter as a "process of materialization that stabilizes over time to produce the effect of boundary, fixity, and surface we call matter" (Butler, 1993, p. 9). Butler outlines five underlying principles necessary for a reformulation of the materiality of bodies:

- recasting the matter of bodies as the effect of power;
- understanding performativity as the reiterative power of discourse;
- the construal of sex as a cultural norm which governs the materialization of bodies;
- rethinking of the processes by which bodily norms are assumed; and
- linking this with identification. (Butler, 1993, pp. 2–3)

The Performativity of Bodies

The notion of performativity is described by Butler (1993, p. 12) as "a reiteration of a norm or set of norms" that "conceals or dissimulates the conventions of which it is a repetition". Simply put, Butler suggests that our identities — whether or not considering gender — are the dramatic effect of our performances, rather than the cause; and that this does not express an inner core or essential self as humanist accounts propose. As such, all 'interior' determinations of identity are denied. In this way, we learn to 'fabricate' and gain proficiency in presenting acceptable cultural and public norms. This performative approach is considered by Bordo (1992, p. 168) to be:

> enormously insightful (and pedagogically useful) as a framework for exploring the ongoing, interactive, imitative processes by means of which the self, gender (I would add race as well), and their illusions of authenticity are constructed.

Such notions of materiality and performativity are useful for researching home economics teachers as an embodied field of pedagogical work in which performances are closely related to matters intrinsically connected with the physical state of bodies. Home economics teachers and students are commonly stereotyped as 'doing' bodies, engaged in cooking, sewing, cleaning and so on — all of which are very active (and low status) physical pursuits.

Discourse and Body Theory

As has been made clear, discourses constitute both subjectivity and power relations, in that they embody meaning and social relationships. The interrogation of practices as discourses, that is, "ways of speaking and thinking and knowing and writing which inform us about who we can and should be" (McWilliam & O'Donnell, 1997, p. 2) is now an accepted means of exploring social theory. But what is the interplay between discourse and body theory?

The power of discourse to constrain the possibilities of thought derives from the capacity to order and combine words in particular ways, changing their meaning and their effects through deploying them in ways that exclude or displace other possible combinations. Butler (1993) argues that language and materiality are not opposed, as language is, and refers to, that which is material, that there is materiality which characterizes language and also that which is associated with body's physicality. But it must be emphasized that discourse is more than language use. For Foucault, and Foucauldian theorists, discourses are practices, not simply a group of signs, inasmuch as they "systematically form the objects of which they speak" (Foucault, 1972, p. 49).

From a body theory perspective, Shilling (1993, p. 16) argues that, while Foucault has provided social theory with profound insights of the body — there are many examples of analyses of Michel Foucault's work in relation to the body. For elaboration, see for example the work of Turner (1997) who provides a description of Foucault's interest in the production of bodies, the regulation of bodies, and the representation of bodies within a context of disciplinary surveillance — and is perhaps one of the most radical and influential social constructionists, one who has encouraged theorists to "take the body seriously" — his view of the body as existing only in discourse is a "hindrance". Foucault considers that the "body is not only given meaning by discourse, but is wholly constituted by discourse" that the body is produced and constituted by discourse (Shilling, 1993, p. 74), in effect causing the body to vanish and become a product of social construction. This fails to overcome the dual approach of mind/body but rather has reproduced it in a different form (Shilling, 1993, p. 81). Angel (1994, pp.

64–65) also argues that Foucault's work actually makes an over-sight of the body, suggesting that Foucault "operates on a model which excludes the body by separating or devolving it from the order of discourse. The devolution of the body into a site for the operation of discourse is operative in much of his work". Bordo (1992; 1993) supports Shilling and Angel's view that Foucault, who has been credited by many as 'discovering' the pol-itics of the body, has played a significant but not singular role in the development of body theory. Instead, she argues that a number of contemporary feminists (e.g. Butler, 1993; Grosz, 1994; Halberstam & Livingston, 1995) have played a significant, but often unacknowledged role in recognising that the body is more than anatomy AND more than socially constituted. In this way, feminists can make "use of the radical potential of the theo-ries of Foucault" but will have to "fill the gaps left by Foucault" as he was "not especially interested in feminist issues" (Bailey, 1993, p. 118). This is not to reject Foucault's work but to indicate that is has been written over by a number of 'postmodern' femi-nists including Mary Russo (1994), whose work is of such impor-tance to this thinking.

Body Theory and Feminism

The relationship between discourse and body theory is made clear by Halberstam & Livingston (1995) who add a new depth to an old understanding of discourse analysis and simultaneous-ly incorporate a feminist perspective. The following paragraph outlines their position with regard to a 'feminist' theory of the embodied subject (of discourse):

> Posthuman bodies are not slaves to master discourses but emerge at nodes where bodies, bodies of discourse, and discourses of bodies intersect to foreclose any easy distinction between actor and stage, between sender/receiver, channel, code, message, context. Posthuman embodiment, like Haraway's feminist embodiment, then, is not about fixed location of the reified body, female or otherwise, but about nodes in fields, inflec-tions in orientations … Embodiment is significant prosthesis (Halberstam & Livingston, 1995, p. 2).

This notion of 'nodes in fields' developed by Donna Haraway (1991) refers to the extreme localization and intimately personal and individualized body which is situated in a larger 'field' and that this situation is not fixed by assumptions about master discourses. This partiality of location and not universality is the condition of being heard to make rational knowledge claims.

Feminist philosophy is attributed by some philosophers (e.g. Bordo 1992; 1993; Davis 1997), as playing a significant role in the emergence of body theory. These theorists argue that through a feminist recognition of the body as a politically inscribed entity, the development of a political understanding of the body has become possible. However, for some feminists there are tensions around feminist thought and body theory (McWilliam, 1996a; Davis, 1997). Butler questions the adequacy of feminist approaches that do not incorporate body theory thinking, noting that "the discourse of 'construction' that has for the most part circulated in feminist theory is not quite perhaps adequate to the task at hand" (Butler, 1993, p. xi). She argues that accepting a construction model of gender assumes social meanings without contestation, and it is 'not enough' (p. 8). Instead, she recommends a re-examination of the notion of matter.

Grosz (1994, p. vii) too, argues that feminists have tended to ignore the body or to subordinate it and that with some notable exceptions "remain uninterested in or unconvinced about the relevance of refocusing on bodies in accounts of subjectivity". She suggests a non-essentialist feminist approach is necessary to reclaim body theory for a feminist perspective, stating:

> [I]f feminists are to resuscitate a concept of the body for their own purposes, it must be extricated from the biological and pseudo-naturalist appropriations from which it has historically suffered (Grosz, 1994, p. 20).

In this way the body can move beyond scientific and naturalistic explanations which typically marginalize and empower certain bodies over others, and into a range of disparate discourses. This involves rethinking the body in terms beyond the dominant assumptions which exist and which have the potential to avoid the impasses of traditional theorizing about the body. Moreover, in more recent work, there have been calls from some areas of feminist thought to retrieve the body from the 'linguistic idealism' of poststructuralism (Butler, 1993, p. 27). Davis (1997) encourages the use of (post)feminist theory of the body as a means of transformation, where subversion through the body can be taken seriously as an alternative body politics.

Some of the recent notable exceptions who do undertake feminist research on embodiment and gendered subjectivities include Jennifer Harding (1997) and Liz Eckermann (1997), who draw on the approach of Foucault to the body, but with a feminist take. Harding's work in the area of hormone replacement therapy argues that feminist and medical discourses converge in their reference to an 'already sexed' body in that they both presuppose the existence of 'sex' as a fixed category. Eckermann examines self-starvation through an analysis of embodiment and gendered subjectivities. In particular, she draws on Foucault's concepts of surveillance and confession. These concepts are developed in Foucault (1980) and have been utilised by other researchers in the field of self-starvation. For example, Spitzack (1987) employs Foucault's concepts of surveillance and confession to analyse the discourse of weight loss. Kathy Davis (1997) brings together a number of (post)feminist theorists using body work in her book *Embodied practices: Feminist perspectives on the body.* Her collection contains two sections, the first a set of contributions showing constructions of female bodies and how this creates power relations. Included are constructions of the female body in classical ballet; medicalised bodies including those with osteoporosis, and disabled bodies; ethnic bodies and related cultural practices such as genital excision. The second section of this book explores different kinds of strategies for transformation. Included in this section is the work of Julia Edwards and Linda McKie who look at the apparent absence of women's public toilets and the reasons for this; Joanne Finkelstein who considers the liberating and conservative aspects of women's fashion; Kathy Davis who theorises using as her subject radical body art in the form of face surgery; along with other scholarly pieces.

Carnivalesque, Grotesque Bodies

The use of parody and irony of the carnival is a particular interpretive lens for posthumanist body theory. This interpretive lens has been utilized in Projects by researchers interested in pursuing analysis that "offer[s] another way to think through problems of reproduction, resistance, and transformation" (Grace, 1996, p. 5). The following section develops an understanding of grotesque bodies of the carnival, since this is the interpretive tool utilized in later chapters of this book.

Fun

Just what is fun, and what does it mean to take pleasure? The idea of having fun and taking pleasure is assumed to be reserved for those short moments of leisure and recreation in our lives and seems contradictory to our work ethic and our education systems. Confirming this view, the notion of 'fun' and taking of pleasure is explored in Harvie Ferguson's work, *The Science of Pleasure* (1990) where he argues that "[T]he bourgeois order, like any conventional order, is built first upon the renunciation of fun" where the notion of taking pleasure and having 'fun' "has been conceptualized as the opposition between reason and unreason"(p. 67). It is 'unreasonable' to have fun, and since reason is the basic philosophy of modernism, fun and reason would seem to be oppositional to each other. However, Ferguson argues that "fun playfully insinuates itself into the life of reason itself" (p. 67), so that fun is in fact troubling to reason and rationality, and is not unreasonable. Indeed, Ferguson (1990, p. 67) suggests that 'fun' is "a subversive germ we cannot live without". What is 'carnivalesque' and from where does this interpretive lens emerge?

Carnival

The term 'carnival' conjures up images of fun, festivities and games; with an offering of a smorgasbord of 'believe it or not' activities. But this rather superficial view of carnival is all that remains of a once powerful tradition of carnival as a parodic and pleasurable space. To retrieve this understanding, the writings of Mikhail Bakhtin are useful because they illuminate the historical role, description and importance of carnival since its popularity in early modern Europe (Ferguson, 1990). Bakhtin (1968) developed his theory of the carnivalesque in the book, *Rabelais and His World*, in order to theorize the differences between the lives and pleasures of the bourgeoisie and the common people. According to Bakhtin's explanation, carnivals were popular and common in the early modern European era with some towns devoting up to three months of each year to festive public spectacles that cumulatively were called carnivals. Bakhtin documents the genuine popularity of carnival for all stratum of society, with both the 'downtrodden' who used carnival as a form of parody, protest and exaggeration of the politics, people and practices of the day; as well as with the 'privileged' in society, who also participated in carnival and acted out the role of the carnivalesque.

Bakhtin illustrates the domain of carnival as public festivities which "made outrageous fun of orthodox and authoritative opinion" (cited in Ferguson, 1990, p. 107), with grotesque realism, exaggerated and typically degrading and mocking of the human society and body with respect to the norms and practices of the day. Grace (1996, p. 5) further explains that:

> [F]or Bakhtin, the carnivalesque represented freedom, creativity, invention, and the possibility of being other in the world. Whether the effects of the

carnival were fleeting or sustained, its participants experienced an altered sense of reality that held potential for renewal and change.

In this way, with potential for renewal and change, Bakhtin's work and ideas have been recognized as having a broad range of applicability. However, Bakhtin stresses that carnival is not just an inversion of the dominant, normal way of life as it "refuses to surrender the critical and cultural tools of the dominant class, and in this sense, carnival can be seen, above all, as a site of insurgency, and not merely withdrawal" (Russo, 1994, p. 62). In this way, carnival is "…a world closed in upon itself: an exhaustive reality which criticizes the more profoundly by its indifference to, than by its caricaturing of the official world" (Ferguson, 1990, p. 108). So, carnival is seen as a space for parody and the bodies engaged in the carnival — carnivalesque bodies — as tools of parody.

Mary Russo, author of *The Female Grotesque* (1994) draws upon Bakhtin's notion of 'carnival' and 'fun' to look closely at the carnivalesque body, arguing that it is the materiality of the body that is the site of the carnivalesque.

The Carnivalesque, Grotesque Body

Typically, people performed in carnivals, their bodies engaged in parody, protest and exaggeration. Hence, the carnivalesque body emerges from Bakhtin's work on carnival as a "grotesque that moves" (Russo, 1994, p. 29) — the masked, excessive, grotesque body that performs the work of the carnival, which is a grotesque parody of 'normal' life. Hence, the masks and voices of the grotesque body resist, exaggerate, challenge and destabilize the norms of society through the vehicle of carnival. The grotesque body of carnival is recognizable in relation to a norm, that is, it emerges as a deviation from the norm but not just in opposition to the norm (Mellor & Shilling, 1997).

Building upon Bakhtin's writings about carnival, Mary Russo explains that the grotesque body of carnival is:

> … open, protruding, irregular, secreting, multiple, and changing; it is iden-
> tified with non-official "low" culture or the carnivalesque, and with social
> transformation (Russo, 1994, p. 8).

Russo argues that the grotesque body is a risky space, suggesting that "exceeding the norm involves serious risk" (Russo, 1994, p. 10) and hence grotesque performances in which grotesque bodies engage are risky activities (Russo, 1994, p. 22). This view is supported by Mellor and Shilling (1997, p. 10) who suggest that the grotesque body is within us all:

[T]he significance of grotesque bodies was not simply that they represented the threat of the 'uncivilized' Other in Western society (an Other which manifested itself variously in the form of race, the female sex, and the dangerous classes), but that even white, male elites could only become and remain civilized while they suppressed the grotesque passions and bad manners lurking inside themselves.

Hence, the task of *modernist* work is to work towards "suppression of the uncontrollable, of the grotesque" (Mellor & Shilling, 1997, p. 11), rejecting the irrational and excessive and instead seeking rational experiences and explanations. The work of *postmodern* projects by contrast, is to look at the grotesque bodies that have been ignored and suppressed in this process. Russo suggests that it is this work on carnival and the carnivalesque which has "translocated the issues of bodily exposure and containment, disguise and gender masquerade, abjection and marginality, parody and excess, to the field of the social constituted as a symbolic system" (Russo, 1994, p. 54). She further claims that carnivalesque is important to contemporary feminism in that "it sets carnival apart from the merely oppositional and reactive", suggesting opportunity for "redeployment or counterproduction" (Russo 1994, p. 62). In her work, Russo (1994, p. 12) argues that the category of the female grotesque that emerges from Bakhtin's explanation of the grotesque body of carnival and carnivalesque, is 'crucial' for a transformative shift from the norm to identity formation for both men and women. Russo's notion of female grotesque emerges from the position that it is "the feminine as the body marked by difference" (1994, p. 13) so that 'male grotesques' are produced in association with this.

The grotesque — like carnival — also is "necessarily incomplete" (1994, p. 13). However, it is through the practice of risk and the incomplete nature of the body that possibility becomes available. As Russo explains:

[W]ithin the expanded spatial dimensions of late twentieth century spectacle, the female spectacle which emerges as a de-formation of the normal suggests new political aggregates — provisional, uncomfortable, even conflictual coalitions of bodies which both respect the concept of situated knowledges and refuse to keep every body in its place (Russo, 1994, p. 16).

Bakhtin transposes the notion of carnival to today's world, such that carnival may become a potential site of transformation in a "world as regenerative and (with) incomplete projects" (Ferguson, 1994, p. 33). In this way, there is an embodiment of possibility and error. These carnivalesque moments and the body as grotesque represents the other-than-normal body. These are risky, freakish bodies engaged in risky activities that parody officialdom and refuse order and folkloric normalization. These are the bodies which refuse to be tidied and kept in place, but instead provide "an altered sense of reality that [holds] potential for renewal and change" (Grace, 1996, p. 5) and for "social transformation" (Russo 1994, p. 8). Hence, the grotesque body can be utilized as an interpretive lens to re-look.

The next section of this chapter provides glimpses of the possibilities that radical (post)feminist embodied scholarship on the body — in education — can offer.

Applications of Postmodernism and Posthumanist Body Theory in Education

Postmodern approaches to theorizing and researching in education settings are advocated by a number of contemporary writers including Kiziltan, Bain & Canizares (1990), Greene (1994), and Hamilton (1994). Education can be seen as a modernist social enterprise, which makes the field open to scrutiny from a postmodernist perspective. However, as Kiziltan et al., (1990, p. 355) acknowledge, "educators, practitioners, and theoreticians alike, have managed for the most part to seal out or to dismiss the issues emanating from the post-modern". However, education is not immune to the effects of postmodernity and there is an increasing awareness of the threat to education of its loss of cultural significance and legitimacy which is naturally embedded in the grand narratives of modernist thought that are challenged by postmodernism. The implications for education can be profound. As Kiziltan et al. (1990, p. 359) explain:

> the post-modern condition involves more than a change in attitudes toward public education or the birth of a new type of student, teacher, parent, or administrator ... rather, it points to the emergence of a new (dis)order, no longer bound to or legitimated by the systematic set of relations organized by the metanarratives of modernity.

There is a growing field of literature which reports upon research which does just this. This research re-thinks thinking about education and teaching and learning through postmodernist lenses. Of particular interest in this book is work where posthumanist body theory has been the approach for re-thinking pedagogical events. A brief reflection upon some of this literature shall focus upon, but not be confined to, examples of body theory applied to teaching and classroom scenarios.

Erica McWilliam (1996d) for example, has utilized postmodernism and particularly body theory to re-look at the education field. For her, this approach stems from a lack of attention to the body in recent education literature, suggesting that it "ignores the teaching body altogether, speaking of it, if at all, as 'facilitating'" (McWilliam 1997b, p. 228). In this work, extracts of accounts from a series of narratives were used with body theory to demonstrate that the teacher's desiring body is material to the pedagogical relationship between student and teacher. Drawing on Angel (1994), she inquires into the importance of teachers as bodies of knowledge and considers the body as a site/sight of inquiry, rejecting the mind/body duality that invalidates such an approach. McWilliam (1996d, p. 11) explains:

> the body of the teacher is crucial inasmuch as it performs what it looks like to have a love affair with a body of knowledge, and this performance is enacted and observed as erotic, a manifestation of desire which is necessarily ambiguous and duplicitous within the pedagogical event.

This approach emphasizes that the body must be interrogated as unfinished or incomplete as a site of cultural production, and as the literal sight of a knowing body. In related work, McWilliam and Jones (1996) give focus to the body — of the teacher and of the learner — in the educational setting of universities. They note that the body is a powerful component of the teaching/learning experience, the body being "elated by the experience of powerful pedagogical moments" (1996, p. 128). In this way, the learning context may be eroticized, in ways that are not simply reducible to pedagogical abuse.

For further work, McWilliam (1996c), raises the issue of the importance of gendered bodies in the construction of the 'great teacher' as a cultural phenomenon. This questions the relation between gender and pedagogy and insists on the embodiment of pedagogical work, where the material body of the teacher is acknowledged. An example of performativity is presented by McWilliam (1996b) who discusses the performative dimension of teaching, suggesting this incorporates aspects such as text, utterance and bodily gesture. Using these performative dimensions, she links teachers bodies to posthumanist performances of pedagogical work, rejecting the modernist narratives of pedagogical work being conducted by and on no/body. She argues for the use of seduction as a legitimate metaphor for understanding the pedagogical work of successful teachers.

McWilliam and Palmer (1995, 1996) utilize body theory to investigate the effect of open learning on pedagogical events as performances. The researchers explored issues raised for teachers by the shift to an 'open' pedagogy, based on the very real effects this new and increasingly common pedagogy had by demanding a change in the anatomical presence of students and teachers. What was found is the need to understand new possibilities and problems which may emerge, and the differing capacity of teaching bodies to be "more malleable and permeable" (1996, p. 170).

McWilliam encourages researchers to 'take on' radical projects in education and teaching, always insisting that "pedagogical work demands material engagement" (McWilliam, 1997b). As she states:

> I continue to ask how the teacher's body is material to a radical pedagogy. The exploration of the pedagogue as a "body of knowledge", one that is facialized as a political surface/body subject, invites examination of pedagogical bodies as both the site and sight of pedagogical display.

The work of Malcolm Vick (1996) draws upon posthumanist concepts of the body and particularly the work of Shilling (1993) in his analysis of three manuals of classroom teaching method produced within modernist notions of mass schooling. In particular, it considers the way the 'pupil' is constructed and the self is constituted in terms of the mind/body dualism.

Along similar lines and providing a new way of thinking about body research is the work offered by David Kirk (1997), which constitutes a detailed historical investigation of students' bodies by focusing on the emergence, consolidation and reconstruction of the school practices of physical training, medical inspection and sport, between the 1880s and the 1940s. Using a Foucauldian lens, he presents an argument that demonstrates how school processes have contributed to schooling young people's bodies by constructing and constituting the body in modernity. Kirk concludes his work by highlighting the future benefits of taking the body seriously, and beyond the limitations of a modernist framework. He states:

> [O]ne way in which these forms of schooling bodies may have been improved in the past and may still be improved in the future is for social and educational theorists to begin to take serious note of the social construction of the body through schooling. ... By bringing these school practices under detailed examination, by seeking out the connections between these practices and other related practices, by taking seriously the effects of these practices on young people, and by providing means of educating teachers, policy makers and the general public about the whole range of consequences of school practices, perhaps the processes of schooling bodies may be less likely to be oppressive, negative, and alienating and more likely to be fulfilling, enabling and in the most hopeful sense of the word, liberating (Kirk, 1997, pp. 177–178).

In her paper *Text as Body, Body as Text*, Barbara Kamler (1997) explores the embodied nature of language practices used by two sets of students, these being first year university law students, and students in their first month of primary school. Her work aims to "make visible the practices that discipline both groups to engage in performances that shape the body and mind into predispositions for behavior as part of a larger group or corporate body" (p.369). This analysis of embodied practices reveals how everyday practices of schooling such as the monitoring of posture, movement and visual gaze of the students by the teacher, operate to discipline the student body. As a consequence of this Project, Kamler (1997) raises a number of issues regarding the methodology of undertaking such work. First, she insists on the reading of embodied text rather than linguistic text alone, thereby capturing the embodied performance. Moreover, she argues that contradictions and inconsistencies should be identified as an effect of discourse rather than as the failure of the individual teachers; and that the performativity of the body is recognized to be a struggle which is constantly being remade. And finally, that issues of subjectivity would benefit from more thorough linguistic analyses.

This chapter forms a basis for conceptualizing how the work of this book will proceed. Of course, the notion that a view from a body, as an ongoing project, is useful for (post)feminist embodiment theory and research means that research methodology is a difficult matter, since it is shifting and fluid as an object of analysis. Pillow (1996, p. 20) elaborates on the importance and difficulty of applying such theory to research methodology suggesting it is one way to engage in interruptive analyses of modernist practices:

> [E]mbodied analysis seeks to exploit rather than cover or conceal the discrepancies not only in the corners of the Master's house but question and implode the perfect facade of the master's house — to question how its foundation is laid, by whom, to whose benefit and why; to methodologically work both within and against this house.

At the commencement of this chapter the need for a shift in approach to studying home economics was stressed. The shift required is one away from the essentialism, individualism and epistemological assumptions of modernism that have been hegemonic in the theorizing of home economics. The need for this shift has emerged from an exhaustion of Enlightenment epistemologies and the limitations of theoretical approaches faithful to them, including structuralist analyses, behavioral studies, psychological and attitudinal studies, and so on. These studies all inform on educational work as a humanist project by drawing on modernist notions of human capability.

It is argued that a shift to postmodernist forms of enquiry, and particularly embodied scholarship on the body, is required. There is a need to re-think thinking about home economics teaching as located in physical culture at disciplinary sites; and as embodied, where home economics teachers perform as body subjects, engaged always in a labor of reinscription of themselves and others. In this way, home economics teaching and teachers can be seen as textual/material subjects of pedagogical work, continually shaped and shaping the site of their pedagogy. This shift constitutes a departure from the traditional mind/body duality and makes possible the sort of thinking about home economics that can lead towards a new order which is at the same time a new disorder.

The dilemma a postmodern approach poses for the researcher is how to go about doing research work in this area, including making the transition from theory to method. Central to this dilemma is an acknowledgment of the difficulty of doing any research 'guided' by postmodern theorizing. For example, a criticism leveled at feminists, and in particular body theorists, has been the complex and dense writing styles used to develop their frameworks for analysis. Bordo (1992, p. 174) argues that unless such philosophical approaches are presented in accessible, non-elitist language, the potential benefits offered by these perspectives will remain the domain of a "handful of academic sophisticates". McWilliam (1993, p. 201) concurs with this view, suggesting that some writers in the area of contemporary social theory are "legendary in achieving the status of unreadability" with the subsequent outcome that "potentially exciting ideas in social theory are often corked up so tightly in ... academic bottles that they remain inaccessible when cast out in search of an audience". McWilliam (1993) argues that difficulties in conceptualizing and presenting research in the current climate of contemporary social theorizing go beyond the inaccessibility of terminology and writing, inventing her own term for the phenomenon. She suggests that PMT — post-modernist tension — is typically experienced by those "who seek to do compelling contemporary work, informed by current social theorizing" (McWilliam, 1993, p. 199). The 'symptoms' of PMT include: difficulty in being theoretically contemporary, given the hasty pace of emerging theory; the inaccessibility of theorizing writing; the constraining assumptions underlying theorizing writing, particularly thesis writing, which is at odds with postmodernist thinking; the difficulty in determining and defending a 'theory'; among other 'symptoms' (McWilliam, 1993, pp. 199–204). This research must be informed by such insightfulness given that the researcher works hard not to fall victim to PMT — whilst acknowledging that it is impossible not to do so.

Debate rages about the possibility of doing postmodern research at all. Connor (1989), for example, raises questions about the critical debates which surround postmodernism, particularly the argument that it absolves itself of value at the same time that it discredits 'legitimate' research, and suggesting that such debates about postmodernism constitute postmodernism itself. This is supported by others, such as Pillow (1996, p. 1), who notes that some consider postmodernism to be "a place from which no work can be done", and warns that the challenge of doing feminist posthumanist work is that "activists and theorists who challenge the master's house often have to face charges of their own intellectual and/or moral incontinence".

Nevertheless, Hatcher (1993) argues that postmodernist research is possible and desirable because it requires researchers to work beyond positivist epistemological assumptions by embracing postpositivist enquiry. In her own research, she argues that three conceptual shifts are essential in order to produce 'postmodern' research. These are: a focus on the local rather than the general as a source of understanding, the foregrounding of the research process, and, the notion of data as 'vivification' rather than as proof (Hatcher, 1993, p. 13). The shift from the general to the local is a shift from grand narratives to the local cultural production of individuals. Narratives become more precarious multiple texts which tell a variety of different stories with different points of focus.

The notion of data as 'vivification' rather than as proof emerges in the work of Lather (1991), who, in elaborating postmodern approaches to methods in educational research, argues that the point of 'post' research is "not to substitute an alternative and more secure foundation, but to produce an awareness of the complexity, contingency, and frailty of historical forms and events" (Lather, 1991, p. 6). Hatcher (1993) describes this as a shift from positivist to postpositivist research, noting that it is a shift "from certainty to uncertainty" (1993, p. 16).

So, how does one go about doing the uncertain work of postmodern inquiry and critique? What does it look like? What methods are acceptable in order to undertake an embodied analysis of home economics as a site/sight of pedagogical activity? What are the means by which research can work methodologically both within and against the 'masters house', the characteristics Pillow (1996) asserts are essential for an 'embodied' analysis such as is being attempted here? Lather (1996) warns that it is not methodology that holds the key to better research, but more fundamental issues of epistemology, that is, the theory of the method and what counts as knowledge. Lather defers to Viswasnaran (1994) when she warns that no longer should the feminist researcher be the hero of her own story, and that much feminist research fails not at the level of method, but epistemology — the move is away from falsity rather than towards truth.

As already pointed out, the answers to the questions of method are not easy, and there are many who debate these dilemmas. As the above example from Lather shows, much of the work takes us back to considerations of 'knowing' rather than forward to considerations of 'doing' and this makes enacting such research very difficult. Fraser and Nicholson (1990) suggest that Jean-Francois Lyotard, author of The Postmodern Condition, (1984) rejects certain methods, because their "illegitimate genres include large-scale historical narrative and social-theoretical analyses of pervasive relations of dominance and subordination" (p. 25) with this view based on the premise that philosophy should not be grounded by a foundationalist metanarrative which institutionalizes inequality. This reinforces Lather's (1996) and Hatcher's (1993) point about epistemology — that foundational notions of the nature of knowledge will not do. However, Fraser and Nicholson (1990) contest this wholesale rejection of genres, arguing that an array of different methods and genres is appropriate, dependent upon the nature of the social object under observation. In particular, they argue that feminists have a case to challenge this, given their claim that feminist research continues modernist epistemologies, as outlined in the following statement:

> ... [V]estiges of essentialism have continued to plague feminist scholarship, even despite the decline of grand theorizing. In many cases ... this represents the continuing subterranean influence of those very mainstream modes of thought and inquiry with which feminists have wished to break. (Fraser and Nicholson, 1990, p. 33)

It may therefore be appropriate for feminist research to incorporate genres now located in mainstream modernist techniques, in order to view influences that cannot be ignored. Hence the task of the researcher is to work out of an appropriate epistemology, arguing its case on the grounds of the requirements of a particular research project.

Fraser and Nicholson (1990) suggest that postmodern feminist theory tailor its methods and categories to the specific task at hand. They suggest that research should look more like a tapestry where multiple categories are used when appropriate, and that single 'feminist method' or 'feminist epistemology' should be avoided. In this way, what emerges is "a practice made up of a patchwork of overlapping alliances, not one circumscribable by an essential definition" (p. 35). This tapestry approach is evident in much recent research applying posthumanist body theory, an example being the work of Kennedy (1996) where specific reference is made to the weaving together of ideas and theories to offer a tapestry of desiring positions from which to think — in this instance — film experience.

Whatever it does look like as a research design, the features of this woven tapestry design for a post-feminist approach would, according to Fraser and Nicholson (1990), include:

- a rejection of the suggestion that large scale theoretical tools be abandoned;

- an 'explicitly historical' view of culture, society and time;

- a non-universalist but comparativist perspective, noting changes and contrasts but not establishing laws; and

- a rejection of the unitary notions of woman and feminine gender identity, replacing it with plural and complex constructions of social identity where gender is only one strand among others.

In an attempt to provide further direction for research method, Grosz (1994, pp. 21–24) has identified six criteria by which thinking a feminist corporeality or embodiment as a particular approach to postmodernist research is possible. These are to:

- avoid mind/body dichotomies which categorize, thereby refusing the duality;

- avoid the association of body with one sex or race such that they must bear the burden of corporeality;

- refuse singular models of the body which are based on one type of body as the norm against which all others are judged — a "field" of body types is preferred;

- reject any essentialist accounts of the body, recognizing that the body is the site of inscription, production or constitution;

- include physical representation of the subject's lived body; and

- problematise binary pairs such as private/public, nature/culture, physical/social, instinct learning, genetic/environmentally determined; and instead, stress the body as a cultural product.

Such 'direction' is hardly a manual for undertaking body work — but rather, what not to do. This may be historically and politically appropriate but it is nevertheless frustrating to the novice researcher. Having developed these generally cautionary criteria, Grosz (1994) is ready to acknowledge that there is yet a considerable amount of thinking in order to develop a feminist understanding of the body which is not constrained by patriarchy. She states that "no one yet knows what the conditions are for developing knowledges, representations, models, programs, which provide women with nonpatriarchal terms for representing themselves and the world from women's interests and points of view" (Grosz, 1994, p. 188).

The work of Butler (1993) and Grosz (1994) as (post)feminist theorists of the body "embraces queer theory as a radical perspective for rethinking feminist body theory and developing an alternative politics of the body" (Davis, 1997, p. 13). Davis (1997, p. 13) explains that queer theory originally developed in response to the pathologisation of same-sex desire but has now "moved on to become one of the most potent critiques of modernist thought ... [because] ...[I]t attacks all forms of binary thinking, including dualistic conceptions of sex and gender".

If this is the terrain of the approach taken, then Pillow (1996) argues that an embodied analysis should be both disruptive of modernist discourses and master's tools and "taking up/taking on the master's tools and (re)tooling them for different uses" (p. 3). She explains that this embodied analysis can engage in a disruption as it encompasses a doubleness, that is, it "can both transgress and elude the master discourse because it knows and understands this discourse and yet is both proliferated and silenced by it" (p. 3). Similarly, Lather (1996) argues for a 'double science' approach, refusing the binary of scientific/anti-scientific approaches to research. In this way, it is a notion of inquiry that is "both/and and neither/nor science and not-science" (Lather, 1996, p. 5).

Historically, there are two major research 'traditions' — the quantitative/ experimental/ normative/ positivist/science tradition and the qualitative/ phenomenological/ interpretive/ antiscience tradition. Hamilton suggests that the concept of traditions can be explained through an investigation of three elements: practitioner-guardians, practices and artefacts and that the "history of traditions, therefore, is as much a narrative of diaspora as it is a chronicle of successful parallel cohabitation" (1994, p. 62). The quantitative approach is "concerned with discovering natural and universal laws regulating and determining individual and social behaviour" (Cohen and Manion, 1985, p. 6). The positivism paradigm is the basis for the quantitative methodologies and the

empirical science mode of research. The strength of the quantitative approach depends on how effectively the research questions
reflect the reality of the human systems and environments being
studied (Bobbitt, 1993). Descartes's work published in 1637
is credited by some as founding the quantitative research field
(Hamilton, 1994, p. 62). The qualitative tradition is "more
concerned to understand individuals' perceptions of the world.
They seek insight rather than statistical analysis" (Bell, 1993).
This mode assumes phenomena can be understood from people's
perceptions of the situation. Its purpose is to understand the perceptions and perspectives of people involved in situations with
emphasis on the micro/macro contexts of relationships.
Qualitative approaches to the study of humans and their environments permits expanded perceptions which contributes to greater
breadth and depth of study. This phenomenological approach
is a study of what is the perceived reality of a particular phenomenon. Research from a qualitative perspective is based upon
an organismic view where the sum is greater than the parts
(Bobbitt, 1993). The epistemology of the qualitative tradition
emerged from "an epistemological crisis of the late eighteenth
century" (Hamilton, 1994, p. 63). Epistemology, the theory of the
method, or grounds of knowledge or what constitutes knowledge,
is an issue of debate between the opposing traditions of research.
The view that knowledge is "hard, objective and tangible" (Cohen
and Manion, 1985, p. 7) is subscribed to by the quantitative tradition — and is known as positivism. In contrast, the anti-posi-
tivism approach of the phenomenological tradition sees knowledge as "personal, subjective and unique" (Cohen and Manion,
1985, p. 7). The positivist approach works with knowledge as tangible and quantifiable, while the anti-positivist takes knowledge
to be qualitative.

According to Lather (1996, p. 4) "the concept of a double
science ... argues the need for a proliferation of eccentric kinds
of science to address the question of practice in post-foundation-
al discourse theory". Following this line of thought, Jane Flax
(1990) suggests that the role of the postmodern researcher should
be that of the 'deconstructive' reader of texts (written, verbal,
material). By this she means a reader who is:

> disrespectful of authority, attentive to suppressed tensions or conflicts
> within the texts, and suspicious of all 'natural' categories, essentialist
> oppositions and representational claims. They are willing to play with the
> text, to disrupt its apparent unity, to rescue its heterogeneous and disor-
> derly aspects and its plurality of meanings and voices (Flax, 1990, p. 37).

McWilliam, Lather and Morgan (1997, p. 30) elaborate this textual perspective, encouraging the researcher to "...open up spaces in which suppressed voices and other stories (including women's) can be set to speak". They suggest that typical practices of textual analysis might include:

- pressing the literal meaning of a metaphor till it yields up to unintended meanings;
- looking for contradictions;
- identifying gaps;
- setting silences to speak;
- focusing on ambiguous words or syntax;
- demonstrating that different meanings can be produced by different readings;
- reversing the terms of a binary pair and subverting the hierarchies; and
- the use of irony.

Greene (1994) concurs with many of these suggestions, emphasising the need for education research to disregard long-standing conflicts between the scientific/anti-scientific or quantitative/ qualitative debate. The traditions of qualitative and quantitative study provide differing perspectives and opportunities for research. It is important to recognise that the traditions of research are legitimate mechanisms in theory development, application and testing and for contributing to a more holistic, detailed framework for understanding humans and their environmental interactions. Qualitative methods can benefit from quantitative approaches, and vice-versa, and together they can provide a depth of perception or a binocular view that neither can provide alone. As Burgess (1985, p. 3) explains "it is not a question of the superiority of one method over another, but the appropriateness of a method of investigation for a particular research problem". By acknowledging the value of qualitative and quantitative research, home economists can make contributions toward meaningful data interpretation by "demythologizing" the quantitative-qualitative dichotomy — as Bobbitt (1993) suggests, a holistic profession requires holistic approaches, including research. There is no doubt that research will be considerably enriched as qualitative and quantitative researchers learn to integrate their approaches. Greene (1994) urges the use of metaphor and the imagination as a method to link theory and experience together for new and dynamic approaches. Greene links the conceptions of imagination and metaphor, suggesting that imaginative thought can be best represented in terms of metaphor in language. Imagination provides the opportunity for human beings to construct alternative ways of going beyond 'given' experiences to alternative projects and solutions, and this can be expressed metaphorically. In this way, she (1994, p. 458) explains "the postmodern imagination is ... poetic as well as critical: rich, free, playful, confronting open possibility".

Investigating Home Economics as a Site/sight of Pedagogical Work

From these discussions and guidelines from researchers in the field, it seems possible to undertake a feminist posthumanist project in home economics where the body is interrogated as a text that speaks home economics as a cultural pedagogical practice. This (post)feminist work "offers a way of celebrating a politics of creative subversion without retreating to identity politics or the tactics of collective rebellion" (Davis, 1997, p. 13). The characteristics of such study draw upon the characteristics already noted in the previous section of this chapter and guides the course of this project. Its features are:

- recognition of pedagogical work as 'embodied';
- a shift from metanarrative to the local site;
- a refusal to reject large scale research tools (if they are argued as appropriate);
- a shift from general theorizing to practice;
- a refusal to establish 'laws' but to acknowledge the boundedness of truth claims;
- an emphasis on bodies as the site of lived experience;
- a rejection of binary constructions and unitary notions of gender;
- incorporation of reflexive engagement with the language of the reporting data (for example, identifying gaps; focusing on ambiguous words or syntax etc);
- the unsettling of familiar accounts; and
- the weaving together of ideas and theories into an 'unfinished' tapestry of analytical elements.

This is achieved through an exploration of the body of the text (that is, how the home economics body is written or situated by themselves and how it is erased, ignored and overwritten — the site of the home economics body); and the body as text (where the performativity and materiality of the body is available as a subject of discourse as well as an object of external gaze — the sight of the home economics body). The performativity of the profession as represented by symbols and icons, photographic records and so on, can be scrutinised and the actual bodies of a number of 'atypical' home economics teachers will be 'read' as culturally inscribed sites. These readings will work to reconstitute home economics as a 'body' of knowledge.

The inquiry documented in the following chapters explores how home economics teachers perform as bodies of knowledge. To do so, I attempt to document the sites and sights of their bodies as disciplinary display. The intention is to blur clear distinctions between the home economics body of knowledge and the material bodies of home economics teachers. In contrast with previous research, I regard it as unhelpful to separate the sites and sights of home economics. Maria Angel (1994) provides a useful way to understand this blurring in her explanation of 'facialisation', which she uses to describe the blurring of distinctions between a body of disciplinary knowledge and the material body. She argues that the phrase 'face to face' which is often used in educational research to describe embodied pedagogical events, need not be an impoverished view of the work bodies do in pedagogical spaces. To her, bodies can be 'facialised' in and through pedagogical work, thereby acknowledging both the site and the sight of pedagogy.

It is important to note that this approach is not seeking to give home economics teachers a 'voice', as has been the intention of much critical redemptive research. This project is not redemptive unlike much of what passes for critical and feminist educational reform and research. The notion of redemptive culture is explored by Popkewitz (1997, p. 91) who asserts that the basis for educational reforms in the latter part of the last century "are inscribed in pedagogy as a culture of redemption — pedagogy is to save the child for society and to rescue society through the child". This is a shift from the early part of the last century where "the school was to rescue and save the child through making that child a productive citizen. The rescue was from the economic, social and cultural circumstances in which the child lived or to which the child aspired" (Popkewitz, 1997, p. 96). In this way, the redemptive culture of pedagogy at the start of the last century "embodied a social, collective project" (Popkewitz, 1997, p. 99), and this was the climate in which home economics as a field of study was established and thrived. However, the redemptive shift at the end of the last century was toward "the participatory, constructivist teacher who works with flexible identities in multiple communities (students)" (Popkewitz, 1997, p. 100). Popkewitz (1997, p. 92) argues that the practices of teacher reflection, empowerment, and decentralization of school policy making with which we have all become so familiar, join with constructivist pedagogies where students and teachers " 'make' knowledge and negotiate meaning" — in other words, the problem solving approach to education where the teacher is flexible, but still in the role of redemptive agent. Thus, Popkewitz (1997, p. 108) concludes, the governing practices of schools and their students and teachers exist in a culture of redemption where "reform and post-modern educational discourses utilize a similar image of the teacher and child that relate to the self-monitoring and self-motivated individual".

This work is about reconfiguring how to think about home economics as a cultural practice by documenting the practices deviant and normalizing certain teachers are engaged in, teachers whose bodies are rendered invisible in more orthodox inquiry. In this way, the purpose of the research is to reconfigure how to think differently about home economics teachers and the profession of home economics as a cultural practice.

There are three separate studies which each form part of an account. Study One and Study Two are surveys of collectively three hundred home economics teachers in which they provide a written account of home economics as a location of their pedagogical performance. This is in keeping with the advice of Fraser and Nicholson (1990) who argue for a rejection of the suggestion that research genres with modernist epistemologies be abandoned, but rather support the need to incorporate genres now linked with modernist techniques as a way of viewing influences which cannot be ignored. The 'typically' disciplined, governed body of the home economics teacher is located in this data. Following this, the data is re/searched using a postmodernist lens that disallows universalist perspectives. For Study One and Study Two, orthodox analytical methods were employed to read the qualitative and quantitative data collected.

Study Three comprises interviews with home economics teachers who identify themselves as 'marginal' or 'atypical'. However, the study does not simply accept this categorisation as 'the Truth' about these teachers. It refuses singular models

of the body as a norm against which all others are judged, drawing on the poststructuralist feminist idea of a 'field' of bodies
(Grosz, 1994). In support of Grosz's (1994) advice for undertaking
embodied postmodernist research, physical representations of the
subject's lived body are included as elements, moments, shreds
of home economics culture. The textual and contextual analysis
that follows heeds the advice of Flax (1990) and McWilliam,
Lather and Morgan (1997) documented earlier in this chapter
to open up disruptive, pressing, ironic, contradictory and disre-
spectful possibilities in the analysis. Specifically, the embodied
analysis utilises the theoretical work of Bakhtin's (1968) carnival
in Russo's (1994) *The Female Grotesque* as the interpretive lens.

   This analysis of 'marginal' home economists teaching
practices is undertaken by:

- documenting and describing some specific teaching sites;
- indicating how the existence of such practices unsettles
  the idea of home economics as a monolithic culture; and
- demonstrating the possibilities such marginal activities/
  identities might offer to home economics pedagogy.

The point of the analysis is to produce readings that are attentive
to the possibilities that exist within marginal identities for enacting a politics of difference in home economics. The analysis therefore inquires into particular home economics teaching bodies as
constantly 'in trouble', oscillating between attempts to be 'normal'
and to embrace their 'deviant' status. For this book, it is interesting to consider if these 'deviant' bodies are radical or subversive
to the home economics culture? The way of considering this question is by turning to the work of Michel Foucault (1985).

   In his book, The Use of Pleasure — The History of Sexuality
Volume 2, Foucault provides a way of considering the ethics
in which these atypical bodies are engaged. Foucault explains
how ancient Greek society recognized the struggles involved
in the production of the ethical individual — and the way pleasure is derived — by noting the use of terminology in certain texts.
This terminology distinguished between being 'moderate' and
'continent', and being 'immoderate' and 'incontinent'. According
to Foucault (1985, pp. 64–65), the ethical individual is 'moderate',
choosing the "right mean between insensitivity and excess" and
thus deriving "pleasure from the moderation he (sic) displays",
whereas the immoderate individual is "shameless and incorrigible", "taking pleasure in bad conduct". The continent individual,
as distinct from the "moderate" individual, experiences pleasures

"that are not in accord with reason, but he (sic) no longer allows himself (sic) to be carried away by them, and his (sic) merit will be greater in proportion as his (sic) desires are strong". In contrast, the incontinent individual deliberately chooses bad principles, allowing themselves to be "overcome in spite of himself (sic), and despite the reasonable principles he (sic) embraces". From Foucault's perspective, continent people are thought to have more virtue than moderate people as it is harder for them to restrain themselves. In the case of the modern teacher, the desirable ethical position is that of the moderate individual, or if not this, the continent individual — that is, either with the correct balance of reason or with the capacity to reject urgings for pleasure. What ethics do these atypical home economics teachers have, and therefore, what potential for subversion and radical change, by unsettling the mainstream culture of home economics?

Further Thinking

Conduct a thorough literature review to identify recent postmodernist research of relevance to home economics. As explained in this chapter, one of the challenges of postmodern thinking is the challenge of undertaking the task itself, that is, what is postmodernist research. In what ways did you determine that the research is postmodernist? How does this research contribute to the study of home economics?

The notion of 'fun' is one that is rarely used in conjunction with the idea of paid work. Why is it that fun and paid work are seen as incompatible? What understanding of fun is produced in a modernist theoretical framework? Why are the teaching profession and 'fun' seen as incompatible?

In this chapter the grotesque body of the carnivalesque is introduced as the theoretical point of interest as a way of re-thinking home economics. Referring to the relevant sections in the chapter, explain why such a conceptual 'tool' would be chosen in order to re-look at home economics teachers bodies that have been ignored and suppressed. What is the relevance of 'risk'?

Disciplining the Body of Home Economics Teachers

This

chapter provides a poststructuralist reading of corporeal pedagogical identity — specifically of the self-production of the disciplined body that is the home economics teacher. This feminist posthumanist approach is intended to interrogate the body as a text that speaks home economics as a cultural pedagogical practice. The analysis here and in the following chapters is framed by:

- ⌣' recognition of pedagogical work as 'embodied';
- ⌣' a shift from metanarrative to the local site;
- ⌣' a refusal to reject large scale research tools;
- ⌣' a shift from general theorizing to practice;
- ⌣' a refusal to establish 'laws' but to acknowledge the boundedness of truth claims;
- ⌣' an emphasis on bodies as the site of lived experience;
- ⌣' a rejection of binary constructions and unitary notions of gender;
- ⌣' incorporation of reflexive engagement with the language of the reporting data (for example, identifying gaps; focusing on ambiguous words or syntax etc);
- ⌣' the unsettling of familiar accounts; and
- ⌣' the weaving together of ideas and theories into an 'unfinished' tapestry of analytical elements.

An interrogation of home economics teachers as particular sorts of docile bodies, self-governing according to versions of 'proper' professional practice that are made available in the culture of home economics teaching are presented. In keeping with this, the data under scrutiny are provided by two large surveys administered to home economics teachers. The analysis reveals two key themes in texts written *about* home economics teachers *by* home economics teachers — that is, that 'normal' home economics teachers are 'skilled' bodies, but also they are 'suffering' bodies.

The 'Normal' Home Economics Teacher

Modernist research techniques are commonly used as normalizing practices by constructing 'typical' features of various categories, characterizing those who are the same and thereby dividing and positioning the others. Popkewitz (1997b, p. 25) explains that this "ordering of difference from sameness is a pervasive quality of contemporary social and educational theory" and is a "deeply embedded" approach. Home economics teachers, like other professional groups, conduct research which is complicit in producing a particular sort of docile body, self-governed and disciplined according to the versions of 'proper' professional practice that are made available in the culture of home economics teaching.

Two surveys of Queensland home economics teachers (Study One and Study Two) provided written accounts of home economics teaching from within the profession. Each survey was administered to home economics teachers in order to provide an account of the area as a location of pedagogical performance, as expressed by home economics teachers themselves. In this way the data generated from Study One and Study Two form a grand picture of home economics teachers, building upon orthodox methods. The surveys worked within methodological conventions of 'modernist' quantitative and qualitative modes of analysis.

Background to Study One and Study Two

The surveys used in the studies were designed for the purpose of collecting descriptive data, as opposed to analytical data that are concerned to test hypotheses about relationships between variables (Kidder & Judd, 1986). Descriptive surveys are designed to "portray accurately the characteristics of particular individuals, situations or groups, and to determine the frequency with which such behaviour or attitudes occur in the population being sampled" (Bulmer, 1984, p. 54). Since the purpose of the surveys was to give home economics teachers the opportunity to describe their identity and role as home economics teachers, descriptive surveys were appropriate. This approach has many precedents for use with professional groups, ranging from characterizing such professions as health information managers to scuba divers, to nurses and so on. For example Wilks and Austin (1991) considered the stereotype of the heroin user; Smith, Weinstein and Tanur (1991) considered the stereotype of women karate experts; and Wilks (1993) considered the stereotype of Australian scuba divers.

The collected information locates home economists by way of the language they use to name themselves. In essence, it provides a plain language account of home economics teachers. Both surveys were administered to 302 home economics teachers respectively. The first study collected demographic information including years of teaching experience, gender, location of workplace (country/metropolitan), and the number of teachers in the department in which the respondent worked. Next, the survey asked respondents to list up to 5 adjectives they would use to describe a home economics teacher. This data was also analyzed using SPSS and formed the foundation for the development of Survey Two. This technique has been used by other groups to enable them to gain an understanding of their members and how their members perceive their profession. This methodology is also used to determine stereotypes, that is, behavior for certain groups. For example, a study by Wilks and Austin (1991) to determine stereotypes of heroin users held by university undergraduate students resulted in the adjectives: dependent, insecure, addicted, unstable and desperate being generated. The final section of Survey One asked respondents to list advantages and disadvantages of being a home economics teacher; and finally, how they could recognize a "good home economics teacher". This data was analyzed using content analysis to generate a picture of overall trends through the identification of categories of responses.

The comprehensive findings of this study, and that of study two, are published elsewhere (see Pendergast, in press). In brief, Study one found that only 4.41 adjectives (of the total 146) were required to account for half of the participant's responses when asked to list terms describing a home economics teacher — this represents a strong stereotyping of home economics teachers by home economics teachers. The words included in the first 4.41 are: creative, hardworking, and organized; with the remaining one to two adjectives from caring, dedicated and practical, each of which scored the same percentage of selection (17%).

An interesting finding from this study emerged when the number of years of teacher experience was used to group the five adjectives to describe a home economics teacher. It was found that with increasing years of teaching experience, there was increased consensus around certain words to describe a home economics teacher, those being: organized, hardworking, creative and dedicated.

In terms of advantages and disadvantages of being a home economics teacher, three main advantages were identified: advantages emerging from the nature of the subject itself; advantages seen to offer benefits for the teacher; and advantages seen to offer benefits for the students, and thereby have a positive effect on teachers of home economics. For each of these categories, a number of common themes emerged and these were grouped into subcategories. For advantages relating to the subject itself, the five sub-categories included: the relevance of home economics for life; its vocational links; the challenging content; the variety and interest of the subject; and the practical, 'hands-on' nature of the subject. With respect to the second category, the perceived benefits to the teacher, six sub-categories were generated from the data. These are: positive student interaction with the teacher; the opportunity to engage in practical aspects in which the teacher is interested; the variety the subject offers teachers; the linkage between theory and practice; pride for teachers seeing students achieve; and the opportunity to consume food. With respect to the third category, that is, perceived benefits to the student, six sub-categories were generated from the data. These are: students freely choose the subject therefore they want to be there; students see they can achieve; students enjoy the practical components; students develop positive relationships with teachers; students develop a sense of satisfaction and pride; and students are positive about home economics.

In response to the request to state up to three disadvantages of being a home economics teacher, six main types of responses were identified in the data and categorized as: physical demands of the job; continual change and disruption; gender issues and politics associated with the gendered nature of the field; negative perceptions of the field; safety, hygiene and legal issues; and resource problems.

For some of these categories, a number of themes emerged and these were grouped into sub-categories. In some instances, further breakdown of these sub-categories was also possible. For others of the categories above, that is: continual change and disruption; gender issues and politics associated with the gendered nature of the field; and safety, hygiene and legal issues, there were no further sub-categories. For disadvantages because of the physical demands of the job, the four sub-categories were: the exhausting nature of practical classes; the physical demands of lifting heavy weights; stress; and demands associated with limited time. Time issues were further categorized into four types of time demands: professional development; preparation for practical classes; lunch and after school demands; and time demands associated with expectations of running functions for administration and for classes.

For disadvantages because of the negative perceptions of the field, the five sub-categories were: the public perception of the field as cooking and sewing; the perception by others that the field is not academic; the perception that home economists are 'jack of all trades, master of none'; the constant need to justify the existence of the field; and negative attitudes to home economics. The negative attitudes sub-category can be further broken into negative attitudes by school principals; students; and others, including parents and other teachers. For disadvantages because of the resource problems, the four sub-categories were: the demands placed on teachers due to the maintenance of equipment; the need for specialized rooms; lower ability students were often enrolled in the subject; and the high financial cost of the subject.

Survey respondents were asked to complete the following statement "I could recognize a *good home economics teacher* by...". Three main types of responses were identified in the data and categorized as: personal dimensions of the teacher; looking to the students; and other.

For responses related to personal dimensions of the teacher, there were two sub-categories: specific characteristics and descriptions of the teacher; and secondly, the teacher as a role model. The specific characteristics of the teacher were further classified into ten categories: physical appearance; respect; outgoing personality; management and organizational skills; positive approach; pride in their work; confidence; caring nature; enthusiastic approach; and a high degree of professionalism, evident in the areas of a commitment to and willingness to change, a commitment to students, a commitment to the philosophy of home economics, and a commitment to accepting difference.

For responses related to recognizing a good home economics teacher by looking to the students, there were five sub-categories: the teachers capacity to cater for the range of students; success for all students is possible; quality end products; enthusiastic students; and happy, enjoyable learning relationships between students and teacher.

The purpose of the second study was to consolidate, refine and validate findings from Study One regarding home economics teachers' perceptions and understandings of themselves. Just 6.37 adjectives were required to account for half of the participants' responses and this is considered to be a high index of uniformity. The six most frequently selected adjectives were: multi-skilled; professional; organized; resourceful; practical; and hardworking.

Survey Two also asked respondents to complete a semantic differential bi-polar comparison measure (Kane & Snyder, 1989) to describe their perception of a 'home economics teacher'. A semantic differential was chosen to assess current perceptions of home economics teachers by home economics teachers because it is a recognized and effective technique for measuring attitudes and perceptions of particular topics, issues or people (Isaac & Michael, 1981; Kane & Snyder, 1989). This method is often used to characterize the perceptions and stereotypes of professional groups (Kane, 1989). An example of this method is presented by Wilks (1993), who asked introductory divers to complete a semantic differential scale on 27 items, to describe the 'typical' scuba diver'. Findings revealed that the adjectives used to describe a typical scuba diver included: pleasant (unpleasant), good (bad), friendly (unfriendly), rugged (delicate), exciting (boring), happy (sad), energetic (lazy) and enthusiastic (unenthusiastic) (biploar adjective not selected is shown in brackets).

The adjectives which were strongly preferred to describe home economics teachers (the undesirable polar pair follows in bracket) were: hardworking (lazy); caring (uncaring); professional (unprofessional); dependable (undependable); and organized (disorganized). These were closely followed by: good (bad); pleasant (unpleasant); friendly (unfriendly); intelligent (stupid). The remaining adjective pairs provided no clear direction of preference.

This confirms preferred terms used by home economics teachers to describe home economics teachers as a collective, throughout Study One and Study Two. There is a repeated and persistent use of terms including: professional, organized, hardworking, caring, and multi-skilled. Other words that are favored include: resourceful and creative.

In addition to this very neat, modernist reading of the data produced out of these studies, further analysis of the data was conducted around the key themes identified. The reading that follows is organized around key descriptors of the 'typical' home economics teachers, as expressed in the teachers' texts. These are:

- multi-skilled, professional, organized, resourceful, practical, hardworking, caring, and creative;
- 'dishpan hands, varicose veins and stooped shoulders';
- the 'right' body; and
- 'women's work'.

Multi-Skilled, Professional, Organized, Resourceful, Practical, Hardworking, Caring, and Creative

When looking to the data to generate 'truthful categorizations' it is necessary to bear in mind that home economics teachers belong to the larger category of 'teacher'. 'Teachers' are already normalized as a collective, so home economics teachers exist within an already discursively produced domain. There are rules for performing as a teacher, and these are governed by folklore about what is recognizable as a teacher. In their book, *That's Funny, You Don't Look Like a Teacher*, Weber and Mitchell (1995, p. 11) note that "teachers are figures of such impossible familiarity that they are apt to vanish beneath the general and the particular disparagements such taken-for-granted phenomena may attract to themselves". This is evidenced in the data where teachers render themselves 'properly' invisible. Weber and Mitchell (1995) go on to demonstrate that the teachers body is culturally inscribed by "items of clothing ... glasses, hairstyles, makeup, tattoos, body decoration, jewelry, accessories and the like" (p. 55), explaining that through the use of such materiality, teachers bodies become normalized:

> Teachers are not supposed to look attractive or sexy or 'different'. They are not supposed to look aristocratic. They are supposed to reflect prevailing social standards of middle class respectability. If teachers do differ from the norm, they are expected to differ in a more negative manner that is somehow considered to be more true to life: teacher-as-spinster; teacher-as-absent-minded-bumbler; teacher-as-bossy-matron. (Weber & Mitchell, 1995, p. 60).

Given that 'teachers' as a broad category are produced in such ways, what are the particularities, if any, that make a 'home economics' teacher? In the surveys, home economics teachers were asked to list words to describe a typical home economics teacher, that is, to list the words commonly used to represent 'proper' or appropriate intellectual and/or behavioral work practices and personality characteristics of home economics teachers. The findings revealed the following words were the most frequently used by home economics teachers to describe 'normal' home economics teachers. In brackets are the percentages of the respondents (from one hundred and ninety-one respondents) selecting these terms: multi-skilled (70%); professional (43%); organized (39%); resourceful (35%); practical (30%); hardworking (27%); caring (26%); and creative (26%).

These words have an important function in producing a universalizing 'identity' for the home economics teacher — a norm or an ideal against which home economics teachers can judge themselves. In so doing, they reinforce the existence of dualities, inferring what a home economics teacher may not be, that is, they may not be unskilled, unprofessional, disorganized, lazy, uncaring, lacking resourcefulness, be impractical nor lacking creativity. These descriptors are not unique in that they privilege what would be expected in terms of any professional, paid worker. Further, predominantly the mind of the home economics teacher — not the body, is also privileged in these terms. Identity is thus produced as a result of working on the cognitive domain — and the work of teaching is thus rendered largely a mind-to-mind matter.

This privileging of the mind can be shown to be a product not simply of home economics research but of the epistemological assumptions that have underpinned this thematic as the prevailing view of knowledge, action and of theory in the field. For example, research by Banes (1992) characterized home economics as a female dominated profession whose teachers focus on developing career oriented skills and life management skills. Terms Banes used to describe home economics teachers included 'multi-skilled' and 'professional', both words correlating with the findings of Study One and Study Two. In this way, to be professional is to be 'skilled'. Another example is a study conducted by Jones (1994) where home economics teachers were asked to comment on the future directions for home economics. The directions most frequently advocated included: the maintenance of a survival/life skills approach; to ensure the practical does not become subservient to the theory; to become vocationally oriented; and to move the focus of study from the home to the wider world of industry and commerce. Again, in this research by Jones, the words used by home economics teachers to describe typical home economics teachers are consistent with current research, incorporating concepts which can be linked to the 'professional', 'caring', 'multi-skilled' nature of home economics teachers.

While these outcomes are of interest for reaffirming familiar narratives, the task here is to 're-member' (Shapiro, 1994) the material body of the home economics teacher. So what, if anything, do these written texts (in the form of respondents replies to survey questions) indicate about the *body* of home economics, beyond words used as basic descriptors? How do they describe the site/sight of the 'normal' home economics teacher?

Dishpan Hands, Varicose Veins and Stooped Shoulders

As already discussed in the previous section, in Study One and Study Two the key words used by home economics teachers to describe a 'typical' home economics teacher were gathered and analyzed. These words do not draw attention to the corporeality of teachers' work. When asked to list the advantages and disadvantages of being a home economics teacher and how a home economics teacher might be recognized by others, however, teachers did make reference to the fleshly body of the home economics teacher. This text is of particular interest in this study. One teacher suggested a home economics teacher is recognizable by:

> the bags under her eyes, dishpan hands, varicose veins, [and] a great sense of humor (they need it). [The home economics teacher] can leap a stove in a single bound [and] wears a superwoman t-shirt.

This is a powerful visual image of the literal sight of the home economics teacher. As an embodied vision, it speaks the gender of the teacher and implies that the body is a product of practices associated with being a home economics teacher — practices which produce and reproduce a particular sort of body. The tenor of this comment is repeated by other respondents in the survey who insist, for example, that "she has stooped shoulders from bringing in bags of groceries" or that "she is exhausted and downtrodden from cooking for the principal".

Many of the comments which were given as disadvantages of being a home economics teacher are in a similar vein. Rather than commenting on the body, most texts explain ways 'she' is likely to be identifiable to others. For example, home economics teachers are "seen as the school's general cook and bottle washer", "the stitch and stir lady", "the expert cooker and sewer" involved in and expected to "do the dishes", "washing up and the laundry", "fridge cleaning, kitchen checking, washing and drying and folding", "cleaning, housekeeping, shopping, budgeting chores", "equipment maintenance", and "mending kids shirts". Moreover, there is an expectation that they will "cater for functions in the school" and "make costumes for musicals", "give up all lunch hours" and "starve", and "lug sewing machines around". This leads to the home economics teacher being "exhausted", "stressed and in poor health". It is little wonder home economics teachers are described as "need[ing] to be 'superteacher[s]' " but are characterized by others as "expert[s] in drudgery".

The body of the home economics teachers produced in the above text is that of a docile and malnourished female in a traditional Western domestic setting. The text reinforces what Weber and Mitchell (1995, p. 60) argue is typical of teachers who may differ from the norm, that is, they are "more negative" and "more true to life" than a "typical conservative, middle class" teacher. Because the home economist is located within the domain of heterosexual normativity for women — cleaning, shopping, washing, cooking and sewing in the home or as a support in the school setting — she exists as a more 'true-to-life' and negative production than other female teachers. This normalizing spectacle of the home economics teacher is symptomatic of a repressive politics which can and does marginalize home economics teachers in schools — and outside them.

When commenting on the advantages of being a home economics teacher, a small number of references were made to the teacher's fleshly body. For example, the expression "hands on" was sometimes used to describe the applied nature of the area. To be "hands on" was seen as a positive; teachers described their appreciation of the "hands on" nature of the work in which they are engaged. To them, this was a pleasurable aspect of their work, and, in fact, they literally describe the practical nature of home economics as "getting your hands dirty".

The 'Right' Body

The text from the studies reveals that home economics teachers engage actively in disciplinary techniques for producing the 'right' body; — many express guilt and remorse if their body is 'not right'. Again, Weber and Mitchell (1995, p. 64) note that for teachers, having the 'right' and 'normal' body of a teacher is important to maintaining the "image of teachers as moral guides and upstanding members of society" and that "a certain type of personality is inevitably assumed to accompany a given choice" of body appearance.

That the home economics teachers body should be a "positive role model for students" was frequently stated as a way of recognizing a good home economics teacher. For example, one respondent insisted that home economics teachers should "practice what they preach, dress creatively, be polished, eat nutritious, home cooked food". The version of the 'proper' home economics teacher that emerges from such texts is of a person who painstakingly disciplines their body, "tak[ing] care in their appearance and so pride in their work". They should be "well groomed", have "great dress sense" and "set personal examples that match his/her expectations". In this way, home economics teachers use their body as a site to perform the home economics curriculum which (apparently) promotes such values. These comments indicate that careful bodily management is a way of recognizing home economics teachers.

Careful management is also necessary in the eating practices of the teacher in the classroom. Survey respondents make specific mention of how physical pleasure was gained through the "consumption of samples of food" which students offered to teachers. But this always introduced a risk because there was "too much food to be sampled" and this was potentially a problem because "home economics teachers can't be fat". This text reveals that home economics teachers govern themselves, self-regulating around the idea of a body that is not too fat and not too thin. This means a constant struggle between their role in testing food, and their need not to overindulge. It is only by getting the balance right that they can be a positive role model for their students both in terms of their physical appearance and their eating patterns.

Testing of food 'within reason' (McWilliam, in press), implies self-monitoring and abstinence, with the home economics teacher at times taking on the attributes of a martyr. They must rein in their appetite for food and give students 'affirmation'. In this way, home economics teachers govern themselves, controlling their food intake with a denial of appetite whilst still meeting the expectations of their work, thereby creating a well-governed body that is 'proper' for pedagogical display.

Home economics teachers also see it as their responsibility to "change/convert students with eating/diet problems". The idea that home economics teachers should play a redemptive role in the lives of students was reiterated in the texts many home economics teachers wrote about their ideal selves. This is in keeping with Popkewitz's (1997) argument that the governing practices of schools and their students and teachers are situated within a broader culture of redemption where the self-monitoring and self-motivated individual is valued. This role of the teacher is also supported by Weber & Mitchell (1995, p. 113) who argue that "[f]emale teachers are supposed to be selfless and sexless, adopting a 'leading from behind', child centered pedagogy". Home economics teachers, through their textual descriptions, suggest that they conform to this late twentieth century version of the teacher as self-denying savior.

Women's Work

From the text produced by the home economics teachers, it is apparent that home economics teachers are doubly produced — first as 'female' teachers, then as 'home economics' teachers. They are women, working in the domain of women, and as such, are strictly governed entities.

Many of the comments made about ideal and real home economics teachers' bodies indicate either directly, or through the use of gendered terminology, that the home economics teachers' body is gendered — that is they are "all female". Weber and Mitchell (1995) suggest that there are certain rules for the self-production of the female teacher (not just home economics teachers) that are not necessary for male teachers. They found that female teachers are produced as a 'certain kind' of woman, one who wears "long skirts, with their hair pulled back in severe buns, evoking the stereotype of an 'old maid' " (p. 45). Women who aim to be 'good teachers' are pushed to take part in this cultural production that has the effect of negating or effacing their sexuality. Not to do so is to risk being considered deviant.

The gendering of home economics in teachers texts goes beyond characterizing the home economics teacher's body as female. Home economics is viewed as a "women's subject"; "the girls [students] love it". This reinforces and parallels the widespread view that home economics is a gendered field of study and therefore necessarily lower in status as 'women's work'. As one teacher puts it:

> Being a so-called 'woman's' subject means people view it as unimportant, so we are continually having to prove the importance and get rid of the myth of 'just cooking and sewing'. We are often asked to do trivial work.

The dilemma named here is that 'cooking and sewing' is seen by outsiders as the main act in the performative dimension of home economics teachers, and this is more likely to be oppressive than status-enhancing. Home economics is impoverished because it is seen as 'women's work'. The lingering perceptions of home economics as 'cooking and sewing' remains a troubling legacy for home economics as a set of Australian educational practices, and the struggle to push beyond this folkloric perception towards legitimation has been ongoing and continues today, both as a struggle over content to be delivered to students, and as a struggle for a new location near the center of the politics of school knowledge. For example, the Mission of the Home Economics Institute of Australia (HEIA) (the peak body for home economics teachers in Australia), is to "enhance the professionalism and legitimation of Australian home economists" (HEIA, 1997). So home economics teachers find themselves at an impasse, where the performances and products of their field become the means to characterize the discipline in negative terms. This is what people see — the performance — (cooking and sewing); and the products — (the scones, cakes, shirts and skirts), all of which are understood to be material traces of women's work in the private sphere.

Because home economics is framed by its repressive classification as 'women's work', home economics teachers feel compelled to validate their existence in the school curriculum. As one home economics teacher in the study explains:

> [T]he principal of my current school constantly denigrates home economics and refers to it as the 'dying art of cooking and sewing' — my status in the school suffers greatly as a result. There is a real stigma because of this. I feel that I'm constantly having to justify home economics continued existence. I'm always 'soapboxing' and they see me as a dragon who is only good for doing the catering for all the functions and sewing costumes for the play.

Such comments were not rare, with respondents often referring to their necessary role as advocate for the subject. They sometimes created images of themselves as fighting for survival: for example the "soapboxing dragon" in the text above along with others including "superteacher", "superwoman", and "the bitch from 'H' block".

Home economists are not alone in suffering from status problems and trivialization of their work. As Madeleine Grumet (1988) argues, the struggle for legitimation of women's work is to be expected in all Western models of schooling given that education is dictated by male experience, ignoring women's lived experience as of no account. She argues that education has been distilled into an economic system that purposely ignores "experiences of family life, of bearing, delivering and nurturing children" (1988, p. 15) because they have no measurable economic value. The consequence is that where the struggle for legitimation begins and ends within the production of home economics as 'women's work', it will always be relegated to the margins of what is considered to be valued and valuable since it refuses to challenge the social production within which it operates.

Summary: The 'Two Bodies' of Home Economics Teachers

What does the preceding analysis, when taken together, tell us about home economics as a body of knowledge? What body work is being done in and through the body of the text?

It seems there is nothing 'new' offered in this account, simply a rehashing of already existing accounts of home economics. It is evident that many of the 'findings' presented in this section were already laid out in the literature, and this textual analysis simply spotlights the particular body work being done. This is to be expected given the orthodox tools utilized in these studies.

What can be argued is that there emerges from this analysis 'two bodies' for home economics teachers to inhabit. These bodies work together to produce the normalized home economics teacher. To be normal is to possess what can be termed the 'ideal body' (professional, organized ...) and the 'real body' (stooped shoulders, exhausted ...). This idea of the 'two bodies of home economics' is not without analytic precedent. In 1996 Ernst Kantorowicz (cited in Carrion, 1996, p. 45) introduced the 'two bodies' concept in order to explain the "complexities of the figure of a monarch". He argued that there were a number of "irreconcilable parts that had to be coordinated in order for the king to rule properly over all other bodies under him" and that in order for this to occur, the two bodies of the king represented 'private' and the 'public' interests. Similarly, the social production of the two bodies of home economics derives from and adds to myths and folklore value, and this is part of the normalizing tradition of being a home economics teacher, where seemingly irreconcilable parts remain in tension to facilitate the teaching of home economics.

Like the king in this dual scenario, the 'ideal' home economics teacher is a disciplined body — a member of a profession who is also organized, hardworking, caring, multiskilled, resourceful and creative. She is assumed to be a positive role model, with the 'right' weight, willing to perform as the redemptive savior, to produce quality products, and so on. The 'real' is the ruined body — with dishpan hands, who is: cleaner; cook; and martyr. She has black rings under her eyes, is starving, stressed, and in poor health, exhausted and wrecked from home economics work. These two bodies of home economics are in some senses both symbolic and irreconcilable, as dualisms always are. The real, ruined body of the home economics teacher is the physical effect of 'normalizing' — the sight of the 'good' home economics teacher at work. Both of these bodies also carry the weight of the gendered rules for the production of female teachers as an entire category (Weber & Mitchell, 1995). Hence, home economics teachers are doubly produced — first as 'normal' female teachers, and then as 'normal' home economics teachers. These real and ideal bodies are the disciplined bodies of home economics that are produced (and reproduced) out of the textual data produced from Study One and Study Two. The ideal can be described as a 'skilled' body and the real as the 'suffering' body. The home economics body suffers because of the marginalization of the field and everything that goes with this.

It is not surprising that the analysis undertaken thus far leads to a cul-de-sac in thinking about home economics teaching as necessarily dualistic. However, dualistic thinking (real/ideal, suffering/skilled) is a limited way of understanding the nature of home economics teachers. It is precisely this reductionist way of thinking about home economics that has stimulated me to push further in this research task. This 'known' position of 'truth' becomes my starting point for engaging in new ways of thinking about home economics teaching (Davis, 1997). Because postmodernist projects reject the notion of 'truths' and 'binary dualities' which typify such modernist work (Weiner, 1993), their first step is to look beyond the dominant assumptions in the field, and in so doing, to "exploit rather than cover or conceal" discrepancies or discontinuities in cultural practices. In this way, there is more to be gained by seeking out the aberrant than by reaffirming familiar narratives, such as this has done.

Further Thinking

Conduct your own survey of teachers, students or practitioners in the area of home economics (or another subject), attempting to locate a stereotype. Ask participants to generate a list of words they would use to describe a home economics——(e.g. teacher, student). Compare this to the findings presented in this chapter. Are the findings consistent? Explain reasons for similarities or aberrations.

One of the interesting comments the teachers in the surveys reported was their attempts at having the 'right body', to serve as a 'positive role model' and 'moral guide' for students. Do you consider this to be an essential role of home economists? What about other teachers? Explain your position, and extrapolate upon the effects of this stance.

Many of the stereotypical associations of home economics teachers presented in this chapter represent negative aspects of the work of home economists. In your view, are these truly negative aspects, or are they merely represented as that by our societal structures? Do you consider that home economics teachers would agree these are negative factors? Explain.

Four Odd Bodies: Home Economics as Carnival

Can home economics teachers do other than produce the hegemonic body of the skilled and suffering home economics teacher, and if so, how? This chapter documents four 'atypical' home economics teachers, examining how these potentially 'transgressive' bodies trouble the conventions of the profession. This is undertaken by providing a postmodernist reading of the body of the text, provided by interview data.

The questions which drive the reading/analysis of the atypical teachers are:

1.   How do the texts generated about the atypical teachers give shape to a body, which is both 'normal' and 'aberrant'?

2.   What body work is being done in and through the texts?

3.   How are these bodies 'atypical'?

4.   What relationship is there, if any, between these atypical teachers and the skilled and suffering body of 'normal' home economics teachers?

The four interviewees, and the order in which they are analysed in the section, are: John Brown; Valerie Archer; Marilyn Moore; and Elle Manson. These names are pseudonyms. Each of these home economics teachers are 'atypical' in a range of ways. In broad terms, John Brown is an atypical home economics teacher partly because of his gender. Valerie Archer steps outside the enclosures of the home to include the outdoors. Marilyn Moore's sexy, 'groovy' body is atypical. And the fourth subject — Elle Manson — is atypical because of her willingness to touch students. The work of this analysis is to read how interview and related textual data frames these four teachers as embodied discursive subjects.

Subject 1: John Brown
— Hypermasculinity in Home Economics

This teacher is introduced by way of my own reflections upon first meeting him as a student home economics teacher at university. I was a lecturer in the area of home economics and in most of the eight semesters during which John completed his Bachelor of Education (Home Economics — Secondary), I was a unit co-ordinator in at least one of his four subjects. My memories of him are strong because of the extent to which he 'stood out', challenging the norm whenever the opportunity arose:

> I met John on his first day at university as a student home economics teacher. His first words to me were "I didn't know the lecturers would be young Sheilas like you". John must be in the wrong class. He was male, obese, ex-army, tattooed, smoking heavily, coughing a heavy smokers cough, wearing a black t-shirt, and riding a motor bike. His face was aggressive.

> At the end of his first year of study he gave me a card that said "For a feminist you're not a bad chick", along with the gift of a cigar. He said he would have given flowers but that would have insulted me.

> At the end of his degree he gave me a card that he had sketched from a photograph of himself. The photograph showed him holding a placard which read "Home ec rules okay ... or else!" with a very aggressive face and fist thrust forward. He drew a sketch from the photograph for use as a Christmas card, and in his determination, as suitable for promotional material for use in schools. In this sketch, he is holding the placard which in this case is pinned to a baseball bat. The threat is clear. He gave me a carton of beer and said I was "a good bloke for a Sheila". He wanted to take me on a pub crawl as a sign of appreciation. I went.

John was invited to participate in this book as an atypical home economics teacher initially because of his 'atypical' gender. He is a home economics teacher and his role as a home economics teacher is complicated by his maleness because, as we have seen, home economics is defined as 'other' to him, with feminine experiences and perspectives presented as the authentic experience of home economics. John's presence as a male home economics teacher positions him as 'working out of' home economics texts, not 'working outside' of them. Being other to the norm of the properly produced home economics teachers provides opportunity to consider how the atypical bodies cut across, as well as augment, the mainstream body of home economics. This documentation draws on what John's students had to say about him when asked to comment on how he looks, sounds and acts in a typical home economics class on a typical day, along with interview text.

White Female, Well Dressed

John self-identifies as an atypical home economics teacher. To him, a home economics teacher "must be female, white, upper to middle class" (John, Line 14). In his eyes, he therefore cannot be a typical or proper home economics teacher. When provided with the opportunity to elaborate further, he indicates that the clothing worn by home economics teachers makes these women distinguishable from other female teachers. He also notes behavioural differences, as in the following interview extract:

16 John   [Home economics teachers are] ... well dressed and usually with fairly expensive clothing ...

18 John   ... that's what I would say would be typical.

19 Donna   Right, and how would the public distinguish her from other women?

20 John   I think probably the way she dresses would be a lot of it. I've found most home economics teachers I've ... the older ones I'm talking about now ... one's that have been teaching for, you know, say over 10 years, are usually very well dressed and um (laughs), might sound a bit funny but you know, I mean a little bit fussy. If you know what I mean ... like they fuss around, do things like cook a few little scones here and a few little things like that, you know, and just do the little things around the staff room that, you know, not many other people sort of do.

27 John   Yes. I'd say you should get a very well dressed white upper to middle class female running around making sure they've got plenty of biscuits in the staff room and if we need coffee and tea and milk then yes, straight away, that would be the home economics teacher.

John is familiar with what it means to be a typical home economics teacher, and how this includes being a female teacher of a particular sort (Weber & Mitchell, 1995). To him, the home economics teacher is recognisable by gender, race, socio-economic status, standard of dress, age, "fussy" nature, and her role as provider of food. Her public image as the "morning tea lady" reinforces what home economics teachers indicate in the surveys to be a disadvantage of the field — and yet that is how those from within the field identify as the public persona of the home economics teacher! It is immediately obvious that John cannot conform to this embodied vision because the mere fact that he is a male home economics teacher makes him atypical — his anatomical body does not fit the norm.

But there are other reasons he and his students consider him to be different. As one of his students stated:

> Mr Brown is really good. He is the greatest and different type of teacher to work with. He's not a typical home economics teacher. (Male student, aged 16)

The proposition here is that John's 'difference' is what makes him 'good'. This proposition troubles the norm (typical is good). In this way John's identity appears to cut across assumptions about 'good' teachers.

A Man – Overweight, Big Belly and Mustache

John is a man … and he is a home economics teacher. This point is insisted on by his students who state clearly that he is not normal because of this fact. The students' written texts which follow show how students link his male gender and his role as a home economics teacher:

> Mr Brown doesn't look like a normal home economics teacher because he's not precepted (sic) as one because he's not a woman. He's a good teacher and we can understand him and he helps us with our work without us feeling stupid. I think he's a great teacher. (Female student, aged 16)

> Mr Brown does not look and act like a normal home economics teacher, because he's a man. Unlike other home economics teachers that I have had Mr Brown helps us cook and doesn't say that our cooking isn't good enough. He doesn't put our work down. (Female student, aged 16)

> Mr Brown is not the stereotypical home economics teacher. Most people think that it's weird that when I talk about my home economics I say "Sir said this, Sir did that" instead of "Miss". During practical lessons he walks around singing old songs in a really bad voice, but we enjoy it. I think there should be more male home economics teachers if they are like him. (Female student, aged 16)

These texts indicate what John Brown does not look like and why — that is, he doesn't look like a home economics teacher because he's not a woman. 'Home economics teacher' and 'male teacher' are dualities. In this binary, one is clearly privileged by the students and by the normative discourse. This comment is repeated frequently by the students and is for many, the foremost reason this teacher is different.

Students elaborate on this difference in terms of the physical aspect of John's body. For instance:

> Mr Brown is fairly tall and is a bit overweight, he's got a big belly, sort of medium build. He talks normal. He has a short beard and a mustash (sic) and always wears long shirts and long pants. He has black hair and a deep voice. (Female student, aged 16)

These descriptions of the physical body of the teacher highlight the 'masculine' features of the teacher. He has a mustache, beard and deep voice — masculine characteristics which set him apart from being the norm. He also has a "big belly", a point reiterated in the following student text:

> My teacher is a white male with a mastash (sic). He's a bit overweight for a home economics teacher. But he's a good teacher. He acts like a pretty normal human being. You would never think of him as a teacher. (Female student aged 16)

The 'body work' being done through this text is of particular interest. The student texts describe their teacher as "normal", "good", "overweight" and so on, and note that this is at odds with his role as a teacher —"you would never think of him as a teacher". What seems to be implied here is that someone cannot be a "pretty normal human being" and also be a teacher.

The texts draw attention to a body that is not an appropriately disciplined body for a home economics teacher — he is a "bit overweight, he's got a big belly" and this is not usual "for a home economics teacher". John's fat, fleshly body with its big belly cuts across the expected body of a 'proper' home economics teacher. The sight of his excessive body is not typical in such a context. As indicated in the earlier analysis of texts from Study One and Study Two, home economics teachers are expected to have bodies which are disciplined role models for their students. That is, they are expected to have the 'right' body — not too fat and not too thin. To quote from the text of a teacher in Study One, "home economics teachers can't be fat". John's body contradicts this expectation. How then does John reconcile his obese body with that of a 'good' teacher? The following text explains his efforts to do so:

134 John	(Coughs) Excuse me, I haven't got … the body that I had like ten years ago as it were but (laughs) I often sort of refer to that … and if I go down to the tuck shop for example I know I'll buy a can of coke or something and the kids say "Oh, you shouldn't be doing that Sir". I say "No", you know "and if you drink that you'll end up looking like me".
136 John	… because I taught you this sort of thing, you know. I sort of refer to that a bit. You know, if I eat the wrong foods they always say yes, and that's why I look like I do … "Sir's a big fat fella because he eats pies and coke". You know, there's a lot of other home ec teachers … we haven't got any very svelte, is the word svelte?
138 John	… home economics teachers in there but they always seem to be eating the right things like salad rolls and all that sort of thing … whereas I probably seem to be eating the wrong things, but, as I said, I just refer back to it and I don't sort of try to say look "okay, I'm fat but I eat the right things so I'm good". I say, "look, I eat all the worst things and all the

things I shouldn't be eating and that is why I'm fat". So I use my body that way.

John talks about using his body to model what not to do. This contrasts with what home economics teachers in Study One say good home economics teachers should do — that is — to be "positive role models for students", "practice what they preach" and "eat nutritious, home cooked food". Instead, his body is a parody of the 'right' body, and he uses it as a negative exemplar in his teaching. In this way, he can "eat ... the wrong things" and still maintain his redemptive role. He understands the importance of right foods and wrong foods, using his body to do 'good' pedagogical work by naming it as a failed project of governance. In this way he remains orthodox, working within, not against, the orthodoxy of home economics knowledge.

However, John expresses neither the guilt nor the self-denial which so often accompanies failed body projects, especially for women. He acknowledges that his literal sight is far from orthodox, but without apparent distress or self loathing. He describes his physical body and the clothing which adorns it as follows:

30 John   ... probably overweight, clothes probably not well fitting, basically because of body shape ... probably doesn't care about the external appearance as maybe other home economics teachers do, for example, the shirt hanging out a little bit at the back, or ... one of the things I've noticed about myself when I looked at myself on a video for example is I usually have my belt sitting underneath my beer belly as if it were, you know, right really hip, really sitting on the hip.

32 John   ... with the crutch of the trousers away down near the knees somewhere, you know what I mean.

34 John   ... usually with a crew cut but not always ... very short hair, but you know, often with a crew cut and a beard ah, depending on every now and then like, I just take most of it off and just regrow it again, rather than shave it every day. I just take most of it off and then I just regrow it for a couple of months and then I just take it off again and regrow it. So probably ... half a beard perhaps.

The text above addresses the sight of his body. He acknowledges that his clothing and his way of wearing clothing is not the norm for a home economics teacher, that he "probably doesn't care" as much as "other" home economics teachers do about these issues. This is evidenced for example, in "the shirt hanging out a little bit at the back" and "the crutch of the trousers away down near the knees". He refers to looking at himself on video, and observing that his "beer belly" causes his belt to "really sit[ting] on the hip". Again, the physicality of this teacher cuts across the expected body of the home economics teacher. John's students also comment on his lack of concern about external appearance, but they are also careful to point out that this does not detract from him being a good teacher. Indeed, quite the reverse is true:

> He's a good teacher, but he looks a bit scruffy and untidy. He is always polite and concerned about students. He doesn't lose his temper very often and his lessons are fun to be in. He hardly yells at students for doing something wrong. (Female student, aged 15)

> Another positive is his dress standards. He is relaxed is (sic) which makes us feel relaxed and by him feeling relaxed he is less stressed. And he doesn't have to worry about ruining his clothing while demonstrating food to us. (Female student, aged 17)

In earlier discussions certain dress standards of home economics teachers were identified as characteristic of normal teachers. John also notes that clothing is a way of recognising a typical home economics teacher, given his comment that home economics teachers are "well dressed and usually with fairly expensive clothing" (John, Line 16). From his interview transcripts and the texts of his students, it appears that John rejects this normalising strategy of being "well dressed". Students note that because he is "scruffy", it does not mean that he is impolite or unconcerned about students. His 'dress' is described in one text as "relaxed", and this is linked to students feeling relaxed as he is "feeling relaxed [so] he is less stressed". This is a literal sight which students see as different from other teachers. Students even advocate for John's 'style', arguing that he is more appropriately dressed because his clothing cannot be ruined in class.

Sing, Dance and Cook

There are other characteristics beyond his relaxed and unruly body which make John different: he doesn't perform like a home economics teacher. One student claims he "helps us cook" and "doesn't say that our cooking isn't good enough. He doesn't put our work down". This student text suggests that this student may have been the recipient of criticism from other home economics teachers, where he was made to feel "stupid". Moreover, John claims in his interview that he is not a typical home economics teacher because he is not judgmental and that such an attitude seems to come from a typically conservative, "sheltered" background (which is the background he believes most home economics teachers to have) unlike his own:

> 94 John   I think there's too much judgmental factors come into ... in particular home economics teachers and I think this is

based on what I perceive ... I would say the background home economics people have. I think in general most home economics people come from a fairly sheltered background and I mentioned before upper to middle class, middle class up rather than say middle to lower.

96 John   And I think with that fairly sheltered background with the family structure, fairly stable ...

98 John   ... and I don't think they can relate to a lot of the students who we have here who don't even live at home, like they live in different places. We've got people in this school who live in shelters. We've got students who come to school for a week and haven't been home because they had to live under a bridge because their parents have been drinking.

The conservative culture of home economics and home economics teachers has been discussed previously. In this earlier discussion, it was explained that the original purpose of the field was to provide the necessary skills to prepare women for life roles through the production of desirable (conservative) feminine identities for the home and workplace (Eyre, 1989; Brown, 1988; Badir, 1990; Logan, 1981; Pendergast, 1991). These conventions were achieved by the training of women using curricula selected as appropriate for these roles, including preparation for varying roles of servitude. Because of this historical past, home economics as a field of study has been indicted for perpetuating conservative, middle class values as social norms (Thorne, 1980). According to John, the legacy that remains is the judgmental attitude held by home economics teachers, and this, in turn is linked to middle class conservatism which rejects risk taking.

John also acts differently in the home economics classroom. His body performs for the students pleasure, and also for his pleasure:

My teacher is a male home economics teacher. I have had female teachers in the past and I prefer him. He sounds like a good Aussie bloke. He acts like a friend and is one. He will always make us laugh. He can sing and dance and cook, which all home economics teachers should do. In conclusion, he is a terrific teacher with a heart of gold. (Female student, aged 16)

Mr Brown is a very intelligent man and I also know he's a great Dad for his children. He is very entertaining, we never need a radio because Mr Brown sings his favourite 'oldies' songs. He doesn't look like a typical home economics teacher because there aren't many male home economics teachers. (Female student, aged 16)

Mr Brown can sing really good. He is a good person and can help people. He's a good bloke and a good chef. (Male student, aged 15)

Mr Brown does not look like a home economics teacher because he's a man. But he's a good teacher, knows a lot about the subject and he's easy to get along with. He teaches the class clearly and can easily be understood. Mr Brown sings and jokes around in class which makes it fun. He's a great teacher and every class gets better every lesson, you don't know what to expect. Even the theory lesson's are worth goin (sic) to. (Female student aged, 16)

The students talk about the teacher as a friend and an entertainer, singing, dancing and joking, making students laugh and having fun — this is his atypical performance of home economics. This performance is acknowledged beyond the home economics classroom, as is evidenced by the senior school song penned by the 1997 grade 12 students, which contained a stanza about him:

Mr Brown and his singing

Makin' us all go deaf

Mr Brown and his singing

We're gonna take his voice box out

John considers each home economics class to be a performance, and that his singing, dancing and joke telling are his trademark, providing mutual pleasure for his students and himself. He 'performs' in his home economics classroom. He describes this aspect of his teaching in the following interview text:

168 John   And when you're actually sort of cooking I often sort of walk around singing, I just sort of walk around and they hate my songs because I sing a lot of country and western (Laughs) but I walk around and ... now they use radios in the block and that sort of thing but we don't actually seem to use them. I just walk around singing and that sort of thing and ... I thought I'd just sort of liven them up and they said "Oh yea, that's terrible" and that sort of thing. I say, "okay fine we'll have a nominated singer" ... every lesson you know like I'll nominate one student who will sing throughout the lesson and so I've nominated them and they'll say "oh no no no no, I'm not going to sing", "shame", you know, that kind of thing. So I say, "oh well, if you don't want to then I'll keep singing" (laughs) and the kids bear it in good stride ... so I get to sing whatever. I find it makes for a pretty good working relationship with the students, cause they know I'm not ... I don't know I just find it relaxes the kids.

John integrates his singing and dancing into his overall teaching style, i.e., into the "physical postures, poses and persuasions" (McWilliam, 1996b, p. 16) that are enacted here as a teacher. John argues that his approach "makes for a pretty good working relationship with the students" (Line 168), that his embodied performances lead to an enhanced pedagogical relationship with students. He also sees his singing and dancing as "relax[ing] the kids", another reference to the pedagogical posture he performs often but not always. Embedded in his overall classroom management style is a preference for the didactic, which he admits is "wrong" because it is contrary to his teacher training instructions at University. He says he does "everything that I've been told not to do", going on to explain that his class is run on a military style, in what he calls the "old army spiel". He yells instructions such as "line up", "march in", "stand up", *"you will be able to..."*. In his own words:

142 John   I either go in and I'll set up I'll ... I sort of do everything wrong, you know what I mean, I sort of do everything that I've been told not to do.

143 Donna   (Laughs) like what?

144 John   Well, I was told I need this structure and that sort of thing. And you come in and you do the first ten minutes and you ... you must know and make sure the students understand the first two minutes and like, and I agree with that, you know, and I'm not saying I shouldn't be doing that, I just don't ... I do the old army spiel, the kids come in, and I line them up and we march in basically and I sort of stand them up and say "right AND THIS LESSON YOU WILL LEARN HOW TO MAKE CABBAGE STEW, BY THE END OF THIS LESSON IF YOU DO *NOT* KNOW HOW TO MAKE CABBAGE STEW THEN YOU HAVE NOT LISTENED TO ME", that sort of thing ...

John makes excuses for his classroom management style, knowing that it is not the right (orthodox) way to teach. He is aware of his departure from the 'good' rhetoric of student-centred pedagogy. He describes this approach more fully:

152 John   That's the introduction and then with them I ... do the demo or whatever ... I often use the kids, give them the instructions... I know I've got to go in there and I've just got to set up all the classroom and I've got to have my ingredients and that sort of thing in front of me. And then come in and the students are going to come in and they're all going to have everything ready to go and everything's going to be lovely, but I come in and I'll say right and I've actually got nothing on the bench and there might be say ten kids there and I'll just rattle off the ingredients so you know, "Frank" ... "get the self raising flour; you get the sugar; you get the butter; you get this; you get that" and they just go booff.

John explains that this is not typical home economics teaching practice. The teacher-centred didactic methods he uses and practices (the old Army spiel — marching, drilling, ordering) are contrary to the model he was encouraged to use as a student teacher at University. Instead, he falls back on what he knows from his previous career in the Army — Army drills. He "knows" this is not the norm, even agreeing that his approach is "not right", and suggesting that "I'm not saying I shouldn't be doing that" (the 'right' student-centred pedagogical approach advocated at University). This insistence on the 'wrong' performance is a tricky pedagogical posture.

McWilliam (1996b) explains that "teachers display their disciplines at work in the culture by rehearsing and enacting particular poses or 'positions' in relation to knowledge". Their positions are:

... manifest in the performative dimension of teaching, whether as text, utterance or bodily gesture. Through 'performances' ... teachers ... indicate a range of positions in relation to a 'body' of disciplinary knowledge. [They] model knowing by striking a range of scholastic poses through which the learner is mobilised to desire to learn, to reject the seductive power of ignorance. (McWilliam, 1996b, p. 17)

John enacts a certain 'mock' military positioning in his home economics pedagogy and this is embodied in his utterances (the old Army spiel) and bodily gestures (singing and dancing). The pedagogical message is that pleasure and regulation come together in his performance. The effect on students seems to be that they are mobilised to engage in the disciplinary work. And yet, earlier in this analysis, students referred to John's "relaxed" and "unruly" style, particularly with regard to his dress. John is both relaxed AND disciplined, blending the Army discipline with the relaxed dress of the unruly teacher. However, John's pedagogy is far from being radical. It disturbs usual conceptions of home economics teaching, but recuperates the "teacher as ultimate authority, male in power" (Weber & Mitchell, 1995, p. 98) which is characteristic of traditional teaching.

A 'Blokey' Kinda Bloke

It is evident from their texts that students do not see John as a typical home economics teacher. Instead, they recast him in two ways. The first is as a "normal, typical", "good" (male) teacher (but not a home economics teacher). The second is as a chef, and in particular, an Army chef. The following student texts demonstrate examples of how John is depicted as a "normal, typical" and "good" teacher:

Mr Brown doesn't look like a home economics teacher — he looks like a normal, typical teacher. Most people think it's weird when we say that our teacher is male but to us he is one of the best, if not the best teacher in the school ... I personally think there should be more male home economics teachers like him because if they were all like him I know that their (sic) would be more people doing these subjects. He's a good bloke. (Female student, aged 16)

Mr Brown looks like a good teacher. He is better than all the other teachers I had for home ec. He is funny and he sings a lot. We learn a lot from him and I enjoy going to his class. (Female student aged, 16)

Mr Brown looks like a good teacher and he is a good teacher. He is funny and makes jokes all the time. If you are bad he will get up you, but not in a mean way. (Female student, aged 13)

In these instances, John is characterised as a 'normal' male teacher. According to Weber and Mitchell (1995, p. 58), male teachers work out of a set of cultural rules about what is recognisable as a male teacher:

[They wear] nondescript clothes, sometimes a suit, usually a shirt or sweater and pants, occasionally a beard, often with heavy glasses. These male teachers are often a bit scruffy, and occasionally covered in chalk dust.

John's body — evidently — complies with this socially produced version of what male teachers are supposed to look like. He embodies the heterosexual masculinity expected of 'relaxed' male teachers — "a beard", "a bit scruffy" and wearing "nondescript clothes". But producing himself as a typical, normal male teacher in the field of home economics is rule breaking because typical males in home economics are non-hegemonic males, they are exceptional in that they are not typically heterosexual males. 'Real men' do not frequent the domain of the home economics classroom, and yet John does.

Another way John's pedagogical body is made visible in the home economics classroom is as a chef, as the following students texts indicate:

Mr Brown looks like a chef. He's a good singer and he makes the class interesting. In other words, he is a 'legend'. (Female student, aged 17)

Mr Brown is the best. He is a good bloke and a good chef! (Male student, aged 16)

The text indicates that John "looks like a chef" and acts like a chef. He is not merely a "cooker and sewer" like other female home economics teachers, but is elevated to the higher public status position of "chef". This provides a form of legitimation for John in his role as home economics teacher. It is okay for a man to be a chef. This is an honourable vocational outcome for a heterosexual male, so teaching in this area can be validated within such a framework. He is 'normal' in this sense. Often he dresses in chef's apparel, reinforcing this role as chef. John confirms in his interview that he is more comfortable being recognised as a chef than as a home economics teacher and that he promotes this understanding in his students, believing that "most of the students ... see [him] as a chef" (John, Line 58). In this way, his skills in catering move the domain from the private space of the home kitchen to the public space of the restaurant.

42 John	... So I think most people do recognise that I'm sort of stronger in the food area ... and in particular in the food area, the hospitality side of cooking bulk, cooking functions etc.
44 John	... I think I'm not saying, I'm not trying to blow my own trumpet or anything like that, but most people if they sort of talk about me and sort of usually mention one of the functions I've catered.
46 John	At the school using the students, rather than any shirt or anything like that I've ... the one's the students have made, it's always referred back to, "oh yeah, it was a great night that the cooking kids did the other night", or something like that. It's usually referred back ... something I've catered for the school, or within the school.

It is interesting to note that John acknowledges that he is recognised and valued by the school community because of his contribution as caterer, performing for and at school functions. The text he employs to describe this food preparation with students is driven by employment related terms such as: "hospitality"; "cooking functions"; "cooking bulk"; and "cater". This is the language of public authority, of legitimation and power, of a chef in professional role, and can be contrasted with the home economics language of private home "cooking". The positive recognition John gains from this role as chef, performing his public catering role, appears to be the antithesis of the recognition brought to home economics "cookers". In the teacher texts from Study One and Study Two about home economics teachers roles, the image of the home economics teacher as 'cooker and sewer' is a derogatory image. Teacher texts speak of the negative association with this image, being seen as "the school's general cook and bottle washer", "do[ing] the dishes", "catering for principal's morning teas" and being "expert[s] in drudgery". These were disadvantages of being a home economics teacher. Performing the same roles but by a different name and with a male chef (instead of a female home economics teacher) in a 'public' context, removes the negative connotations. This is because John is seen to be a legitimate chef (e.g. "cooking in bulk"), not a home economics teacher playing at it (cooking in quantities for the home). The private/public divide is the issue. This is not surprising to Grumet (1988), who argues that the marginalisation of the private is to be expected since education and curriculum is dictated by male experience, ignoring women's lived experience as of no account. Grumet argues that education has been distilled into an economic system which purposely ignores the work of the private domain because it has no measurable economic value. Hence, the private work of the home economists is marginalised, whilst the public work of the professional chef is considered to be valued and valuable since it contributes to the economic system. The text which follows reveals John's need to validate his role as home economics teacher by this more legitimate role as cook and chef:

48 John   Yeah, a lot, another reason for that I think as well is ... I've heard that since, ever since I've entered university for example, if I've told someone "Oh yes, I'm a home economics teacher" the eyebrow sort of shoots up and they sort of look at me a bit funny and then I'll say "well see, I'm a chef by trade" and then they go "oh yeah, well that's okay", I mean, they don't actually say, but you can actually see it in the body language. Oh, okay, there is a reason why you are doing a home economics course being a home economics teacher in that you are a chef, that it's okay.

52 John   If I don't say, "yeah, look I'm a home economics teacher and I cook and I teach sewing and cooking or whatever", not that I'd do that because I learnt all this stuff at university that we don't say that, but, if I was to say "yes, I'm a home economics teacher" and I just decided to be a home economics teacher with actually no prior background and I had a chance to be say, an English or a history teacher but I chose home economics, then I often get some ah ... you know as I said some strange looks ... as if to say what the hell are you doing that for ... and as I said, I say, "well, look, I was a chef by trade so you know I wanted to teach cooking", and that sort of seems to be, in their body language, that it's perceived to be okay then. Do you understand what I mean?

54 John   Okay, yeah, well, that's okay, well, if you were a cook, yes. Now I understand why you chose to do that, whereas before when you just said you were a home economics teacher I could not understand why you were in that position.

56 John   But now it's okay. You know, and that legitimises me. You know what I mean?

In this text John explains the way he validates his decision to be a home economics teacher, emerging out of his more legitimate role as a chef. It is not 'valid' to be both a 'normal' heterosexual male and to be a home economics teacher. John's positioning of himself in the home economics landscape as a cook or chef with a vocational orientation in this area reworks this problematic. His description of the situation where "the eyebrow sort of shoots up and they sort of look at me a bit funny" is suggestive of a judgment being made about his masculinity. The raised eyebrow introduces a questioning gaze — is this man strange/ 'queer'? This is a very important matter in such a homophobic culture as Australia and in such a homophobic context as the school, and within such a female dominated sphere as home economics.

John's ability to reclaim his heterosexual masculinity is evident in many of the student texts, where reference is made to him as a "bloke", and a "good Aussie bloke" at that. For example:

> Mr Brown is a typical Aussie bloke. Home economics wouldn't be fun without him. (Male student, aged 15)

> He looks like, sounds like a great guy, which he definitely is. He is a *great person and a good bloke*. (Female student, aged 17)

'Blokes' have certain rituals and performances. Further, being a bloke removes the other possible role for a man in home economics — the effeminate male whose sexuality is immediately brought into question, the androgynous man — the not heterosexual male. Being a 'typical bloke' suggests that John is a heterosexual male. Perhaps the strongest confirmation of John being seen in the role of a bloke is evident in the student text which follows:

> He looks like a truck driver, bouncer guy, but has the heart of a (????) caring. He's a good bloke. (Male student, aged 17)

The imagery of the truck driver and bouncer confirms John's heterosexuality. And, according to John, being a "good bloke" also works as a positive role model for the male students. He explains:

72 John   ... a lot of the lads, especially, as I said, in practical home economics class, they're not rocket scientists, you know what I mean?

74 John   ... and probably never will be rocket scientists, you know, no matter how much study they do they probably never will be rocket scientists, but I think by having me as a teacher it's okay. They see it as okay.

76 John   You know, to do it, well, it's okay. Look, you know, our teachers a bloke you know, and I think ... then again, kind of you know, sounding my own trumpet, I think they would like to see a blokey bloke there rather than a non blokey bloke, if you understand what I'm saying then.

In his text, John is making a distinction about the type of bloke he is. That is, he is not a "non-blokey bloke" (homosexual, effeminate, strange, non-heterosexual etc) but a "blokey bloke", a heterosexual and a hypermasculine male. In this way he can be "okay" in the eyes of his students in that he is blokey (heterosexual) that is, he can be 'different' in culturally normative ways. He suggests that this is what his students "like to see", just as women are heterosexual in terms of a performance of the body of home economics. It is interesting to see what John means by being a "blokey bloke". That is:

78 John — Someone they can relate to, if you know what I mean. Like they come in and say "g'day how ya goin", and I'll say, "how ya goin" back, they can relate to that. You know, if they come in and say "g'day, how ya goin" and I said "Good morning class and take your seat now and let us ..." You know, they just can't relate to that, if you understand what I mean.

79 Donna — Uh huh.

80 John — ... and I think they're looking for someone who's sort of down a bit, bit down to earth, someone who can understand where they're coming from as well.

He considers that being a "blokey bloke" is evident in his language, his manner, and his "down to earth approach". The use of slang, his example being his return welcome to students of "how ya goin", is evidence of the "blokey" culture being enacted. He contends that a formal response would be inappropriate because students "just can't relate to that". By being "someone they (students) can relate to" as a 'normal' male this makes it acceptable for his heterosexual male students to be in the home economics classroom and there is no threat to heterosexual normativity.

Another dimension of John's production of heterosexual normativity is his use of swearing — which is part of the broader folklore about 'blokes'. And this is embodied in a physical form which is clearly recognisable as a blokey form, a hypermasculine form.

82 John — ... and I think they feel fairly comfortable with that ... I make a lot of mistakes as a teacher. For example, I swear every now and then I'll say "oh shit", when something goes wrong. And the students know I don't allow swearing in my class but because I swear every now and then they'll always pick me up on it and say "Sir, you swore you know you'll have to do five minutes detention" that sort of thing and then I just turn around and say "you know, you're right". I do, "I shouldn't have swore blah blah blah so now the whole class has to come up at lunch time and make sure I do my five minutes detention" and this sort of thing, and they accept that.

John speaks of "making mistakes" as a teacher and places swearing in class in this category. His text implies that he considers swearing in class to be unorthodox for teachers. However, from these 'contrived mistakes' or deliberate 'slip ups', he quickly redeems himself by taking perverse pleasure in reversing the role of teacher-as-disciplinarian-of-student to student-as-disciplinarian-of-teacher. In recuperating in this way, his strategy of dealing with his own swearing institutionalises discipline as foundational to the classroom. He normalises his behaviour within the frame of acceptable classroom behaviour for a teacher, noting his own transgression and offering a 'remedy' for his students to accept him back into the normative traditions. He carries through the 'charade' and notes that his students "accept that".

84 John   And I think if you get some people who carry on like they wouldn't say "shit" for a shilling the kids just can't relate to someone who doesn't use their language, if you know what I mean.

86 John   My students, even though I don't swear often, they know that I use the same language as maybe their parents do when the occasion warrants it, I'm not a foul mouthed person or anything like that, but every now and then I'll just sort of say something that probably is inappropriate and I think the students can relate to that. So, well, Sir swears. Now, if I do swear, okay I've got to do a detention but I know that I shouldn't do it and Sir knows that I shouldn't do it but you know, he understands me, he understands that yes, that's where I'm coming from and this is the way I speak. I think that is understanding.

John's text describes how he understands that students see his swearing as "using their language" and perhaps "the same language as maybe their parents", thereby validating and making excusable his occasional use of swearing. He states that "kids can't relate to someone who doesn't use their language", thereby further legitimising swearing as a way of enhancing his pedagogical relationships with students. The use of a punishment system which is in place for both himself and the students builds an "understanding" relationship between him and his students.

Fourteen Blokes and a Sheila

In the following interview text, John describes how it feels to be an 'atypical' home economics teacher, but yet still to be a home economics teacher:

202 John   No, I think it's just ... I don't know, like ... I think it's like if you go to football, it's like footy. You're going to have fifteen blokes on a team and if there's a girl comes along then that's just not usual and you're probably sort of, it would

take a long, long time to sort of get used to having that girl in the footy team. Whereas, footy teams are fifteen blokes ... not fourteen blokes and a Sheila. You know and I use that term, Sheila, purposely.

The analogy that John is using is one to express his feelings of isolation in the home economics world. He has expressed this in his blokey way — how would it be to have a Sheila on the footy team — "it would take a long, long time to get used to it". It's just not footy. So too with home economics. The 'team' is women, and a bloke wants to play — so "it would take a long, long time to ... get used to". He draws attention to the specific selection of the term 'Sheila' as the female to put up against the footy males. In this way he reinforces the heterosexual normativity that is central to his way of thinking. John goes on to explain that he does not want to be "difficult" about this as he knows that he is not what is "expected" as a home economics teacher and that he will bear this burden. This is his method of 'tidying' himself to work within the parameters of orthodox home economics teaching.

204 John   ... I'm not sort of trying to be difficult. I used that term on purpose. It's like fifteen blokes and a Sheila. So ... how can I put it ... and I think that's the expectation that we're going to play footy so there'll be fifteen blokes there, and when there's not fifteen blokes there ... then it's always in with a problem. Come on fellows, all you blokes going down to the pub? Yea yea yea we are, oh, are you going too Sheila, or whatever.

He goes on to describe the 'singling out' of the atypical from the norm, because "it just doesn't fit":

206 John   ... you have to always single that person out, whether she's accepted or not, you always find yourself singling that one person out because it just doesn't fit, you know.

208 John   So, that's sometimes how I feel, I'm sure it's not a conscious thing, I mean, for people just (coughs) excuse me, always try to go out of the way to sort of make me feel welcome and everything and as I said I got in very well with the ladies down there but there was always that ... even the lecturers ... were so used to saying "girls" or "ladies", that they'd always have to pull themselves up and say "Oh, and John", you know whatever, you know. It was just like I knew I sort of made to feel, well, obviously, unusual, me being here because they always say, "Okay, ladies, Oh, and John".

210 John   As an afterthought, and ... so even though you sort of feel part of the group you always sort of feel a little bit isolated.

In this text, John alludes to his positioning on the margins of home economics culture. He is not a mainstream player on the

team and he is "singled out" of the main pack. He is not excluded, but nor is he ever really "in". He is isolated. They are the team
and he is the other. They invite him in to the socially produced
world of the home economics teacher where "ladies" and "girls"
are the norm. The use of singularity in this way is acceptable
because he can be singled out in terms of his gender — but not his
sexuality. This feeling of isolation was explained in a further context, where he attended a live-in conference with a group of home
economics teachers. Here, his isolation was physical:

180 John	I always sort of, when you say part of the group, I am and I'm not. You know what I mean. Like I ... I don't know I sort of am and I'm not. I was ... they accepted me and all that sort of thing and we had a great time and I got on well with everybody but there's always this, there's always something different, like, I was in a room by myself you know.
182 John	And I kept asking someone to share it with me but (laughs)
186 John	Yeah. Well, as I said, I was lonely and the only one without a roomy, I want you to be my roomy and all this sort of thing. They just sort of giggled, but no one would be my roomy. But really, there's always that thing whereas say three or four in a room and I was like by myself and even on a different floor.
188 John	Totally sort of away from the rest of the group, you know what I mean?
189 Donna	Right, so you sometimes feel that you're isolated, even physically?
190 John	Isolated physically and I mean, I'm always sort of, well, usually made to feel welcome um ... And you know like I am included in all the things but in a lot of ways I'm always sort of ... I'm always that odd person out. Like, if we went out for a pizza there was eleven women at the table and me see, and like it was always just that, do you know what I mean?

John speaks of there being "always something different" in his
experience of home economics. He is very aware of being the odd
person with the odd body who is "made to feel welcome" — when
it is appropriate. He describes how it is necessary for him to perform as a heterosexual male at the conference to maintain
his position in the culture and to reinforce heterosexual normativity by seeking out a 'roomy'. However, his heterosexuality
is protected by his women colleagues who "isolate" him physically, thereby removing the potential for a dangerous liaison with
the (heterosexual) women. He concludes this discussion by saying "it's always there you know, I mean, there's always something
that really ... you know sets you apart from the group" (John,

Line 196). His body is always there — a constant reminder that he is Othered as a home economics teacher, for better and worse. Being the "odd person out" and "away from the rest of the group" have both positive and negative affects, shoring up his masculinity at the same time as insisting on his marginality within home economics culture.

A Bloke in the Home Economics Landscape

John has occupied his place in the home economics landscape as a hegemonic male — he positions himself as heterosexual male with hypermasculine body and practices. John is "a blokey kinda' bloke" and aligns himself with the more legitimate role of chef to validate this positioning. This assists him in rejecting the other position available to men in home economics, the position of effeminate male whose heterosexuality is challenged. In this way, he has a heterosexual identity and reinforces heterosexual normativity. Further, he conforms to what Weber and Mitchell (1995) argue are the gendered rules for the self-production of the male teacher. Yet the home economics context does not disempower him; his effectiveness as a teacher is illustrated by comments which follow. John provided a copy of a journal prepared by his students as a surprise thank you to him for teaching them home economics. In this journal, there are many comments which refer to John as a 'good' and effective teacher. For example:

> Thank you for being such a great teacher. I have gained so much from being in your class for the past two years and have many memories that I will keep with me throughout my life. (Female student, aged 17)

> Throughout the past two years I've known you, you have been a great friend and teacher. The knowledge you've taught me is invaluable and I'd like to take the moment to say thank you for your help and encouragement. (Male student, aged 17)

> I have enjoyed my home economics class the most out of all and the atmosphere was great. You have taught me a great deal which I will never forget. (Male student, aged 17)

These texts from students show that John stays within orthodoxy in important ways. He is a normal male teacher, conforming to the normalising traditions associated with this. He has taught students "a great deal" and "knowledge [which] ... is invaluable".

From the texts generated by John and his students, a particular kind of body, both 'normal' and 'aberrant' emerges. John is aberrant as a home economics teacher for reasons including his gender, his refusal to have the 'right' body, his refusal to eat the 'right' food and wear the 'right' clothes, his refusal to be a positive role model for his students, and through his pedagogical performance utilising a teacher-centred philosophy. He is normal through his production as a 'blokey bloke' who swears and relates to his students, as a chef, a heterosexual male and a normal teacher. This is the body work being done in and through the texts.

Subject 2: Valerie Archer
— Blurring the Boundaries of Home Economics

The second subject in this study is Valerie Archer. Valerie teaches in a non-traditional schooling environment. This was a school established as a model to determine the educational success of combining students enrolled in traditional post-compulsory secondary schooling and vocational education programs. Concomitant with the success of this model, the divergence of general and vocational education as policy has been adopted in Queensland secondary education. It was through a close working relationship with Valerie in this unique context that I knew her to self-identify as an 'atypical' home economics teacher. In the following reflective statement, I introduce Valerie by way of the lasting impression I carry of her:

> The image I carry around of Valerie is of her hands. When I think of her, it is her hands that intrigue me. She does not have the hands of a home economics teacher. She does not have the hands of a woman. Her hands are large and strong, fingernails clipped squarely. A dark shadow of dirt outlines each nail. There is no polish. Her hands are rough and calloused. Her hands are outdoor hands — not hands for needlecraft or cake decoration. Not hands to put in the food bowl. And yet, these are the hands of a home economics teacher.

Valerie was invited to participate in this project as an atypical home economics teacher because of her refusal to remain within the enclosure of the 'home', the place of 'women's work', which is considered 'normal' for orthodox home economics teachers. To me, her rough, calloused hands are symbolic of this refusal. So, how do the texts generated by Valerie give shape to a particular kind of home economics body, both 'normal' and 'aberrant'? What body work is being done in and through the texts, and how is her body atypical? The textual analysis that follows draws on interview material and visual images provided by Valerie.

Middle-Aged, Well-Dressed, Wearing an Apron

To Valerie, a typical home economics teacher conforms to stereo-types similar to those produced out of the analysis of Study One and Study Two. That is, home economics teachers are typically "well dressed", "concerned about their appearance", often "wearing an apron" and mainly "middle aged". The text that follows appropriates Valeries' conception of a typical home economics teacher:

> 4 Valerie   I probably would expect them to be ... well dressed and presented, reasonably concerned about their appearance ... I don't know the old image that conjures up to mind is per-haps an apron or sort of ... being surrounded by perhaps posters ... about nutrition and (   ). I think they tend to be middle aged probably I wouldn't say short tempered ...

As already disclosed in this chapter, this 'proper' home econom-ics body is a refinement of the norms of any female teacher (Weber & Mitchell, 1995). When asked if she considers herself to be a typ-ical home economics teacher, Valerie defers to the opinions of others to substantiate her view that she is not typical:

> 6 Valerie   A lot of comments are made, a lot of comments are made by people who tell me, that they don't seem to think that I actually fit into that image of a home economics teacher.

When further prompted, Valerie explains why she considers that other people see her as different to "that [orthodox] image of a home economics teacher":

> 16 Valerie   I think it's because I do a whole range of diverse things so that I don't actually fit into what they would consider to be the mould.
>
> 17 Donna   So what sort of things do you do that people see as different?
>
> 18 Valerie   Well, I mean, I teach outdoor activities such as climbing and canoeing and ... I'm interested and also being involved in the military sort of area so they don't expect me to have those sorts of behaviours and be a home economics teacher. They think that they're quite contradictory.

To others, Valerie contradicts the expectation that home econom-ics teachers focus on the home because of the performances in which her body is regularly engaged. It is assumed that the work of home economists is confined to and enclosed by the home. But, for Valerie, her teaching body is engaged in outdoor pursuits that do not conform to the expected "behaviour" of a typical home eco-nomics teacher. In her words, "I do a whole range of diverse things so I don't actually fit". She does not fit the "mould", instead blurring the boundaries of the enclosure of the home.

In her text, Valerie advocates the idea of the presence of a "mould" for home economics teachers which determines 'proper' behaviour and which emerges from certain normalisation rituals. She also contends that her behaviour in outdoor pursuits and her role as a home economics teacher are considered by others to be "contradictory" to what is expected from this home economics mould. So, not only is her body engaged in aberrant performances, but these are antithetical to her role as a home economics teacher, thereby creating a paradox which seems irreconcilable.

In her text, Valerie refers to this expectation that home economics teachers retain the boundaries of the home as being "domesticated":

20 Valerie   And I guess, I suppose they see a home economics teacher as being quite domesticated and involved with what's in the home or around the house and home making and family care and I, you know, I really don't fit into that image at all.

Rather than "fit[ting] into that image" of the normal "domesticated" home economics teacher who is expected to engage in activities "involved with what's in the home or around the house", this home economics body engages in practices which are unexpected, including canoeing, climbing, participating in military activities, wearing rough clothing, and thereby getting dirt under her finger nails. In performing in these ways, she steps out of the bounds of the production of 'normal' home economics teachers that typically means performing within the boundaries of the private sphere.

This refusal to be bounded by the enclosures of the home was also true of John. Both are involved in outdoor pursuits and are members of the Army Reserve. Both make use of these practices in their home economics classrooms. Further, John engages a military style in his pedagogical practice, drilling students in the way in which he was drilled in the Army. As noted in the reading of his text earlier in this chapter, he 'apologises' for this approach, tidying the bits that he has not normalised into the expected home economics teacher mould. But Valerie does not excuse her use of 'outdoor' experiences in her home economics classroom. Instead, she argues that this approach is a positive aspect of her pedagogy. In the following section, she explains how she couples teaching 'norms' with her unique approach.

Valerie's Teaching Performance

Valerie describes teaching as "a bit of a performance" (Valerie, Line 56). She explains that when she does not feel like teaching, "putting on the performance gets [her] into it" (Line 56). This concept of putting on a particular performance for her teaching is depicted by Butler (1993, p. 12) as "a reiteration of a norm or set of norms" rather than as a matter of superficial theatricality for its own sake. In Valerie's text (Line 56), these norms or set of norms can be identified as her 'put on' of "enthusiasm" for what she is doing, thereby creating "motivation" in her students. She elaborates further in the following interview text:

> 58 Valerie Oh, I think I always try to be encouraging and supportive of what they're doing and saying even though I may not be feeling that at the time, and I think they warm to that aspect and I guess to my enthusiasm.

Butler (1993) suggests that our identities, in this instance Valerie's identity as a teacher, are the dramatic effect of our performances, which we learn to 'fabricate' and gain proficiency in presenting acceptable cultural and public norms. That is what Valerie is engaged in here. Her body is performing acceptable norms for a teacher's body, creating an "illusion of authenticity" (Bordo, 1992, p. 168) as a teaching body by being "encouraging", "supportive" and showing "enthusiasm". Beyond 'putting on' her teaching performance in these forms which are accepted as 'norms' for teachers, Valerie considers that her decision to extend the domain for teaching home economics beyond the typical enclosures of the home, have, "enlivened [her] performance as a teacher" (Valerie, Line 76). These applications have provided a new confidence that is respected by her students. She explains how this occurs in the classroom, comparing her performance to those expected approaches of 'proper' home economics teachers:

> 22 Valerie I think it is, and I think it's also the different experiences that you draw on to elaborate things. Say for example, if you're doing human relationships and you're talking about trust you might talk about exercises in trust circles and things whereas I'd probably go and take my students abseiling, you know so that they can feel what trust is and the real consequences of the exercises are. And if we're talking about textile studies, I can draw on experience with, you know the latest developments in technology in terms of climbing equipment and camping equipment and ... textiles for extreme conditions because they're the sorts of things that I'm interested in so I think that I'd probably draw from a broader base. Because of what my interests are,

and that often does surprise people, like when we do excursions I take them to a camping store and we look at the latest developments in nylon, elastic nylons and finishes of the ... and that quite opens up a whole different area for people.

She refers to "real consequences" and "broader base", reiterating the extended nature of her experiences. She engages students bodies in the learning process, there is a physical bodily involvement which has real effects and students "feel what trust is". This is a leap from the mind-to-mind learning which is typical of current learning to the mind-and-body experience of learning, where students are engaged in performing learning. By engaging with the bodies of students in this way, Valerie believes students see her differently from other home economics teachers, and thus she is atypical. Indeed, students are "surprised" by her mode of teaching that involves "different experiences" from normal home economics classes. Felman (1997, p. 23) regards such 'different' pedagogical approaches to be noteworthy because they work outside of what would be, in this case, the conventionally linear 'home economics' application. She explains this approach as:

> proceeding not through linear progression, but through breakthrough, leaps, discontinuities, regressions, and deferred action, the analytic learning-process puts indeed in question the traditional pedagogical belief in intellectual perfectibility, the progressive view of learning as a simple one-way road from ignorance to knowledge.

Valerie's different approach to learning demonstrates her resistance to the idea of a 'one-way' approach to learning in home economics. For example, she explains that her Army experiences provide the basis for a broader application of home economics "[L]ike we'll look at, you know, the use of the equipment and the uniforms in terms of textile studies, or we'll look at the way that you know, the military ... that I've been taught that the military does problem solving and I'm saying that our design process is very similar and so I can relate it to a different context and where it works in a different environment" (Valerie, Line 44), and she considers this to be "quite atypical" (Valerie, Line 46) of 'proper' home economics teachers.

The idea of army in a home economics classroom is surprising. The mothering, nurturing, caring world of the student and teacher in the classroom seems far removed from the macho, sweating, drilling of the army. Nevertheless, like John, Valerie uses Army as a surprise tactic in her pedagogical work. As already noted, both use the pedagogy of the Army, John performing as drill-master; Valerie performing as the problem-solver. Valerie also brings to her performance elements of the physical context of the Army — certain fabrics, clothes and physical challenges. This shift from a student-centred nurturing ethos to the real, hard world of the Army offers a moment of removal from a dominant maternal tradition of pedagogy in home economics.

This different spatialisation of knowledge beyond the accepted boundaries of the home economics domain of the 'home', reconfigures home economics as a body of knowledge. Valerie believes that this approach into real life is a positive shift for the field and for students in the subject as it is "just not restricted to the home". This is described in the following interview text:

62 Valerie   I hope it says to them that home economics is vitally important, but it's just not restricted to the home, it goes out into all facets of life. That maybe that they haven't even considered where they can take what they learn here and apply it to whatever they do, you know, whether it means if they go travelling or um on their holidays or in their workplace situation they can apply some of the theories that we're actually doing into their real life situations. But it's just not meant to be in the classroom or what you do at home.

64 Valerie   And I think that's what I really do try to get across to them that you know home economics is a wonderful subject, it's just got this horrible aura around it I think when people see it as old fashioned and very limiting whereas it's not.

This is a clear break from the normal home economics context, where the site of the home as enclosure (which is not seen to be important) and is "very limiting", is blurred to include "all facets of life" such as workplaces, travelling and real life situations. This is stretching the boundaries — but not breaking them, and she is adamant that by using her approach, home economics can be seen as a "wonderful subject" and can escape the "horrible aura" which surrounds it. This is why Valerie considers herself to be occupying the home economics landscape differently, as she is refusing the "very limiting" and "old fashioned" orthodoxies so evident in other home economics teachers pedagogical practices.

Linked with this limiting approach is the idea of home economics teachers using formulae, recipes and patterns, which was also raised by John earlier in this textual analysis. Valerie refers to this teaching approach as being a "pedantic" approach typical of home economics teachers. This is characterised by the idea that there is a "right way and the only way" to do things — like a formula for correct approaches:

10 Valerie   They are pedantic about things having to be done in a certain way as being the right way and the only way.

Parallels can be drawn between John's text about the "fuss" of the home economics teacher and Valerie's notion of the "pedantic", the "right way" and the "only way". John suggested that the "formula approach" used by home economics teachers is a result of their typically conservative, middle class background. This apparently conservative, middle-class foundation of home economics is performed through the insistence on "certain way[s]" as being the only way. Valerie's text can be contrasted with texts from and about John, where he is praised by students for not criticising their work because he doesn't expect them to follow a formula. This conservative base and the values associated with it, including this dogmatic approach, is noted by Henry (1989), Pendergast (1991) and Brown (1993) as being one of the 'problems' which has led to negative perceptions about home economics as a field of study.

Dressing for Home Economics

Because of her engagement in activities beyond the enclosure of the home, the sight of Valeries' material body, in addition to her performance, is atypical, as Valerie is aware that this:

24 Valerie ... quite often surprises [students]. Occasionally I come in and dress, like, if I've got a climbing class or I've just come in from a class I may come in casual clothes which is not normal to what I would wear for my home economics clothes.

26 Valerie Because of the role I play, and that often surprises them, or if they see me walking around with a *back pack* and *rope* that also surprises them.

Home economics students do not expect to see their teacher dressed in this "casual" way. Nor do they expect to see their home economics teacher engaged in outdoor pursuits, which require the presence of a backpack and rope as accessories to her dress. She admits that this look is "not normal to what I would wear for my home economics clothes". It is this very notion that she has "home economics clothes" that confirms she dresses for home economics in particular ways. For the main, Valerie consciously maintains two dress codes, and this is recognised and appreciated by her students. This is her attempt at tidying the atypical practices in which she is engaged, such that she is seen as 'normal' when she enters the home economics site. Valerie believes that the students are very aware of her behaviour and at her attempts to produce a 'proper' home economics body:

32 Valerie   I think it does, in that my outdoor clothes, for want of a bet-
             ter word, are daggy because they are exposed to getting
             stained and dirty and torn, so they're not particularly good
             clothes, and people see it as a contrast from when I do dress
             better. For, usually what I would wear for their class as
             to opposed for theirs, and a comment was made that you
             know "is that your home economics teacher, she looks really
             daggy", and a student made the comment "oh, she doesn't
             look like that for us, she looks quite different". So I guess
             I do dress for most parts for the part that I'm playing.

Dressing for the part that she is playing incorporates Valerie's performative attempts at conventionality and at producing a typical
home economics body. Her home economics students are aware
of this and note that "she doesn't look like that [wearing daggy,
stained, dirty and torn casual clothes] for us, [but instead] she
looks quite different". When specifically asked how she usually
dresses differently for home economics classes, Valerie explains:

30 Valerie   If I'm just involved in teaching home economics I'd proba-
             bly dress more ... more formally than if I'm doing some-
             thing else during the day.

Here 'formal' dress, which is not casual, daggy, torn or dirty,
is 'normal' dress for home economics teachers. It is "good" and
"better" than her dress for outdoor education. Valerie explains
in her text how she believes that students expect her to dress differently for home economics classes, and they make comments
to her about the selection and care of her clothing:

40 Valerie   And also I mean they'll make comments about whether
             things ... match or whether it's pressed correctly or not.
             I mean, they had that expectation that you will adhere
             to those sorts of principles because that's what they think
             that you should be teaching them.

This expectation that home economics teachers clothing should
"adhere to ... principles" was mentioned in the production of the
typical home economics teacher earlier in this chapter. Home economics teachers consider that they should act as 'proper' role
models for their students, setting appropriate grooming and clothing standards and reflecting the principles which they are teaching the students. Valerie reiterates this expectation, based on what
she sees as an expectation students have of their home economics
teacher. She justifies this expectation as emanating from the subject matter of the field. However, regardless of her awareness
of these student demands about appropriate dress and her own
attempts at compliance with them, Valerie does not believe that
her appearance and her efforts to meet student expectations

is particularly important in her role as an effective teacher. She explains this in the following text:

> 42 Valerie   There is a certain amount of confidence that goes with what I do and I believe the students respect my performance rather than my appearance.

When she speaks of confidence from what she does, she is speaking about the confidence which comes from her body performing, by pushing her body to its physical limits — climbing higher and further; walking longer distances; carrying heavier loads; enduring appalling weather conditions. This confidence is about knowing her body and performing by surviving physical hardship. This gives her confidence that exceeds the limits of confidence that is gained through "appearance" from body adornment in the form of clothing. This dualism where respect is derived from performance not just appearance through dress allows Valerie to be a proper home economics teacher, where appearance doesn't/shouldn't count. This is in contrast to John's appearance that counts as a negative exemplar.

The Removal of Enclosure

From the texts generated out of the interview with Valerie, a particular kind of home economics body — both 'normal' and 'aberrant' — emerges. The body of the text (her interview text) and the body as a text (her physical presence, activities and behaviour), suggests that Valerie is aberrant as a home economics teacher because she refuses the boundaries of enclosure of the home, which is a fundamental principle of 'home' economics. This is evident in her physical body as a site of pedagogical knowledge, engaged in and engaging her students in outdoor pursuits and activities atypical of home economics, and as a sight of home economics, when she sometimes wears daggy, dirty and torn clothing which is not typical of home economics teachers.

However, this aberrant body does not overturn the orthodoxy that produces domestication and the home as the site for home economics. Instead, it works as an anomaly, reinforcing the home as a 'mould' for home economics teachers as the norm, which she is resisting. Hence, Valerie intensifies the production of the typical home economics teacher and the home as the site of home economics by insisting on the uniqueness of her position. She works to maintain a tradition rather than undercut it. She is a 'special case'. In this way, Valerie presents the site of the typical home economics teacher as conforming to the normalised versions we have seen represented previously.

Subject 3: Marilyn Moore
— A Groovy Home Economics Teacher

Marilyn Moore was invited to participate in this project as an atypical home economics teacher because of her refusal to remain within the normal boundaries of the sight of orthodox home economics bodies. Marilyn works hard not to look like a typical home economics. In the following statement, I introduce Marilyn as a subject for this study by way of my reflection. This reflection is focused overwhelmingly on Marilyn's body as text:

> When I think of Marilyn, it is the blond bimbo stereotype that comes to mind. She is very trendy in a sexy kind of way. There is always plenty of flesh to see. She has instant sex appeal and laughs all the time. She is effervescent and fills the room. She strives to appeal in a sexual way. She is often criticised by other women for her outward, flaunting sexuality. Young women, such as her students, respond to her as a sexy, appealing role model. She doesn't fit the normal expectations of what it is to act like a teacher — and particularly a home economics teacher — because she is not serious enough — and too sexy — both in her appearance and her manner.

How does Marilyn occupy the home economics landscape differently because of her blatant sexuality? How do the texts generated by Marilyn and her students give shape to a particular kind of body, both 'normal' and 'aberrant' and what body work is being done in and through these texts? The documentation that follows draws on interview text from Marilyn and written comments from a group of her students.

Mothers and Virgins

According to Marilyns text, there are two orthodox productions of home economics teachers. The first is a "mother figure", whom Marilyn characterises as:

| 4 Marilyn | ... definitely with the somewhat dowdy Osti dress, conservative, one to stick with the rules concerned about the family and how they get on very like caring in that sort of format but not someone that you would label as the huge party rager. (Laughs) Someone who you would go to probably when you're drunk and cry on their shoulder that sort of thing I would type cast them as that. |

The other production of the orthodox home economics teacher is the young virgin, characterised as the "girl that misses out". This is a naive, sexually and socially frustrated position:

6 Marilyn   Or else they'd be, they may be the ... this is horrible saying this ... they may be the girl that misses out on the date scene and they might actually be the friend. (Laughs). Oh dear, cynical, cynical. (Laughs)

7 Donna   And what clothes would they wear?

8 Marilyn   Oh, well it wouldn't be, I doubt very much whether it would be tight fitting clothes, they'd be fairly loose fitting clothes. They'd probably match fairly well, longish, sensible shoes. Could even be like good accessories, I'd, I tend to think that probably the pictured home ec may, sometimes you get the ones that do dye their hair or do something else with dye and then there's your died in the wood natural, no make up.

So it seems to Marilyn that home economics teachers are typically either the somewhat matronly, conservative mother figure in the Osti dress, who provides comfort and care when needed; or the dowdy, younger version, who dresses 'sensibly' in loose clothes with matching accessories – minimising the possibility of sexual interest from others. She is the novice, and her body is protected from sexual gaze, maintaining her single virgin status as the "girl that misses out on the date scene". Marilyn suggests the matron is not a "rager", but is a stickler for rules about families. Not surprisingly, these two productions of home economics teachers are in keeping with what Weber and Mitchell (1995) describe as the larger category of the 'normal', culturally produced female teacher.

Both of Marilyn's versions conjure up images of purity and virtuosity, of martyrdom and sacrifice, and of naiveté and loneliness. These home economics bodies are suffering, virgin mother martyrs who enforce "rules". In this way, Marilyn is complicit in normalising the home economics body. Further, within the virginal condition of the typical home economics teacher, there is no chance of sexual deviance, and so this is another way of maintaining heterosexual normativity. And the mother figure "stick(s) with the rules concerned about the family", thereby maintaining the traditional family form as the norm. With the text from the interview, Marilyn endorses the versions produced in Study One and Study Two as typical.

The Last Bastion – The Oldies and Goldies

Marilyn speaks of these typical mother and virgin home economics teachers as the "last bastion" of the "conservative base" of home economics. To her, virgins and mothers are the 'face' of home economics, and therefore of professional home economics teachers. But she is not critical of their presence. In fact, Marilyn expresses concern at the loss of what she describes as "apron ... and chocolate slice making" conservatism because she is uncertain of what might replace it. In this way, Marilyn portrays her commitment to the skilled body of the home economics teacher, and her concern at the potential loss of it:

> 96 Marilyn   There'd have to be the good core of still the oldies and the goldies in there that still want to do aprons and that still want you to do chocolate slices. And I think that's ... I think it's sad for them in a way. When that last bastion move on I'm somewhat worried about what's coming through because I don't really know who's going to be the, because you need to have some sort of conservative base somewhere along the line so it doesn't go completely radical so it's not looked at as being a Mickey Mouse subject.

In her text, Marilyn is mourning the progressive loss of the orthodox home economics teachers who in her view are the guardians of the field. In this way, she is complicit in producing a certain version of home economics teacher. She argues the need for this "conservative", normalised teacher to ensure the subject does not become "completely radical" or "Mickey Mouse". She scorns the chocolate slice and apron making skills, but she is "worried" about the alternative. She equates the skilled body of the home economics teacher to the 'oldies' and the 'goldies'. Marilyn maintains that there is a need to retain traditional home economics bodies as a means of preserving the field and its integrity. Hence she is not subversive as she wants to protect the subject as it is.

This approach ensures her positioning as 'atypical' since a change to the production of the typical home economics teacher is a threat to her positive identity as 'other'. This is reminiscent of Jane Gallop's (1997) text where she presents the academy as dowdy in order to eroticise herself. If the academy were erotic, Gallop would not be noticed. Similarly for Marilyn, there is a need to maintain the status quo in order to be noticed. Marilyn does not want to be seen to be typical — and in this way she is 'in' but also 'out' of the normalisation process, complicit in normalising but reluctant to be normalised. For Marilyn, the virginal mother figure who wears an osti dress and apron and makes chocolate slice is a reassuring production of the home

economics teacher. And it provides her with the scope to step outside of this orthodoxy in ways that comfort her, since she
is refusing this production for herself, with the reassurance that
it remains intact.

Wearing Supporting Undergarments

Marilyn works hard to produce herself as other than typical.
She refuses to be produced as either virginal or motherly.

To produce this different identity, Marilyn describes herself
as a home economics teacher who has "gone off the rails" and
found herself "in the wrong train station". In the following text,
she describes why she is atypical.

> 10 Marilyn   Okay. (Laughs) Not anything like the one that I just
> described to you. I'm furthest from a mother figure than
> I can think of. Probably the home ec. teacher that had gone
> off the rails, that was somewhat … I don't know, probably
> maybe finally found out that there is a modern world and
> they want to live in it and that home ec is actually a subject
> that can be applicable and I guess dress accordingly, try
> to have some sort of … style is the wrong sort of word
> I guess just to … well, dressed but in a groovy sort of sense
> of the word to appeal, I guess, definitely make up and
> accessories (   ) in that sort of format. I guess they might be
> … I hope for myself to be a bit more of a groover, a bit more
> out there trying to get people together having a good time
> sort of mediator thing rather than the mother sort
> of figure.

Marilyn describes herself as a "groover", "out there trying to get
people having a good time". She regards herself as "furthest
from a mother figure" that she can think of, more interested in
having a "good time". She does not conform to the mother figure
or the virgin documented in her text. These productions of home
economics teachers "miss out", and in the preceding text from
Marilyn, it is clear that she does not intend to miss out. Instead,
she is in the: "modern world" and "want[s] to live in it", to "dress
accordingly" in a "groovy sort of sense" and to "appeal". She
"definitely [wears] makeup and accessories". Accordingly, she
situates home economics teachers bodies as asexual martyrs, and
materialises her own as sexy, seductive and groovy.

Further in the text, she explains that she is "way too loud" and
"moderately obnoxious" and these are not traits that typify home
economics teachers. She believes that this was clear to her when
she commenced study in higher education in the field with one
of the telling signs that she didn't wear supporting (restricting)

undergarments like all the other girls did, hence her sense of being in the wrong place, and possibly letting it all hang out. It seems that from the lack of supporting undergarments to her behaviour as loud and obnoxious, Marilyn is the antithesis of the controlled and constrained body of the home economics teacher, who has appropriate undergarment support to keep the body upright but constrained, supported and controlled; but not sexualised — in order to maintain the virgin position, and with appropriate conservative behaviour, to keep her from being a rager and definitely not appealing on the date scene. She explains:

12 Marilyn   I'd never consider myself as your typical home ec teacher. I always felt ... like ... oops I'm in the wrong place I'm in the wrong train station I really shouldn't be here. But that doesn't mean that I'm not ... I think that the other like typical home ec teacher that most people would still think of, even worth their pinch of salt, I just think that we need to bring the image up into the nineties.

16 Marilyn   We didn't wear undergarments as ( ) undies that was about it. We didn't have supporting garments and we had to have supporting ...

18 Marilyn   I was from a surfing community when I came up here. So I was moderately hippy and hit in with a couple of other people that were like that and we all looked at each other and went "oh dear", and everybody else seemed to be terrible, terribly (little Laughs) ... they were either really shy and quiet and were really good in craft or they were the really fairly well dressed, like moderately rich parents. I can remember one girl in particular who was always like immaculate, she was the ... no you could tell that anything she would have done was like really down to the last tee. And I just always felt I was way too loud I was moderately obnoxious and yeah and ones I did enjoy were the human relationship things but I ... The sewing freaks me right out, and I liked housing at the time but I didn't like the way they taught it. We took turns ... there was five of us, actually there was quite a group because there was five of us home ec students living in the same house and we were like a range from like out there to moderately conservative. We used to take turns going to the lecturers for help because it used to kill us (Laughs). So I don't know ... I stuck at it because I really liked the subject matter and I believe that it had a lot going for it, but the people who taught me apart from one or two people when I come ( ). And most of my other class mates I just thought ... you know this is so scary, whereas the home ec teacher I had down in New South Wales she was terribly groovy, she was great, like she was really ...

Marilyn speaks of her experience with home economics lecturers in tertiary home economics as being "scary", and going to the lecturer's for help would "kill" her and others like her — not in a physical sense but as a humorous episode. She described that she "looked at" others like her and there was a collective resistance to the pressure from home economics university lecturers to normalise their behaviour. For example, attending lectures was to be avoided and elaborate schemes were set up to avoid contact with lecturers.

In her text, Marilyn portrays the typical home economics students in her group as "well dressed", "moderately rich", "shy and quiet" and as "immaculate" — the typical home economics virgins from a conservative, middle class family background. She describes herself in direct contrast to these students, being "moderately hippy" from a surfing community, implying the lack of capacity to be a virgin or a mother and an explanation for her resistance to this body.

A 'Terribly Groovy' Role Model

She contrasts her version of typical motherly and virginal home economics teachers with her own high school teacher, who was instrumental in her selection of home economics teaching as a career. Marilyn refers to her home economics teacher as "terribly groovy", and a "wonderful woman" identifying her as the inspiration to study home economics, and the person she modelled herself on. Consequently, she expected all of the home economics students and tertiary educators would be like her groovy teacher. The risks this teacher took in dress and appearance — her materiality — appealed to Marilyn. According to Weber and Mitchell (1995, p. 58), this is not surprising, as "when we think of a teacher, or remember a specific teacher we have known, it is often the way they dress that stands out". A recent encounter with this teacher reaffirmed Marilyn's confidence in this teacher as a role model:

> 20 Marilyn   I saw her not long ago. We had a reunion and she still was, she wore this really funky wig to the formal which was just ... she was just really good. So I guess I modelled on that thinking that everybody would be the same.

It is interesting to note that Marilyn describes herself as "groovy" and adds a descriptor to the same term to describe her role model and mentor. That is, her home economics teacher was "terribly groovy". Again, the notion of home economics teacher as role model appears in the text, which is a consistent pattern across all the interviews and surveys. In this instance however, the type of role model may be in question by other less groovy home economics teachers who are produced as virgins and mothers. It seems that Marilyn was surprised that all home economics teachers were not terribly groovy as she had expectations that her teacher conformed to a normalised set of practices which ultimately were shown to be atypical. Instead, she found herself in a class of virgins and her response was "you know, this is scary".

Willing to Step Out of Line

Marilyn describes her behaviour as a further reason for being an atypical home economist. She described herself as a student as "radical", with an active social life including drinking (a lot), smoking (a lot), and having boyfriends (a lot). By her social behaviours, she believes she cannot be the typical virgin or mother figure. For her, each moment in her radical approach is used as a form of protest and exaggeration of the traditions of home economics culture, which is so readily recognisable by her. She is making fun of the orthodox traditions of home economics as the antithesis of 'a good time'.

This stepping out of line put her and a small group of other students in an other group of home economics student teachers, where she considers they had an affinity for each other:

22 Marilyn   And I always thought that well my experiences at college from other home ec teachers ... that I saw and when out at prac and them all together was that there was only one or two of them that were really willing to sort of, step out of line ... that were willing to go to the back for things and to be a little bit radical. That they had an active social life other than their family and church and all whatever those sorts of things. Not that that's bad but I just it wasn't what I perceived it to be when I first got in there. And I think for me I always felt that I was fairly crass amongst a lot because I was loud and outspoken and a bit ribald and all those sorts of things. (Laughs). I went out and I'd smoke a lot and I drank a lot and had a lot of boyfriends.

Marilyn found a group of home economics students — "only one or two of them" — who, like her, were willing to "step out of line" and "to be a little bit radical". Having an "active social life other than their family and church" was an indication to Marilyn that she had found an ally in the home economics classroom. From the text, Marilyn has represented typical home economics student teachers as predominantly conservative and engaged in conservative activities and that this is the site of home economics as a body of knowledge.

In this text Marilyn makes attempts at tidying. She was "willing to sort of step out of line" from the 'normal' home economics student role but then goes on to tidy by suggesting "not that [being 'normal' is] bad". In this text there is no attempt to be subversive — but to insist on her special place or unique identity in the field.

I Don't Know These People

Marilyn expresses the notion of being "scared" by home economics teachers en masse. When asked if she attends home economics professional development and the like, she indicates that she generally does not. She considers this to be the site for the mother and virgin bodies of home economics. However, on the rare occasions she does meet with other home economics teachers she is apprehensive. She explains how she copes with this:

> 98 Marilyn   I find a couple of other people who will probably take the piss out of someone and I sit with them and feel okay. But I look around me and think these people, I don't know these people and they're not the sort of people I would choose to socialise with. They scare me. (Laughs). They scare me because they're so like ... they're so Edward Scissorhands, like they're in there with their little categories and they've got the right colours and I don't know ...

"Tak[ing] the piss out of" the mothers and virgins is Marilyn's way of resisting collapse into the norm. Yet, this is not subversive, it is simply removing herself from the threat of being normalised. The reference to Edward Scissorhands is interesting. The idea of 'cutting up' into "little categories" and having "the right colours" suggests the control, accuracy and order of the home economics teacher. The refusal to be risky but instead a desire to conform to the norm. This links back to comments from both Subject One (John) and Subject Two (Valerie), who typify home economics teachers as "fussy" and "pedantic", with formula and recipe approaches. Both John and Valerie regard this as a result of conservatism of home economics teachers.

Likewise, Marilyn is frustrated by the use of formulas and rules in home economics that she believes stifles home economics:

> 102 Marilyn   Look, you can't have an original thought and the fabric and all those sorts of things and leave no room for students creativity. And that's a very creative process. The cooking is a creative process, but sewing garments, putting those sort of fabrics and feel and touch and all those sorts of things, working out what looks good on you. Fair enough

> to sew a perfect garment but it looks like shit why would you, you're not going to wear it are you? Hanging it there if you put it up on the wall in a picture frame, well I sewed that thing you're defeating the purpose and I, I though I did think that was really sad that you've got to do it this way and you can't do anything innovative.

This text again reinforces the conservatism of home economics teachers and their insistence upon rule following. Students not being able to "have an original thought" and "leav[ing] no room for students creativity" are examples of this in Marilyn's text. She also referred to two of her adult friends who laugh about their home economics teachers and their experiences as young home economics students in school. In their experience, the inflexibility and pattern following of home economics teachers "puts students off" and in doing so "they kill it" for their students.

> 98 Marilyn   They were talking about how much they were put off by their home ec teachers. And I felt really sad. Like Mary said, like, the same as me, she only ever did it up to year eight. It was so much, it was so daggy that the thing that I wanted to sew they wouldn't let me sew. They wouldn't let me sew something that I would actually wear and it was useless. The cooking they liked because they got to eat it but that was about it. They can't remember anything else. And Julie who loves and is just unbelievable with fabric, she just has a real penchant for it. She was really sad that in fact the home ec teachers *put students off* enjoying fashion. But they kill it, and they killed it for me. So, yeah, that's the unfortunate bit.

The insistence that certain items be produced in certain ways in home economics classrooms can be seen by some students, as described in Marilyn's text, as producing outcomes which are "daggy" and "useless", leading to student lack of interest ("it looks like shit ... you're not going to wear it"), which ultimately puts students off and "kills" the field of study. This practice by typical home economics teachers of using formulas, recipes, rules and in this instance patterns (sewing), creates certain effects. The effect for the students of home economics is a rejection of home economics and home economics teachers, since students come to reject the very conventions they entrust their teachers to share with them, since this produces "daggy" and "useless" outcomes that are "shit". Hence, the teacher and the subject area are rejected by the students.

A Bit Over the Top

Marilyn is certain her home economics students do not see her
as a typical home economics teacher.

28 Marilyn   God no. Definitely not compared to what their experiences
are at school because they've often said like you're not like
anything that we've had before.

When asked to elaborate on why her students do not see her
as a typical home economics teacher, she suggests that the reasons
are wide ranging. One is her "genuine love of teaching" (Marilyn,
Line 76); her preparedness to be "open and honest" and to "share
a little bit" (Marilyn, Line 72) of herself with her students.

Marilyn believes her body and her performances make her different since she is always "over the top" (Marilyn, Line 92).
The use of this metaphor "over the top" from a military perspective
often leads to the next stage of "being shot down". With her role
of "stepping out of line", this is an interesting use of metaphor
which captures her capacity and willingness to engage in risky
behaviour as a form of protest. For example, she makes conscious
decisions about her clothing and her look:

37 Marilyn   My colleagues will verify that I have one of the largest
wardrobes that they've (Laughs) ever come across, so, like,
I wear different clothes all the time, but yes if like we were
trying to demonstrate some sort of thing it's much easier to
have it on me than to show them a picture. But I don't know
whether I'd necessarily think every day to do that um but I
am conscious of form and like if I was teaching nutrition I
don't think I'd go on a diet specifically to teach nutrition
but I've just probably been lucky that I've always been fairly thin and not in that other category. I think you should
teach a lot by example, but the scary thing is that you can
almost imprint on them to a certain extent — the younger
students, or even some of the older students.

In this text, Marilyn describes the use of her body as a "fairly
thin" model to do the normalising work. She speaks of imprinting
on students appropriate nutrition through the physicality of her
body, which she reports she is "lucky" to have. This is in contrast
to how Subject One (John), makes use of his body in home economics. John is the epitome of poor nutrition practices, with his
big beer belly from eating pies and drinking Coke, and his self
description as a "fat fella". Yet, both use their bodies as 'examples', acting as role models for their students and maintaining
a redemptive role.

Marilyn is forthright in her belief in the role of the home
economics teacher as role model:

34 Marilyn   What you wear and what you look like as a home ec teacher. I always find it super-hypocritical that we were teaching nutrition and fashion and that sort of thing and to get up and to be obese and dowdy and (   ). I don't know how they honestly expect the students to um to believe what they were telling them when they obviously couldn't take that information themselves, and because home ec is a very practical subject as well like you do have to be … I think the performance angle comes into it.

For Marilyn, credibility as a home economics teacher is embodied as part of a complete performance. She believes the home economics teachers body should not be "dowdy" or "obese". She describes as "super hypocritical" those home economics teachers whose bodies do not embody good practice in home economics, arguing that she doesn't know "how they honestly expect the students to believe them". Marilyn expresses her frustration where this is not the case, making links between the body of the teacher and the "performance" which emerges from this. Marilyn appears to echo Barthes' (1978, p. 45) view that "I can do everything with my language but not with my body. What I hide by my language, my body utters", but she sees this as a positive for herself, unlike her peers.

34 Marilyn   As soon as I hit that door it's like *ta-da I'm here I'm here to entertain you* and I'm going to drag you through this in whatever means I possibly can. And if it takes anything from lollies, bribery and corruption through to cajoling all those sorts of things, I believe that it's really important to be very vibrant, to be right in their faces. I don't like classroom situations where it's straight seats, I'd rather it "U" shaped. I'd have to come in and I pace a lot, I throw myself about, I think about, I do think carefully about the things I use, I like to use visuals, I try to use audio, I try to use a number of things in the one lesson. It can get a bit like over the top and I can feel like over-awed. And they're going, oh no not another thing. I like lots of groups work, but I also like holding the floor. I'm at times have to step back from answering questions (   ) because you ask them and then you go (   ) over the top it so that's just ego (   ) nothing there. But I do think that you do have to entertain no matter what you do and no matter what you're teaching. It is like … it is a performance.

In the preceding text, Marilyn likens her teaching to that of a performance, she is there to "entertain" and to "be right in their faces". Her teaching style is high energy and sometimes exhausting, and she "can't sit still in a classroom" with her body "exhausted" by her teaching (Marilyn, Line 51). Marilyn's high energy teaching is self described as "over the top" and she considers she is there to "entertain" her students. She likens her high energy teaching to a wind up toy, "you wind it up and just let it go, that's me" (Marilyn, Line 92). These aspects she sees for teaching in general, not just for home economics. The pedagogical relationship Marilyn has with her students is one where she is anxious to please her students, stating in the interview that "I'd die if … I feel like they [students] really don't want me to be there" (Marilyn, Line 88).

Marilyn works hard to gain the approval of her students. For example, she is very conscious of the first impression she makes on students, and is careful about selecting clothing that is not "dowdy or lacking in confidence, like so many home economics teachers are" (Marilyn, Line 80). This resistance to the conventional home economics 'uniform' and collective pressure to conform to this, reflects a desire to struggle against the normalising traditions. As Weber and Mitchell (1995, p. 62) note: "[C]lothing can be a proclamation of resistance, a mode of innovation or becoming, a reconciliation, a desire to belong, or a surrender". Marilyn has chosen clothing as a proclamation of resistance.

Breasts, Smell and Body

Marilyn's clothing and body are written into some student texts in their comments made to her in thank you notes. For example:

> Your inspiration this year has only been equalled by the invention of the push-up bra. (Female student, aged 17)

> Your happiness and energy all year has been inspirational. May your bodily smell always be sociable. (Male student, aged 16)

> Your inspiration to our minds has only been equalled by our inspiration from your body. Thanks for a wonderful year. (Female student, aged 17)

> Thank you for keeping me awake in class with your humour, cattle prod and that "look", plus much, much more. The greatest thanks though comes for your ability to keep a person afloat when they are sinking. (Female student, aged 16).

The body of this teacher provides invitations to students to think about her in terms of her body. Her breasts, her smell, her body and that "look" defy the usual student/teacher boundaries of body familiarity and sexuality, as outlined by McWilliam (1996b). Marilyn refuses to be seen simply as a disembodied mind, engaged in mind-to-mind pedagogy.

Another student uses the body of this teacher to express her thanks to the teacher:

> For the wonderful support throughout the year — Thank you.

For the shoulder to cry on — Thank you.

For the ears to listen to my tale of woe — Thank you.

For the heart to empathise — Thank you.

For the nourishment to my body in the form of chocolate lollies — Thank you.

And for the nourishment to my mind and for your faith in my abilities, your warmth and commitment — a very special Thank you.

(Female student, aged 17)

These student comments are not about a virgin, but perhaps they are about a fertile mother who is 'productive' in pedagogical terms. The mother figure lurking in this text is merged with a sexualised body. These texts from students show that Marilyn stays within orthodoxy in important and relational ways. She listens, empathises, supports and nourishes her students. In many ways, she is a normal female teacher, conforming to the normalising traditions associated with this.

A Groovy Body in the Home Economics Landscape

From the texts generated by Marilyn and her students, a particular kind of body, both 'normal' and 'aberrant' emerges. Marilyn is aberrant as a home economics teacher as her groovy, sexy body cuts across the sight of the typical home economics teacher. Her pedagogical practices refuse to rely on formulas, recipes and patterns which students are expected to follow in orthodox home economics classes.

The interview text reveals that Marilyn considers she is in the wrong place with the wrong people, and she strives to produce herself as other to these 'proper' home economics teachers, whom she produces as conservative, motherly and virginal, their performative dimension recognisable by apron wearing and chocolate slice making. But Marilyn does not condemn nor reject these orthodoxies as the sight/site of home economics, arguing that it is the role of these 'proper', orthodox home economists to preserve home economics as it is, so it does not become "radical" or "Mickey Mouse" – and thereby allowing her to be the sexy 'other'. Marilyn contrasts her practice as a home economics teacher in terms of both her literal sight and also the site of practice.

Regardless of her resistance to typical home economists and home economics, Marilyn conforms to the conventions of the normal home economics teacher in many ways. Marilyn is not challenging heterosexual normativity in her performativity. For example, she reinforces the site of home economics as the home. She represents the site of the typical home economics teacher as conforming to the normalised versions we have seen represented previously. As such, Marilyn occupies her place in the home economics landscape as a heterosexual female. She reinforces the boundaries of enclosure of the home in ways that are not challenging to the orthodoxy that sets the home as the site for home economics. Her body as text conforms to the production of the typical and 'proper' home economics teacher in the way she strives to present a body of the 'right' weight. She argues that "what you wear and what you look like as a home ec teacher" is crucial to "students believing" (Line 34) what the teacher is teaching them. Marilyn's choice of dress, wearing of make up and accessories are within the context of acting as a positive role model for students and reinforcing the production of the typical, authentic home economics teacher.

Subject 4: Elle Manson — Giving and Taking Pleasure in Home Economics

Elle Manson was invited to participate in this project as an atypical home economics teacher because of her publicly-declared refusal to deny her pleasure for teaching which leads to group episodes of excitement.

How does Elle occupy the home economics landscape differently because of this giving and taking of pleasure through her teaching? How do the texts generated by Elle give shape to a particular kind of body, both 'normal' and 'aberrant', and what body work is being done in and through the texts? The textual analysis that follows draws predominantly on interview material and a video production in which the subject was involved. This video provides an entertaining look at a group of home economics teachers parodying themselves. Their production of home economics teachers is based on their beliefs about how others perceive them. Elle had a central role in the instigation, development and enactment of the parodic play and it supports her views of how others perceive the discipline of home economics and the teachers of home economics to be. In doing so, it presents the literal sight of the socially produced home economics body.

White Apron and Sensible Shoes

Elle suggests that there are three 'categories' of home economics teachers, these being traditional, corporate (or business), and alternative, with the traditional category by far the most common. All three categories are "definitely female — I'm thinking female straight away" (Elle, Line 12) and the dominant traditional category has a material presence which is an easily recognisable sight, with features such as "... an apron, a white apron ... plump, a quiet, reserved, gentle, caring personality ... with flat, covered, sensible shoes" (Elle, Lines 6 and 8)

The apron and sensible shoes have again appeared as home economics icons. Elle also adds a "below the knees skirt" (Elle, Line 20) and couples this with a "plump" body, suggesting at this point of time in Western culture asexuality. The gentle, caring nurturing attributes imply a mother image. Hence, there is evidence of complicity with the normalisation of home economics teachers, and a close similarity to the two versions of typical home economics teachers described by Subject 3 (Marilyn) as the mother and the virgin images. Again, this is confirmation of Weber and Mitchell's (1995) analysis of the social production of all female teachers.

Elle further describes the typical traditional home economics teacher as having the following physical characteristics:

> 16 Elle   ... curly hair, brown hair and perhaps something just tying it back slightly like a ribbon or um hair clips (Laughs). And making a batch of scones.

The morning tea image again appears as a home economics icon. We saw this image in the description of a typical home economics teacher by John (Subject 1). The added detail of the hair, pulled back and tied by ribbon, forms part of the conventions and rules of cooking — hair is removed so that it cannot contaminate the scones being prepared. This implies the conformist rule following behaviour that again, is underlined by other subjects in this project.

A Woman's World

The video which Elle and her colleagues produced works within this traditional imagery of home economics. The video was produced as a within/against analysis of home economics teachers and the subject home economics, and was used as stimulus material at a home economics Head of Department meeting. It is an exaggerated account (though some would argue it is not!) intended through parody to capture home economics pedagogy as a site/sight of practice. The video title is *Home Economics — A Woman's World,* and it presents an overview of the home economics curriculum as four semester units devised around the word *wife.* This is explained in the following dialogue from the video:

> Our main aim in home economics is to teach girls to become good wives. So we've taken the word *wife* and we've devised our four semesters around those. Semester 1— 'W' — is for washing. And we have a specialist in our Department who we're going to see today about washing. Semester 2 — 'I' —is for ironing. We spend a whole semester teaching the girls how to iron their clothes. 'F' is for food and of course you know we all concentrate a lot on food in this area. And 'E' is for embroidery, and we also have an embroidery teacher here in our school. So they're the four units we do: washing, ironing, food and embroidery. ('Bitta Fluff', video presentation)

Heterosexual normativity underpins this production. The video producers blatantly structure home economics pedagogy around this perspective and there is no attempt to substitute an alternative to orthodox heterosexual performances. The statement that the "aim in home economics is to teach girls to become good wives" is the basis for developing the heterosexual conventions which pervade the video and which do not trouble the conventions of the profession.

The main character in the play is "Bitta Fluff", in the role of the home economics Head of Department, who introduces the various specialist home economics teachers in her staff, these being: Wilma Whirlpool (washing specialist); Crispin Starch (ironing specialist); Mrs Muffin (food specialist); and Elna Bobbin (embroidery specialist teacher). The bodies of these teachers are adorned in: sensible frocks (below the knee, shapeless, loosely fitting) or white uniforms; neck scarves; hair pulled back and held by hair band or bows; large glasses; overgenerous make up; sensible shoes and aprons. These bodies reflect many of the typical features that have been described by all of the Subjects in this book. They present 'good girl' and 'motherly' images.

The dialogue presented by each of the specialist teachers is reproduced in a number of monologues. First, the washing specialist teacher, Wilma Whirlpool, who has the added props of equipment typically found in laundries including washing machine, drier, laundry tub, mop, laundry basket, boxes of laundry detergents and she is wearing a large pair of blue rubber gloves in addition to her traditional home economics apparel:

13 Wilma   Well, here I am, in my favourite place in the home economics Department with my favourite appliances — the wash-

ing machine, drier and basin, after whom I was named, Whirlpool, Wilma Whirlpool. Now, what we like to show the little girlies in home economics is how to get those lipstick stains out of their husbands collars, and how to get ink stains out of the pocket. No questions asked, of course. I'd also like to show the girlies in home economics some of our equipment, and some of the resources we use. Now, Napisan, very important for the little ones. We like to stress this to the girlies, you can never learn too early. We also like to show them how to separate their coloureds and their whites — we don't want their husbands having to go along to work and have people laugh at their pink work shirts. Now, we stress that to the little girlies. Now, there are a lot of appliances here that are very, very important and I find this one of the most fascinating things to teach. I could go on for hours and hours but …

The ironing specialist teacher, Crispin Starch, who is standing at an ironing board with iron, starch products and a large pile of ironing, and is wearing a white uniform and apron:

19 Crisp	Well, this is the best place to come, because we teach our girls not only to iron after they wash, but also to get that better finish, to iron before they wash.
20 Bitta	That's excellent.
21 Crisp	Actually, the four main reasons why we teach the girls ironing is that one, it is a great exercise — you pick up the iron in your right arm, exercises the right arm. Pick up the old spray in the left hand.
22 Bitta	And I suppose, fine motor control there, yes, that's great.
23 Crisp	Yes. And therefore it leads on to a good leisure time activity. If you've got leisure time you can always iron. Take those ironed clothes out of the cupboard and you can always iron those again. And of course, that goes on to the third reason, the husband's presentation. This is all about you serving him so that he looks his best.
24 Bitta	Yes, that's right.
25 Crisp	And therefore, this follows on from all of them, you will get such a personal sense of achievement.
26 Bitta	Because we're pleasing him …

The food specialist, Mrs Muffin, who is wearing a white uniform and full apron and is in a kitchen at a bench surrounded by cookery equipment and ingredients:

30 Mrs Muffin	Good morning Bitta. Well, welcome to my kitchen this morning. We are going to make that classic recipe, a batch of scones.
31 Bitta	Ahhh

32 Mrs Muffin	It's so important that our girls learn how to make their scones properly to please their husbands. And there are so many varieties of scones, there are date scones, sultana scones, pumpkin scones and the list is just endless. Well, the first thing we have to do is to sift our flour. It's so essential to making good scones. And we have to measure things accurately otherwise we might make our scones too dry or too moist. So, we measure exactly one cup of flour and we sift it with elegance into our bowl.
33 Bitta	That's beautiful. What skills you have.

And the embroidery specialist, Elna Bobbin, who is situated in a sewing room with a large table with sewing machine and equipment and a wide range of embroidered aprons:

39 Elna	Well, I'm going to do some embroidery here on this lovely serviette. You can see it's a very plain type of serviette so I think a lovely embroidered rose would really set it off.
40 Bitta	Ahhh, lovely. Beautiful.
41 Elna	Yes, I think those lovely little touches really make a difference in our everyday lives.
42 Bitta	And the girls must just love it in here.
43 Elna	Oh they do, yes. You know, we can get just plain, boring old types of aprons and as you can see, with this apron, it has been delicately embroidered around the edges.
44 Bitta	Oh, that is just gorgeous.
45 Elna	Yes, it just adds such a wonderful touch to the whole thing, don't you think?
46 Bitta	You're marvelous.
47 Elna	Thank you, thank you. We do try to impart skills with the girls that will be with them for life. You know, skills they can use on their baby clothes and just little things around the home. It's very important to be a very happy and a very successful happy homemaker.

Throughout the script of the video there is strong evidence of heterosexual normativity at work. What has been presented as a satirised or parodied version of home economics emphasises and reinforces the orthodox view of home economics pedagogy. This is what the intended audience for the video comprising home economics teachers can recognise as an exaggerated view of their own world. Evidence of this is abundant. For example, the basis of the home economics curriculum structure is *WIFE* (washing, ironing, food and embroidery) and these are the areas of specialisation identified to "teach girls to become good wives". The message is that home economics is 'women's work', and is about preparing girls to be wives in traditional patriarchal, families.

This is clearly recognisable in each of the contexts presented: in washing "what we like to show the little girlies in home economics" is "how to get lipstick stains out of their husbands collars — no questions asked". And we "stress this to the girlies" that they don't want their "husbands having to go along to work and have people laugh at their pink work shirts". "We teach our girls to iron" and "if you've got leisure time you can always iron". Ironing is important to enhance "the husbands presentation — this is all about serving him so that he looks his best" and from that "you will get such a personal sense of achievement" "because we're pleasing him". In food "our girls learn to make their scones properly to please their husbands". "We measure exactly". Embroidery skills add "little touches that really make a difference in our everyday lives" and "the girls just love it in here". Home economics teachers "impart skills with the girls that will be with them for life" as "it's very important to be a very happy and a very successful happy homemaker".

The production of heterosexual normativity and affirmation of the conventional roles of males and females is confirmed in this parodic video dialogue. The pursuits of a good wife in order to serve their husband is all that is presented. The enclosure of the home is reinforced, with the contexts offered as the home kitchen, the home laundry and the home sewing room. The text clearly supports the orthodox subject positions of the virginal home economics teacher (good girlies) and the mother figure (caring, washing, ironing etc) that have recurred in other commentaries in this analysis. Further, it picks up on the skilled and suffering body of home economics teachers. The skilled body is able to perform a range of tasks skillfully, to impress and reinforce the husband. The suffering body is the body accepting of the husbands infidelities, who is bored or desperate enough to iron in their spare time.

In contrast to this, there is a brief concluding scene in the video that has all five home economics teachers present — but a radical transformation has taken place. They are dressed in black leather gear, wearing dark sunglasses, and there is exposed flesh. These re-made home economics teachers are holding large knives in an aggressive, threatening pose. The *sight* of the home economics teacher has shifted. The characters point towards the camera and then aggressively shake their fists while yelling:

50 All   We're sick of being called the "Good girls from home economics". From now on we want to be called "The bad girls from block four".

This transition in the *sight* of the characters captures an attempt to remake the *sight* and *site* of home economics. The shift from "good girls" to "bad girls" in the video is authenticated by the literal sight of the characters. It is an attempt borne out of the frustration which pervades the text throughout this project, and which is produced out of a perceived mismatch between the public perceptions of home economics and the home economics teachers perception of how they should be seen. Home economics teachers may be tired of the *good girl*, the *virginal* and *mother* figure imagery, and hence have put this up against the bad girl image. Regardless of this, and ironically, the atypical teachers in this research project confirm that they subscribe to the general perceptions of the typical home economics teacher represented in this video, thereby themselves contributing directly to reinforcing the frustrating assumptions and normalisation about home economics and home economics teachers.

This 'traditional' imagery of home economics teachers is a concern for Elle as she considers this stereotype to have damaging effects on home economics. She explains this view in the following dialogue:

44 Elle	I don't think the traditional image of a home economics teacher actually benefits our subject area.
45 Donna	Uh huh.
46 Elle	I think we need to be seen more as current and I feel that particular look isn't a current look. It's not indicating that we're up there with everything.

Dressing Like the Nanny

Elle says there are two *other* much smaller, marginalised categories of home economics teachers who are "current", one of which she identifies with. She uses the terms "corporate or modern" for this category, and "alternate" for the third group. The *corporate* home economics teacher, which she aligns herself with, has a business image and she describes her own *sight* as a home economics teacher who typifies this category:

32 Elle	... the way I dress. I wear a business ... suit like above the knees short skirt,
33 Donna	So that would give you that look? Is that what you typically wear?
34 Elle	Yes ... yes ... most days I wear a tailored, modern outfit. My hair either up or down it doesn't matter, shoes with a bit of a heel. I wouldn't have an apron.

This active, enterprising image adds a 'shop front' value. In this description, Elle points to a shift from the *traditional* home economics teacher, including skirt above the knee, high shoes, hair that doesn't matter, and importantly, no apron — all of which are the antithesis of the *traditional* home economics teacher which she considers still remains the largest group of home economics teachers. The students notice the clothes Elle wears, and they are "always commenting":

161 Elle   Even though ... I wear business style clothing, the colours I wear are pretty bright. I wear you know those bright lime greens and ... I colour coordinate really well so it stands out.

162 Donna   And the students will comment on that?

163 Elle   Oh yes. The kids are always commenting on my clothes. Like sort of the Nanny dresses but not as way out as she does. Do you know what I mean? But it ... sometimes a little bit different, so you know checkered black skirts, see what I mean, black tops and things like that.

Elle's performance as a corporate individual is a way of making a spectacle of herself. She believes that through the home economics teachers' body presenting in such a *corporate*, shop-front image, that home economics will be reinvented for today's world as a professional area of knowledge, removed from the historical perception of servitude which comes from the imagery of the apron. She continues:

49 Elle   As professionals and as a subject area that's just up to date, not dated, do you know what I mean? So ... I think that sometimes we might give the impression that we're still doing the traditional things and teaching the girls how to do the, you know, the cooking, sewing, home management and all that, when we're not really. There's a lot more we do that's very useful and applicable to today's society.

The link between the *sight* of the home economics teacher and the *site* of home economics as a body of knowledge is clearly made in this excerpt. Elle notes that the pedagogical practices of the field are linked with the imagery which surrounds it, and the iconography which home economics teachers are complicit with. Self-blame is evident in her commentary when she states "we might give the impression that we're still doing the traditional things", but she then argues "we're not really". This suggests a disjunction between the messages that are presented and what she believes is actually occurring in home economics classrooms. She argues the need for self-regulation to redress this mismatch.

It is interesting to note again that Weber and Mitchell (1995, p. 71) concur with Elle's categories of 'traditional' (sloppy and dowdy) and 'corporate' (serious business), not just for home economics teachers but for all teachers. They explain that popular imagery of teachers reinforces:

> ... either the 'serious business' look that so many real-life teachers adopt, or a sloppy, dowdy look that invites indifference, derision, or pity. Both styles reinforce an image of teacher as asexual, concerned only with the mind.

Elle counters this asexual void in her version of 'corporate', modifying it with shortened skirts and bright colours. This adds eros and desire to her business-like materiality. The remaining third category of home economics teacher Elle has named the 'alternative' group, and she describes these home economics teachers as:

73 Elle   Well ... a small group I suppose you know that more towards the drama that look more like the theatrical type. You know black and a little bit more atypical than what the second group is.

Elle's use of the term *alternative* is a marginalizing tactic — this group is *othered* by her text. The suggestion of 'cheap' theatrics emerges from her reference, and the association with 'black' suggests a dark, even sombre body.

Thus, Elle identifies herself as an atypical home economics teacher as she is not in the dominant *traditional* mould. She locates herself as *othered* in the larger of two remaining categories of home economics teachers — the *corporate* category. The third *alternative* group she marginalizes.

Food Passion

Elle is pleasured by her experience as a home economics teacher and is pleasured by exciting students about learning. She explains that her pleasure as a home economics teacher is often strongly derived from her passion for food. She expresses her pleasure as "getting all worked up" and "excited" and this emotion gives pleasure to her students. This is described in the following transcript:

81 Elle   I'm very passionate about food, so I enjoy it whether I be at school or anywhere and people know that because I express myself ...

83 Elle   ... intensely over food. You know, I just love it, so when I'm teaching if the kids can see me, sort of, you know, getting all worked up about ...

84 Donna	So you get a lot of pleasure from teaching in that area?
85 Elle	Oh yes.

Elle indicates that her pleasure for food comes from a range of dimensions, including preparation, presentation, consumption ("I just love food"), and also the reactions of others.

89 Elle	Yeah, I just love food, and eating, and you know, making it and presenting it beautifully so to get a reaction almost from other people as well as to present it that well, and that's what I try and teach students, especially in the catering and hospitality area.

Elle aims to "get a reaction" from her students. She sets up their pleasure and then takes pleasure from their reactions. She sets out to get her students excited. She explains how the students sense her excitement:

95 Elle	My body language, like the excitement I feel. Like, even yesterday I was showing the students one of my most favourite cookbooks and I'm flicking through the pages and I'm getting real excited showing them and they're sort of getting excited watching me you know getting excited over food and they're sort of getting more interested in what we were doing.

Elle is "getting real excited" and the students are "getting excited watching" her. She explains that she gets the most excited and receives greatest pleasure when tasting foods students have prepared:

183 Elle	When they give me their food (Laughs). When they, they get excited about their food and they're really proud of it and they run up and show me and I go oh that's fantastic and they say "Do you want some?".
184 Donna	And they give you ...
185 Elle	( ) Oh yeah and I go Mmmmm okay (Laughs). It gives them real pleasure.
186 Donna	And do you think that gives the students pleasure?
187 Elle	Oh yes. And I know that so I'll ... it's almost like I'll ham it up a bit because I know they enjoy it so much ... mean it but I'll go "Oh, that's fantastic" do you know what I mean? I probably wouldn't do that to one of my friends or my husband when he prepared a meal (Laughs), probably just "Darling that's really nice" (Laughs).
188 Donna	So you return the pleasure to them?
189 Elle	Yes, and I can tell the more excited I am the better they've done I suppose.

This excitement circulates in the pedagogical space moving from the teacher's body to the students' bodies. The students are excited, and they "run up and show" Elle and when she responds in an almost orgasmic way ("Mmmmmm") "it gives them real pleasure". The teacher pleasures her students through the expression of her own pleasure, gained from her enjoyment of their food. She performs her evaluation of the quality of her students work through the amount of pleasure and excitement she receives. This is a very different pedagogical display to that of the 'proper' home economics teacher produced out of the earlier studies in this book, who attempt to control their consumption of food offered by students. Elle's consumption of food risks loss of the 'right' body and the 'right' modelling of food consumption for her students.

Deriving "a lot of pleasure" from students is fundamental to Elle's teaching approach. She explains:

181 Elle   I get a lot of pleasure from students themselves. I enjoy, I just enjoy being with them and listening to them and ... I don't know, it's just youth, they are so different to me I suppose I really thrive on learning about their culture. I enjoy the students who love learning, and of course you know them learning from me so when they learn from me and develop skills that I've taught them, that brings me a lot of pleasure. I absolutely love all the extra curricular activities I am involved in as I get the chance to spend time with students in areas different to my subject area.

This taking of pleasure from students is an expression of teacher-centred pedagogy as subversion. Elle's body as orgasmic, passionate and excited applies in other home economics contexts, not just those where food is involved. She explains that her body is used to create excitement and passion in her teaching of home economics "I think my body gives a message ... of a lot of energy ... and excitement and interest and passion for what I do" (Elle, Line 169 and 171).

Through her embodied performances, Elle models the pleasure of teaching and her students desire to learn is activated. This is a voyeuristic relationship which risks subversion, given that the teacher's desire and the student's desire at times threaten to become outside the bounds of reasonableness. Certainly, the taking of pleasure and having fun is a risky business because "the system militates against this possibility" (Weber & Mitchell 1995, p. 48). Indeed, as Aronowitz (cited in Weber & Mitchell, 1995, p. 48) maintains, "school is an activity, from the point of view of all its participants, that systematically denies pleasure".

Perhaps she is 'saved' by her corporate makeover, which legitimates her excitement and pleasure by framing it within a professional demeanour.

Vanity Yes, But No Hypocrisy

Elle believes that home economics teachers should, through their literal *sight*, be positive role models for their students. This view is common to all of the atypical subjects in this project, and to the view of the orthodox home economics teachers produced from the survey material. Elle argues that this positive sight flows on to the pedagogical practice of home economics, leading to home economics becoming more desirable as a *site* of knowledge. She explains that although she considers herself to be vain, home economics teachers have a responsibility to project a healthy image:

115 Elle		I'm conscious because I'm vain … I think … yeah (Laughs)
116 Donna		So can you explain that a bit more?
117 Elle		I think it's really important to … being a home ec teacher to show that I care about my physical appearance and it shows that I eat well and possibly exercise, not that I'm a huge exerciser but do those things like I promote health and in what I wear, I suppose I demonstrate that. I don't … I would never wear a dress that was you know, unflattering I suppose.

Elle speaks of "conscious" attention to her physical appearance such that she shows she "cares". Through her appearance she regards the messages about the practices that support her appearance are reflected such as eating well, exercising, not wearing unflattering dresses, and promoting health. She regards this as her obligation as a home economics teacher and that she makes conscious decisions about her clothing:

120 Elle	Yes, but that's with vanity as well, do you know what I mean, so … But I also, I'm pleased with the health, the healthy look I achieve.
121 Donna	So that's your aim is it, that health and vitality sort of?
122 Elle	Yes. And I think that's a point, and I feel very confident when I'm teaching things like nutrition to say like you know this is what if you do this you know you do get good results. You know it's not, some, I mean of course it's luck as well but … I think it's very good for students to see that. I suppose that it could look a little bit hypocritical if I didn't do that and if I didn't present myself well at do you know what I mean like … and perhaps I let myself go a bit or and the way I held myself I slouched or whatever.

124 Elle   But I think they would relate that and not probably believe
            what I was teaching them.

Elle is presenting a case for the redemptive role of the home economics teacher. She refuses to be a hypocrite such that her body
as a *sight* — her exterior — fails to reflect home economics pedagogy. Further, this promotes confidence and credibility in her
as a home economics teacher. In this way Elle's embodied practices are those of the orthodox home economics teacher.

A Touchy Matter

Elle uses body contact with students as an important part of her
teaching. Yet, body contact is a 'touchy' matter for teachers with
moral and legal risks involved. Despite these risks, Elle believes
that she uses 'appropriate' body contact by restricting it to head
and shoulder as the safest and least offensive sites. There
is almost a sense of bravado in Elle's claim that she "touch(es)
students all the time". In her words:

142 Elle   I touch students all the time.

143 Donna   Right. Can you explain that?

144 Elle   In fact I'm very, I have a deputy principal and she's very
            warm and touching with students and they respond well
            to it. I learned that from her even though it's probably
            not the right thing to do. Students at our school respond
            very positively, most of them, you know ninety-five per-
            cent, to being touched, and I'm forever ... touching their
            head or their shoulder, male and female, just to let them,
            it's almost like letting them know I'm there.

145 Donna   And you say their head and their shoulder, why do you
            touch them there and not somewhere else? How did you
            decide that was the right place to touch?

146 Elle   Because I think it's the least offensive.

147 Elle   Or the safest places to touch so they're ...

149 Elle   Yeah, anywhere else could be misconstrued.

151 Elle   Yeah, so that's conscious.

She believes that touching students has helped her to "let(ting)
them know I'm there", a common proximity tactic used by teachers for classroom management purposes, but generally without
actual contact. Elle legitimates her behaviour through similar
practices of a higher authority (deputy principal) thus avoiding
special attention, even though she knows "it is not right". When
asked whether she is comfortable with students initiating touch,
Elle responds in the negative:

153 Elle   Actually, I put my hand around someone's shoulder once and they put their arm around me and I got a fright so it doesn't happen that often that they respond back. So I actually took note of it that they did that. It doesn't happen often but they're very comfortable with me doing that, but not the other way. But I've been in the school for a long time too and they know me. If I was a new teacher going to the school and did that they probably would ...

154 Donna   So that's something unique about you?

155 Elle   That I touch students, yes ... yes that's unique, yes.

This retreat from student touch is a retreat to the orthodoxy of the student/teacher relationship. She is aware of the limits to risk taking, reigning herself into 'safe' territory. She is not responsive to student touch, although she uses this tactic to gain attention from students. The touching of the body is also used as a way of demonstrating familiarity and place — new teachers would risk compromising themselves if they tried to touch students. She confirms that although this is "probably not the right thing to do" that this is her "unique" ability. Elle's touchy relationship with students is a spectacle in which she engages and is threatening and risky at a time of moral and sex panic around the pedagogical body. Risk takers such as Elle are highly attuned to the limits of this 'touchy' risk taking.

Giving and Taking Pleasure in Home Economics

The texts generated show that Elle produces herself as a particular kind of home economics teacher in ways that can be recognized as 'normal'. She does not challenge heterosexual normativity in her performativity as a home economics teacher. For example, she reinforces the site of home economics as the home, and as 'women's work'. She represents the site of the typical home economics teacher as conforming to the normalized versions represented previously by other subjects in this study. Elle occupies her place in the home economics landscape as a heterosexual female, adopting a 'corporate' rather than a 'traditional' image as a home economics teacher, avoiding this apron-wearing stereotype. She reinforces the boundaries of enclosure of the home in ways that are not challenging to the orthodoxy that sets the home as the site for home economics. And yet, her 'corporate' imagery makes direct links to the public world, challenging the private/public binary.

Where Elle's body is aberrant as a home economics teacher is in that she overtly takes pleasure from her students. For example, the consumption of food pleasures and excites her, and she refuses to conform to the 'right' role model in this regard. She also touches students, a practice she recognises as being 'wrong' in terms of current policy. In this way, Elle risks subversion.

Skilled But Not Suffering

In previous sections of this book, an account of the normal body of the orthodox home economics teacher was provided from survey data produced by Study One and Study Two. What emerged from this reading was that home economics teachers tended to conform to the culturally inscribed stereotypes of female teachers, as argued by Weber and Mitchell (1995). Home economics teachers appear to be doubly produced, first as female teachers, and then as teachers of a subject that is seen to be for women. As such they engage in close self-surveillance, conforming to the institutions of normative coercion based on their common experience. From these totalising narratives there emerged two disciplined bodies of home economics. The ideal home economics body is the *skilled* body, whilst the real is the *suffering* body.

In this chapter, an attempt has been made to consider what resistance to the hegemonic body of the *skilled* and *suffering* home economics teacher looks like, by interviewing four atypical home economics teachers. In this final section of this chapter, the purpose is to look at the relationship, if any, between these four 'atypical' teachers and the *skilled* and *suffering* bodies of 'normal' home economics teachers. Do these atypical bodies trouble the conventions of the profession and make a shift from the *skilled* and *suffering* home economics teachers bodies?

The *skilled* body of home economics is the body which is technically proficient, promotes actual skills (e.g. sewing, cooking) and products, places importance on the hands on, practical nature of the subject for lifelong learning, and reinforces heterosexual normativity as the context within which this occurs — the site of home economics pedagogy. Words such as *multi-skilled, professional, organised, hardworking, caring, resourceful,* and *creative* characterise the home economics teacher. This is the socially produced view of home economics teachers by home economics teachers and is described as the common experience of home economics teachers.

Do the atypical home economics teachers trouble these conventions of the *skilled* body of home economics teachers? From the descriptions of themselves as home economics teachers given in their commentaries, on the contrary, all four atypical teachers reinforce the idea of the *skilled* body, and they are not defiant of the prescription of normality as *skilled* bodies. John is typical of this reinforcement in the area of heterosexual normativity as the benchmark for home economics pedagogy through his repeated commentaries and actions. For example, his desire for a female 'roomy'; his analogy of being the only Sheila on the footy team; his position as role model to male students and so on. All are reflections of his hypermasculine 'blokeness', in line with the dictates of heterosexual normativity. His skills as a chef are used to validate his location in this woman's domain and his teaching style reflects his masculine role as ex-Army chef. There is also evidence of a lot of tidying in his text in order to be no trouble and therefore not be subversive. Comments such as "I don't mean to complain" act as signs that he is not attempting to subvert or even transform home economics pedagogy. This type of reinforcing of the skilled body of home economics reappeared throughout the descriptions given by Marilyn, Valerie and Elle. Skills for life, the hands on nature of the field, teacher as role model and so on, generate the *skilled* home economics teacher's body. In the eyes of their students, they are *skilled* bodies. Further, these subjects do not trouble the orthodoxies of heterosexuality hence they are not transgressive bodies from the *skilled* body of home economics teachers as they do not trouble this as a, if not the, most prominent convention of the profession. These atypical home economics teachers accommodate the conventions of the *skilled* home economics teacher and are not subversive. They also take on the role of object-of-self-surveillance to conform to this prescription of normality.

The *suffering* body of home economics is the denying role model and the martyr, decentred and genderless, the virgin and the mother figure reinforcing heterosexual normativity, restricted to the site of the home, physically stressed and distressed, mal-nourished and physically exhausted from the work associated with being a home economics teacher. Are the atypical home economics teachers defiant and transgressive of the prescription of normality of the *suffering* body of home economics teachers?

For each of the four atypical subjects there is a refusal to suffer and instead self-regulation to produce a certain sort of *other*, not *suffering* body is evident. Each subject resists the orthodoxies of the *suffering* body in at least one, and often in many ways and thereby discipline their body in order to be against the folklore of the *suffering* home economics body. For example: the *suffering* body of the home economics teacher as the virgin who misses out or the dowdy mother figure is refused by Marilyn, who conceives of herself as a 'groovy' teacher; the refusal of Valerie to accept the enclosure of the home as the boundary of home economics removes her restrictions and opens new and exciting positions for her; the refusal of John to sacrifice his pleasure in food — and plenty of it — yet still to be a home economics teacher; Elle's refusal to resist her taking of pleasure and excitement through the consumption of student's food; and her refusal to resist the taking of pleasure from the flesh of her students.

These teachers resist *suffering* and insist on versions of pedagogy that are not student centred — so they are not *suffering*. However, all of these atypical teachers use normalising tactics to reinforce the conventions of the *suffering* body for the *other* home economics teachers as they like to be in the margins as the *not suffering* home economics body. This is their *otherness*, and the refusal to suffer like *other* normalised home economics teachers makes them atypical. They also differ in their 'Otherness', not producing singular versions of difference.

Being 'atypical' however, is not to be a 'bad' teacher. As McWilliam (1996b, p. 15) argues, these atypical teachers, like other successful teachers:

> appropriately mobilise forces of desire (the desire to teach and the desire to learn) both of which are productive, not malevolent ... teachers often do so in ways that lie outside our cultural norms of legitimate pedagogical exchange.

These atypical teachers are *skilled* but refuse to *suffer*, and as such, create certain desires in students that are outside of what is produced as legitimate, proper and authentic home economics as a *site* and *sight* of knowledge. The following chapter looks to the fun and carnivalesque of these atypical teachers and their pedagogical practices.

Further Thinking

Consider home economists who do not fit traditional stereotypes of home economics teachers. In what ways do these people challenge stereotypes? Have these people suffered victimization or discrimination from work colleagues, students, parents or others because of their difference?

Is it in the best interests of home economics as a field of study to promote one vision of an ideal home economics teacher? Why or why not? How might this ideal look and behave?

The consumption of food is one way in which some of the teachers featured in this chapter admit to taking pleasure in their classroom. In what other ways might pleasure be given and received in home economics classrooms?

The teachers represented in this chapter were characterized as being 'skilled', but as refusing the norm of 'suffering' that is attributed to typical home economics teachers. In what way might these teachers enhance the status of home economics teachers?

Carnivalesque in the Home Economics Classroom

The Undisciplined Body of Home Economics Teachers

The unilateral reading of *typical* home economics teachers presented earlier in this book reveals the production of two metaphorical bodies. These socially produced, disciplined bodies are the *skilled* body and the *suffering* body, evident in orderly accounts of the bodily production for home economics teachers. This bodily production occurs through everyday routines and mundane arrangements, and is maintained through self-surveillance and self-correction (McDowell, 1995).

The reading of the *body of the text* and the *body as text* reveals that certain individuals appear to self-regulate their bodies towards improving/ maintaining *skill,* but do not maintain *suffering.* Consequently, these subjects do not conform to the conventional 'two bodies' of the normalised home economics teacher. These resisting bodies represent themselves as, amongst other things, groovy, sexy, outdoor-oriented, singing and dancing in the classroom, enjoying the consumption of food and generally taking pleasure in the embodied nature of their work.

The atypical teachers appear to insist on pursuing self-interested pedagogy rather than student-centred pedagogy. They appear to offer a route to mutual pleasure — rather than pain — in the pedagogical events they engage in. Nevertheless, each of these atypical teachers are also typical or normal in that they appear to enjoy their marginal positions as non-suffering home economics bodies, and even insist on it, constantly reiterating their understanding of themselves as 'outsiders' for better rather than for worse. Simply put, the margin, like the house verandah, is a cool place to be.

It is apparent that these *skilled,* but not *suffering* bodies occupying the home economics landscape take pleasure and have fun in their work. So, what possibility is there in this cool place, for a radical reconfiguring of the culture of home economics teaching? To frame the inquiry in this way is to ask about the relationship between 'fun' and subversion, something that Ferguson's

(1990) analysis of the carnivalesque addresses. Ferguson (1990) uses Bakhtin's (1968) theory of carnival as the basis for understanding 'fun'. The carnival has been utilised in other projects by educational researchers interested in pursuing analysis that "offer[s] another way to think through problems of reproduction, resistance, and transformation" (Grace, 1996, p. 5). Hence, this project which considers home economics teaching *as carnival* (i.e., the transgressive ways these teachers take their pleasures and have their fun) disrupts neat conclusions about conservative or typical centres and radical or a-typical margins. This serves to provide a new way of re-imagining home economics, which is the broader intent of this book.

The reading that follows in this chapter continues this work by refusing a neat story about two bodies for home economics (*skilled* and *suffering*) and insisting on multiple bodies, constantly shifting and incomplete. It is through the application of the metaphor of carnival, and particularly the grotesque body of the carnivalesque, that this analytical work proceeds.

Re-Membering Carnival and Grotesque Bodies

The domain of carnival is, for Bakhtin (1968), that of public festivities which made outrageous fun of orthodox and authoritative opinion. Carnival contained grotesque realism, which was exaggerated and typically degrading and mocking of the human society and body with respect to the norms and practices of the day. In this way, carnival can be understood as space for parody and the bodies engaged in the carnival — carnivalesque bodies — the tools of parody.

Mary Russo's (1994) argument is the grotesque body performs the work of the carnival, which is a grotesque parody of 'normal' life. The masks and voices of the grotesque body resist, exaggerate, challenge and destabilize the norms of society through the vehicle of carnival. Bakhtin transposes the notion of carnival to today's world, such that carnival is a potential site of transformation. This transposition has allowed writers like Mellor and Shilling (1997) to argue that the grotesque body is within us all.

Russo (1994) insists that the female grotesque that emerges from Bakhtin's explanation of the grotesque body of carnival and carnivalesque, is 'crucial' for a transformative shift from the alternative modes of identity formation. The work of this postmodern project, then, is to look at the grotesque bodies that have been ignored and suppressed in the culture of home economics. Carnivalesque moments and grotesque bodies represent the 'other than normal' body of the home economics teacher. These are risky, freakish bodies engaged in risky activities that parody officialdom and refuse order and normalisation. They are the bodies which refuse to be tidied and kept in place, but instead provide "an altered sense of reality that [holds] potential for renewal and change" (Grace, 1996, p. 5) and for "social transformation" (Russo 1994, p. 8). Something may therefore be learned about escaping the current cul-de-sac of thinking about home economics culture by characterizing the bodies in this study as grotesque spectacles. That is the intent of the following analysis.

Home Economics as Carnival — The Grotesque Body

As outlined, the carnivalesque body is one way of characterising the atypical home economics teachers, and it is important to any project where the mind/body duality of modernist thought is rejected. What I am pointing to in this book is the notion that the carnival is already part of the home economics landscape, rather than elsewhere or absent, and the effects of this should not be trivialised or ignored. The grotesque, the excess, the risk, the refusal, the freakish — these things are already part of home economics. The home economics classroom *is* carnival and the grotesque body *is* the fat person with moustache who touches children and has dirty fingernails, who wears no undergarments and abseils, who is sexy and playful, singing and dancing and generating excitement. This is a present reality in our home economics classrooms.

An unsettling of orderly accounts and familiar traditions is possible through this exposure of the disorderly bodies occupying the home economics landscape, "allowing alternative interrogations of present practices" (McWilliam, 1997b, p. 229). In the analysis in this chapter, there is also a shift from the identity politics where each atypical body is identifiable as an assembled body, to the notion where identity is assemblage. This approach is supported by Mellor and Shilling (1997, p. 10), who argue that "grotesque bodies resist easy classification, and refuse to be individualised or separated from their natural environment". Hence, the bodies are disassembled as individual identities and reassembled as grotesque assemblage with transformative potential where identities are masked, thereby refusing individual identity politics.

John, Valerie, Marilyn and Elle are not analysed as individual identities in this re-working, but rather, composite assemblies of their performance create grotesque assembled bodies. Their individual performances are drawn upon in the creation of the grotesque body assemblages. This notion of disassembly and re-assembly is in keeping with postmodernist body theory as it allows that bodies are amenable to completion, constantly undergoing change, and are not seen as simple, anatomical fleshy bodies. Indeed, as Russo (1994, p. 78) claims, the "grotesque body was exuberantly and democratically open and inclusive of all possibilities". What can emerge therefore is a re-assemblage that masks individual identities and is inclusive of any possibility.

The carnivalesque home economics teacher disrupts the many categories of body norms which exist within the culture of home economics, and which often reflect conservative middle class culture and traditions. This characterising of the atypical bodies opens up possibilities for grotesque bodies that refuse normalisation (Russo, 1994) as *suffering* home economics bodies. The bodies which *refuse to be kept in their place* as typical home economics teachers are assembled in this chapter as:

- fat home economics bodies (refusing to be governed by health with the 'right' body and fitness norms);

- sexy, groovy home economics bodies (refusing to be governed by norms of a-sexual nurturance);

- outdoors home economics bodies (refusing to be bound by the enclosures of the home);

- playful home economics bodies (refusing to restrict themselves to student-centred pedagogy); and

- touching home economics bodies (refusing the norms of pedagogical probity in relation to student engagement).

These are temporary assemblages of my own making — a fiction emerging out of my analysis. Here the atypical teachers can perform at their most grotesque, parodying conventional productions of home economics teachers. They perform in these carnivalesque moments that are experienced as brief, temporal spaces that parody officialdom and normalisation, thereby unsettling orderly accounts of the body of home economics. These moments appear in home economics classrooms, they are moments of 'surprise'.

The important issue is that all home economics teachers perform as body subjects, engaging in a labour of reinscription of themselves and others, continually shaped and shaping the site of their pedagogy.

Performing as a Fat Home Economics Body

The 'fat' home economics teacher is recognisable in the data of the 'atypical' home economics teachers. The utterances of the fat body confirm recognition and acknowledgment of performing as a fat body in a domain that advocates the 'right' (not fat) body. The fat body is self-described as "big", "fat" (John, Line 134) and "overweight" (John, Line 30). But to be both fat and a home economics teacher is recognised as unexpected and freakish, by both home economics teachers and their students. Indeed, as the fat teacher confessed, he "shouldn't be eating" (John, Line 138) the foods he does consume.

Another of the atypical teachers however is most orthodox in arguing that fat bodies are unsuitable as home economics teachers. Her argument — which is well supported in Study One and Study Two as representing the norm — is that it is "super-hypo-critical [for home economics teachers] to be obese" (Marilyn, Line 34). The rationale for this view is that teachers "obviously couldn't take that information themselves" (Marilyn, Line 34), hence fail as role model and martyr. The fat home economics body also seems to comply with this view — by admitting to using their body as an example of what not to do. It is interesting to see that this is how the fat body has learnt to perform as a home economics teacher, maintaining the norm through insisting on the 'inappropriateness' of fatness.

Students regard the fat home economics teacher as freakish, telling the fat teacher "you shouldn't be doing that [eating pies and coke]" (John, Line 134). And yet, with their knowledge of food and weight control through the very subject matter of home economics, this unruly body refuses to conform. The fat body refuses to comply with the expectation that home economics teachers' bodies must be self-monitoring and practice abstinence in order to create a well-governed body that is proper for pedagogical display.

The shape of the fat body, and therefore the way clothing adorns it, is also freakish for fat home economics teachers. The "belt sits underneath [the] beer belly", with the result that "clothes [are] not well fitting, basically because of body shape" (John, Line 30). This is not in accord with the proper home economics body. The proper body is neat in clothing and overall appearance. Their clothing is expected to exemplify the "principles ... that [the teacher] should be teaching them" and students have the "expectation that [the teacher] will adhere to the principles" (Valerie, Line 40). As Marilyn advocates, "what you wear and what you look like as a home economics teacher" is vitally important (Marilyn, Line 34).

This obsession with the 'right' body in home economics makes the fat body a freakish sight. But this obsession with fatness is not restricted to producing 'proper' home economics teachers' bodies — it is evident in whole cultures. Indeed, fatness is one category of what Russo (1994, p. 23) describes as bodily distribution and valuation. She explains why the excessively fat body can be grotesque, particularly for women:

> Fatness ... functions as an extremely significant differential in separating off women of different classes and ethnicities (sic), placing them in different fields or markets of representation. (Russo, 1994, p. 23)

Russo (1994), like Lupton (1996), argues that this is a phenomenon in contemporary western societies, where fat women are thought of as "repositories of shame and repressed desire" (Russo, 1994, p. 24), and this places them in a certain market of representation. Lupton (1996, p. 16) suggests that "bodies [thus] become potent physical symbols of the extent to which their 'owners' possess self-control ... an overweight body speaks of gluttony, lack of self-discipline, hedonism, self-indulgence, while a slim body signifies a high level of control, and ability to transcend the desires of the flesh".

The interesting difference for the fat body represented in this book is that it is a male body, and a home economics body. So, is the gendered fatness allowable, that is, can a male body get away with being fat? It seems that home economics is a microcosm of this cultural precedent, where the fat teacher is criticised as failing to act as an appropriate role model for their students and is chastised for lack of control. So the male body does not get away with being fat in the home economics context. Home economics teachers are self-regulated to demonstrate appropriate resistance, denial, and control of food, regardless of their gender. The fat body becomes the site of anxiety and shame, of guilt, frustration and anger. Thus, the excessive, fat body of the teacher is a grotesque body that is forced to adopt the protocols of exclusion and invisibility to survive in the field. The fat body is a freakish, mutant anatomy in the home economics landscape and thus is a risky body that can parody normality. The grotesque, fat body contrasts with the 'civilised' body that is "constructed as the body that is self-contained, that is highly socially managed and conforms to dominant norms of behaviour and appearance" (Lupton 1996, p. 19).

This fat, freakish body also performs exaggerated desire, and displays of excitement and passion when involved with the preparation, presentation and consumption of food in the home economics classroom. The risk this body engages in is that of potentially becoming 'fat'. For example, Elle admits that "I just love food, and eating" (Line 189). She is unashamedly "passionate about food" (Elle, Line 181), "getting all worked up" (Elle, Line 183). Students are likewise encouraged to display their pleasure and excitement. They "run up and show [Elle] … and they say, 'do you want some?' " (Line 183). Elle reacts with excitement, indicating that "the more excited I am the better they've done" (Line 189). This is in keeping with Lupton's (1996, p. 31) argument that "food stirs the emotions" and that "for many, the pleasures to be gained from food are the high points of their everyday sensual experiences". Lupton argues that there is pleasure to be gained from transgressing the norms of self-control with respect to food and pleasure, but that these embodied sensations fall outside of safe territory. In this instance, this safe territory is of 'proper' home economics teaching.

Performing as a Sexy, Groovy Home Economics Body

As Weber and Mitchell (1995) argue, and as this research also suggests, teachers — and even more so home economics teachers — are expected to be asexual, motherly and dowdy. Hence, the presence of bodies clad in sexy clothing, with drinking and smoking as self-professed habits, is carnivalesque. These freakish, risky bodies of sexy teachers are dangerous to the norms associated with the culture of home economics.

One of the ways of performing as a sexy, groovy home economics body is through the clothing worn by the teacher. There is no doubt that the clothing teachers wear is integral to the stereotyping and normalisation of teachers, contributing to the materiality of the body. Teachers use fashion and clothing as public claims for inclusion within their social category (McDowell, 1995; Finkelstein, 1997). McDowell (1995, p. 89) found this to be common across various social categories. For example, women in professional positions in large merchant banking corporations dressed "exceedingly carefully and conformed to the norms that insisted that they did not mark themselves out as 'the other'". Similarly, Weber and Mitchell (1995, p. 71) note that teachers "know how to dress". For women in particular, this means a de-sexualising of their attire and with that, a de-sexualising of their body.

The sexy home economics teachers also 'know how to dress'. However, in this case, it is as a show of parody. They use their clothing as a means of resisting being produced as the 'proper' virginal and motherly teacher, instead sexualising their attire and hence their body. This is a powerful mechanism, because, as Finkelstein (1997, p. 157) argues, "whenever these styles [in this case the teacher style] are toyed with, then fashion is reiterating its ability to influence human subjectivity ... [so that] [F]ashioning the body becomes a practice through which subject positions are also fashioned". The home economics body that refuses to hide its sexuality — which steps out of the asexual, motherly, virginal norms — flaunts this through their attire. Marilyn wants, through her choice of clothing, to "imprint on them [students]" (Line 37), that she is 'other' to a typical home economics teacher.

Just as certain freakish home economics teachers consciously work against orthodoxy, McDowell (1995, p. 89) found that some respondents in her study on merchant bankers deliberately flouted the conventions and blurred the boundaries of dress in order for it to become a "more pleasurable performance that could be used to create or subvert a particular image". Like McDowell's subjects, the carnivalesque bodies of the sexy, groovy, home economics teachers are freakish and extremely risky, perhaps attempting to subvert the image of the typical home economics teacher, in the double production of being a teacher *and* specifically a home economics teacher. However, Weber and Mitchell (1995, p. 71) note that the strategy of dressing a little differently to the norm — but within the boundaries — is common practice. That is, it is 'normal' for teachers to be a little 'not normal' in their dress, viz:

> ... each teacher has a distinctive style that peeks through that first-glance uniformity, offering a counter-text, proclaiming a rebellious conservatism or a conservative rebellion. In dressing , we exert our right to be ambivalent, and we reveal our individual attempts to both 'fit in' and be ourselves in many ways ...

So there is 'normally' a little paradox in teachers dress. But how much beyond normal is not 'normal' for a home economics teacher? The unruly bodies both 'fit in' and yet do not 'fit in'. Elle's 'corporate image' seems not to be radical — until her version of short, sexy and in bright colours is seen. Valerie's outdoor, Army, rough clothes are a 'surprise' but this freakish body soon returns to 'normal' in the presence of students and knows not to present this way in order to 'fit in'. John's chef uniform in some respects offers a more authentic production of home economics than home economics teachers can, parodying the home economics teacher with new authority and legitimacy. These are all grotesque bodies in carnivalesque moments. Marilyn's groovy, sexy body is very risky indeed in its refusal of certain undergarments — a grotesque, perverse body which is a de-formation refusing to be 'supported' by garments that speak of virginal mothers.

These examples are beyond the 'normal' extent of individuality in teacher dress, evoking 'surprise' in students. The 'surprise' which emerges out of the parodic materiality and performativity of the sexy, groovy home economics bodies is registered by the home economics students. Marilyn's students feel free to respond to her invitation to be seen as sexy. The students speak of "that look" (Student, aged 17) and of the "inspiration from [Marilyn's] body" (Student, aged 16). Marilyn is self-consciously an embodied teacher, engaged in mind and body learning with her students. Many teachers pay a large penalty for 'surprising' students, but these teachers do not. This is because they are normal in many other ways which makes this surprise interesting and fun. These teachers perform in classrooms which are not chaotic, but where work is done and where learning goals are achieved.

Weber and Mitchell (1995, p. 71) make a link between the attire of the teacher and their performance, suggesting that the teacher who wears "lacy underwear ... although outwardly invisible, somehow changes posture or appearance". So these unruly bodies of the home economics teachers also engage in grotesque performances beyond the inscription of their bodies through the materiality of their clothing, which further parody the institutions of home economics.

Performing home economics does not normally include evidence of smoking, drinking, and being sexually active, as these are performances in which 'redemptive martyrs' are not meant to participate. As Judith Butler (1993) argues, the cultural norms of the female home economics teacher are transgressed by such performances. Indeed, any female engaged in sexual activity creates moral panic based on the unequal and traditional double standards for judging women's sexual activity, with "implications for her reputation" and deviancy accepted as the ramification of such behaviour (Davis, 1997, p. 38). Perhaps the sexy home economics body becomes victim of this dilemma, where there is a risk of the perception of deviancy, in that making a shift from the virginal and/or mother figure to the desirable sexy body may create a moral panic. Yet it may also 'pay off', breaking some of the cultural stereotypes which have marginalised home economics. Whatever the implication, both bodies (virginal and sexy) conform to heterosexual norms of femininity and attract the male gaze (McDowell, 1995). The ways in which women discipline themselves to conform to notions of heterosexual attractiveness and particular expectations of feminine behavior are well documented, appearing, for example, in the work of: Bordo (1992; 1993) and Butler (1993). Finkelstein (1997, p. 156) argues that such transgressions are risky because "at the moment women are seen as self-producing, what they are often producing is the constrained and subjugated image of the heterosexually desirable female". This is a dilemma for the sexy home economics body.

Nevertheless, the sexy body of home economics is a seductive, appealing body, designed to be noticed by the students. As Weber and Mitchell (1995, p. 122) note, this is not unusual as utopic texts of popular culture, society and academic scholars have paid attention to the many "vivid images of teachers, many of which carry with them, either implicitly or explicitly, themes of romance, sexuality and power". For example, the popular culture of cinema has presented many vivid and heroic images of teachers, including those produced in *Stand and Deliver; Dead Poet's Society; Kindergarten Cop; To Sir With Love*; and *Lean on Me* to name but a few. Theorists in the field of education invariably refer back to the dilemmas and heroic feats, or radical disasters of these extreme productions of teachers and their pedagogical relationships with students. The vividness of the home economics body without undergarments, with short skirts, engaged in activities such as smoking and drinking, offers seductive, sexy images that may have transgressive appeal to students. Care must be taken however, to limit this so that sexy does not become 'whorish'. These bodies gain applause for their otherness and assume power for their otherness from their students. For example, one of John's students stated that "you would never think of him as a teacher" (Student, aged 16), another that they "have enjoyed home economics class the most out of all" (Student, aged 17), and they will "have many memories [to] keep ... throughout [her] life" (Student, aged 17). These risky bodies are seductive and can lead to the type of '(s)education' which offers pleasure to both students and teachers. This term is borrowed from McWilliam (1996b) who theorizes about the combining of pleasure and teaching in an attempt to reclaim seduction and thus (s)education as a legitimate metaphor for the work teachers do. The argument is that seductive pedagogy need not be abusive pedagogy (McWilliam, 1996c).

Performing as an Outdoors Home Economics Body

The 'outdoors' home economics teacher is recognisable in the data of the 'atypical' home economics teachers. Activities include abseiling, canoeing, camping and other outdoors and 'Army-like' escapades. These are 'freakish' performances for home economics teachers, whom we have seen characterised as "well dressed white upper to middle class female[s]" (John, Line 27) who "cook a few little scones" (John, Line 20) and are "quite domesticated and involved with what's *in* the home" (Valerie, Line 20). Further, in Elle's parodic play, home economics teachers are produced as the 'W.I.F.E.' — the acronym standing for washing, ironing, food and embroidery – again, the indoors home economics teacher, confined to the enclosures of the home.

Contrary to these 'proper' home economics teachers, the outdoors bodies are engaged in risky activities, both in terms of physical danger and also in terms of the pedagogical conservatism of home economics. The classroom pedagogy of the outdoors body has parallels with a military model of instruction and activity — drilling, marching, lining up, yelling orders, and swearing, (see John, Line 144, 152). It also involves: "the latest developments in technology in terms of climbing equipment and camping equipment"; "taking students abseiling ... so that they can feel what trust is"; and "excursions to a camping store" (Valerie, Line 22). It is these strategies that are utilised rather than "exercises in trust circles and things" (Valerie, Line 22) in the classroom, which typify home economics as a nurturant pedagogy.

This shift from the nurturant, student-centred classroom to the hard, sweaty, masculinist world of the Army and outdoors clearly cuts across the cultural traditions associated with and expected in home economics classes, and particularly, conformity to the enclosures of the home. The cloistered, feminised world of home economics is exposed to, and reinscribed by, the hard, masculinized world of the public and the outdoors. Students are enrolled as co-performers and co-authors in a play with new scenery and thus a new site for home economics. The students may be enabled to 'see' other possibilities than the normal home economics domain through the transgressive site and sight of the outdoors body engaged in such an active, experience based pedagogy. Valerie insists on "apply[ing teaching] ... into real life" (Valerie, Line 62) in the hope that students recognise "home economics [as] vitally important ... not just restricted to the home, [but] to all facets of life" (Valerie, Line 62).

The performance of outdoors home economics bodies includes dirty fingernails and physical adornment in 'daggy', dirty clothes, and this denotes a further shift from the civility of the normal home economics body. Again, it must be acknowledged that the clothing worn by teachers 'produces' a particular pedagogical performance. After an examination of teachers' clothing choices, Weber and Mitchell (1995, p. 71) note that dressing as a teacher:

... involves reconciling, suppressing, ignoring, or dealing in some way with the ambivalence and tensions between different ways of living one's social and personal self under the banner of 'teacher'.

These outdoors bodies sometimes appear to reconcile, to suppress, to ignore and to deal with tensions associated with this conflict. Valerie, for example, deals with this dilemma by consciously maintaining two dress codes. This could be thought of as a type of cross-dressing (Russo, 1994), making quick costume changes between home economics attire and outdoors attire, but occasionally being caught out and having to 'wear' the taunts and giggles of student surprise if caught wearing the latter in traditional home economics classrooms (see Valerie, Line 24). The expectations of the students are ruptured by the teacher, because her outdoors clothes are "not normal to what I would wear for my home economics clothes" (Valerie, Line 24).

The outdoors performance demands an admission that the pedagogical practices in which such teachers engage are "everything that I've been told not to do [at University]" (John, Line 142). Hence, to perform as an outdoors body in home economics means to acknowledge that such practices run counter to the 'proper' teaching of home economics. In many ways, the outdoors body adopts the protocols of exclusion and invisibility to survive in the field. This is a freakish, mutant anatomy in the home economics landscape and thus is a risky body that acts as a parodic performance of normality.

Performing as a Playful Home Economics Body

Playful home economics teachers are recognisable in the data of the 'atypical' home economics teachers. This whole idea of having fun in the classroom offers the potential for subversion through irony and parody. Playful home economics bodies provide temporal moments where fun is possible, even central in pedagogy. This is at odds with the rationality of the 'proper' home economics teacher, who is produced in folkloric terms as: "conservative" (Marilyn, Line 96); "domesticated" (Valerie, Line

20); "fussy" (John, Line 20); "middle-aged" (Valerie, Line 4); "from a fairly sheltered background" (John, Line 94); who "wouldn't say 'shit' for a shilling" (John, Line 84) and who does "not relate to a lot of the students" (John, Line 98). In fact, Marilyn argues that typical home economics teachers lack any sense of fun, stifling students creativity and sense of adventure by relying on formulas and instructions for everything. In her words, "you can't have an original thought [there is] no room for students creativity [and this is] very sad" (Marilyn, Line 102). Indeed, she insists that typical home economics teachers are so lacking in fun that they "put students off … they kill it" (Marilyn, Line 98).

It is a very seductive idea that one can be the only bright light in a dull pedagogical place. This means framing the pedagogical place as "so boring, dreadful, so irrelevant and the learning so meaningless that only some superhero heroic deed can save the day" (Weber & Mitchell, 1995, p. 82). The playful teacher becomes the hero, releasing students from the mundane predictability of the recipes, formula and patterns of 'proper' home economics classrooms. Marilyn certainly performs in this role, as superhero to students to enable their escape from the boredom of 'proper' classes. As she says, "as soon as I hit the door, it's like *ta-da I'm here, I'm here to entertain you*" (Marilyn, Line 34). She claims that she uses whatever it takes to make her classes fun for students, including "lollies, bribery and corruption through to cajoling" (Marilyn, Line 34). Her students recognise this embodied performance, noting her as having "humour, happiness and energy" (Student, aged 16).

The playful home economics teacher self-acknowledges as willing to "step out of line … to be a little bit radical … to be crass, outspoken and ribald … to smoke, drink and have boyfriends" (Marilyn, Line 22). Each moment in which students *and* teacher make fun of the orthodox traditions of home economics can work as a form of protest countering and exaggerating the traditions of home economics culture.

In one instance, the playful teacher is worthy of a stanza in the graduating students' song (John), because he dispensed with the conventional teaching practices that dominate the prescribed pedagogy of home economics. Johns propensity to "sing and dance and cook, which all home economics teachers should do" (Student, aged 16), and "joke around in class which makes it fun" (Student, aged 15) was seen to be a transgressive and pleasurable performance.

Elle gets excited with and by her students in her playful pedagogical performances — for a teacher. She admits that she "ham[s] it up a bit because I know they [students] enjoy it so much" and "it gives them real pleasure" (Elle, Line 187). The imagery Elle creates through the video production 'W.I.F.E.' parodies home economics from the comfort zone created by this 'playful' identity. Such playful teachers often win admiration from the students, but they also condemn their teaching counterparts to a less attractive identity as 'orthodox' or boring.

Performing as a Touching Home Economics Body

The touching home economics teacher is clearly recognisable in the data of the 'atypical' home economics teachers. To take pleasure in touch is problematic, risky and grotesque. Such teachers engage in tasting, looking at and smelling food to gain excitement and pleasure (Elle and John), as well as actively, knowingly and freely touching students (Elle) as part of this embodied performance. The touchy, sensory body refuses to reject feelings of passion, love and pleasure, instead performing desire, excitement and passion in their pedagogical performance. The pleasured teaching body in turn encourages students to touch, taste, look and use other sensory means to display excitement. As Elle explains "it gives them [students] real pleasure" (Line 185), and "they get real excited" (Line 183). The relationship is a mutual circulation of desire between teacher and students, such that Elle "can tell the more excited I am the better they've done" (Line 189).

Mellor and Shilling (1997, p. 5–6) suggest that humans "acquire information *through* their bodies" and that "seeing, hearing, touching, smelling and tasting are activities which, quite literally, 'make sense' of the world in a *variety* of ways", yet, "to smell, to taste or to touch someone or something ... run[s] the risk of spoiling the integrity of one's identity" (p. 44). Hence the sensory body of the home economics teacher runs the risk of spoiling pedagogical integrity. Despite the fact that indulging appetites is improper, Mellor and Shilling argue that "modernity's promotion of cognitive apprehension cannot eliminate the passions and sensations of bodies, however much it has tried to manage or repress them" (p. 156). So the grotesque body of home economics teachers *should* resist the desire for sensual experiences, but instead refuses this constraint and is characterised instead by openness and flexible boundaries.

In this way, the embodied performance of sensory, touchy, pleasured home economics bodies is voyeuristic and carnivalesque since it is outside of the norm of classroom emotions and sensory experiences — for both students and teachers. The surprise, excitement and pleasure of touch is risky business. This perverse, excessive and grotesque performance of eroticism (and its suggestion of immorality) parodies the traditions of the teaching act, and is risky business in a world where erotics and touch are dangerous teaching strategies. Elle rejects this barrier, declaring with pride that "I touch students all the time" (Line 142). And yet, she is aware that "it's probably not the right thing to do" (Elle, Line 142) and "could be misconstrued" (Elle, Line 149). This is a freakish, risky performance which opens spaces for transformation and radical change in the pedagogical relationship, where pleasure is reintroduced into the pedagogical relationship.

It is somewhat ironic that home economics as a field of study concerned with the body — food, clothing, human relationships, housing — demands that 'normal' and 'proper' teachers resist physical contact with their students. It is difficult to imagine how home economics teachers and students can possibly avoid all contact when teachers are, for instance, fitting clothing to students as part of their teaching and learning. The games of truth and error that govern contemporary pedagogical practice have created such panic at the merest physical contact between students and their teachers that it is becoming increasingly unrealistic for home economics teachers to perform their roles without a constant sense of fear, dread and apprehension, should they accidentally 'touch' a student. Home economics teachers are in a vulnerable position should a student decide to threaten them with claims of inappropriate physical contact.

This sense of trepidation is not shared by Jane Gallop. An accusation of sexual harassment was made against feminist professor Jane Gallop, after she engaged in 'touchy' experiences with her students. Gallop argued that by kissing one of her graduate students in a public bar where they could be seen, she was engaged in:

> ... making a spectacle of myself. And, at the same time, I was being a teacher. The performance turned me on and was meant to turn my audience on, literally and figuratively. The spectacle was meant to shock and entertain, and to make people think. (Gallop, 1997, p. 100–101)

Whilst traditional home economics teachers and academic teachers avoid such performances (and with very good reason), parallels can be drawn between Gallop and Elle. Elle admits to working through passion and pleasure to "get a reaction" (Line 89) so that students "get more interested in what we are doing" (Line

95). Both are using pleasure to enhance their teaching, and their student's enjoyment of learning. Both also highlight the need for spectacle — but neither advocate that such practices become the norm. If there were too many 'spectacles', this would disallow their existence and uniqueness such that their difference would be reduced to mere common practice. The parody and freakishness would be lost. Therefore Gallop and Elle need to insist on their difference — their marginality — to claim their uniqueness as a spectacle. In this way, both Elle and Gallop's performances are self-serving. They retain their place in the margins of the margins, which can be an attractive and 'cool' place to be, just like the house verandah. Such performances fly in the face of collegiality as a broad idea since there is a need to challenge traditional professionalism in order to retain their uniqueness. Elle and Gallop insist on militating against the norm in taking pleasure in their classrooms.

The Embodied Grotesque Home Economics Teacher

From the assemblage of parody and fun evident in the performances of atypical home economics teachers bodies, it could be argued the carnival is alive and well in the home economics landscape. The grotesque, the excessive, the risky, the freakish — these are already part of home economics teaching.

The soul of 'assemblage' of the carnivalesque body of home economics illustrated above is a grotesque spectacle that has some parallels with Russo's spectacle of a freak in a freak show. Russo (1994, p. 80) suggests that "the freak is doubly marked as object and other within the world of spectacle". Similarly, home economics teachers are doubly marked as object and other within the world of teachers, who are themselves freaks. This double production emerges out of heterosexual normativity associated with the sight and the site of home economics. As a collective made up of females, and a few males playing out hyper-masculinized roles, home economics is particularly vulnerable to individual spectacles working as they are within the bounds of normative femininity. As Russo (1994, p. 53) notes, "any woman, could make a spectacle out of herself if she was not careful", as:

> [F]or a woman, making a spectacle out of herself had more to do with a kind of inadvertency and loss of boundaries: the possessors of large, aging and dimpled thighs displayed at the public beach, of overly rouged cheeks, of a shrill voice of laughter, or of a sliding bra strap — a loose dingy bra strap especially — were at once caught out by fate and blameworthy.

The home economics teacher as the site and sight of heterosexual normativity is constrained by these norms as few other women are. This is part of the production of a heterosexually normative culture, which assumes a natural shape and conspires to marginalise within patriarchal understandings (Butler, 1993). Importantly, as has been argued throughout this project, home economics teachers are complicit in their own heteronormative suffering. Moreover, this complicity is not challenged or undermined by carnivalesque bodies. Their failure to trouble the orthodoxies of heterosexuality parallels carnivals' failure to trouble the power of the church.

Could the embodied performances of the grotesque home economics bodies be in any way subversive? Is the 'fun' and 'pleasure' in which these grotesque bodies are engaged dangerous? One way of considering this question is to apply a concept proffered by Foucault (1985). In his book, *The Use of Pleasure — The History of Sexuality Volume 2,* Foucault has devised a way to explain his views of ethical individuals in ancient Greece. He refers to individuals as being 'moderate' and 'immoderate'. As previously explained in this book, according to Foucault (1985, p. 64–65), the ethical individual is 'moderate', balancing between excess and deprivation, whilst the 'immoderate' individual takes pleasure in bad conduct. Further, the 'continent' individual, is a category within that of the 'immoderate' individual. The 'continent' individual experiences pleasures but contains these. The greater the temptation, the higher the merit of 'continence'. However, the 'incontinent' individual deliberately chooses bad principles. From Foucault's perspective, continent people are thought to have more virtue than moderate people as it is harder for them to restrain themselves. In the case of the modern teacher, the desirable ethical position might be regarded as that of the moderate individual. If not this, at least the continent individual — that is, either with the correct balance of reason or with the capacity to reject urgings for pleasure.

The atypical bodies of home economics as carnival are at odds with the proper bodies of professional teachers. They frequently engage in immoderate practices. They are excessive, shameless and incorrigible, *taking pleasure* in 'bad' conduct such as drinking and smoking and engaging in sexual practice (though these behaviours are not in the classroom, but are implied to be part of the lives of these teachers), attired in ways which were not 'normal', using military drilling and other undesirable pedagogical practices, touching students, creating desire and excitement. However, applying Foucault's (1985) categories of ethical individuals in ancient Greece to home economics teachers, such unruly embodied performances, whilst immoderate, may be argued to be continent, that is, the bodies are in a constant struggle to stay within the bounds of continence. For example, the fat body explained that appetite was a constant struggle, that the body was not right, and it was used to exemplify poor practice. The outdoors body quickly reverted to the dress of the home economics teacher so as to counter the surprise of the students. The touchy body knew what parts of the student body it was acceptable to touch, and was shocked by the reciprocal touch of students. These freakish bodies demonstrated their knowledge of the benchmark for home economics pedagogy and these are all examples of continence, of tidying within the norms of the production of the home economics teacher, and of self-regulation to produce a teacher's body that is acceptable, though being incapable of being moderate. These are *immoderate yet continent* bodies. In terms of pedagogical performance, these teachers understand where the boundaries lie. They know which rules they can 'safely' break and engage in the 'right' transgressions which do not risk their positioning as a home economics teacher beyond 'surprising' their students. They do not step outside of uncertain matters. Such attempts at continence are, according to Foucault (1985), considered to be virtuous because these individuals are in a constant fight to maintain the bounds of the ethical individual as they are constantly experiencing pleasures that are beyond reasonableness, but they deny these desires and pleasures to remain within the bounds of the ethical individual.

At the same time, they work against tidiness and any nostalgic yearning for the 'docile' home economics body that emerges in the versions of typical home economics bodies produced in this Project. These are the *skilled* home economics body and the *suffering* home economics body — *moderate,* ethical individuals who fit within orthodox prescriptions. The atypical bodies do not conform to the expectations that home economics teachers must *suffer* and must be *moderate,* defying prescriptions of normality. These bodies show that home economics pedagogy has its own space for carnival, for fun, parody and perversion, and above all, pleasure — but those who claim both pleasure and professional status know the boundaries of performance.

Where to From Here?

It is appropriate to reflect upon the value of undertaking thinking such as that presented in this book. According to Cranny-Francis

(1995, p. 113), the importance of a body subject opting for parody and refusal is that:

> ... instead of maintaining old distinctions and their regulatory defini-
> tions, it [the embodied subject] tactically occupies a range of different
> positionings that enable it to subvert those remainders and reminders —
> both institutional and individual — of traditional, inequitable discourses
> and social practices.

This re-working of the atypical teachers has revealed that certain embodied subjects do indeed occupy different positionings to traditional positionings that have come to be expected and assumed of home economics teachers. Nevertheless, the parody-ing in which these atypical and immoderate teachers in this proj-ect have engaged is risky business. The risk is minimised but not expunged in their performances in attempts at continence. This book merely offers a glimpse of the embodied perverse pleas-ures, even naughtiness, some *continent* home economics teachers engage in to escape the *suffering* and *moderation* that has come to be regarded as 'normal' for home economics. Should there be a message in this postmodernist thinking, it is that home econom-ics teachers engaged in a refusal to become 'normal' are having fun and taking pleasure from their teaching, thereby revealing a space for the counter-orthodox to be named and acted. These home economics teachers may not be 'radical', but nor are they 'normal', 'traditional', nor 'moderate'. Their failure to suffer seems to be read by students as a pedagogical plus.

What might this mean for the culture of home economics teaching as a whole? This analysis does not aim to offer an alter-native approach or particular progress (as is the goal of modernist work) for the field. Rather, as captured in the words of Russo:

> [T]he impetus of this project, if not its destination, lies in the direction
> of a reconfigured body politic which recognizes similarity and coinci-
> dence, not as a basis of a new universalism, but as an uncanny connection
> characteristic of discourses of the grotesque. (Russo, 1994, p. 14)

Further Thinking

This chapter purposely shifts from identity politics through a blurring of a neat story about atypical home economics teachers who can be described as skilled but not suffering. It insists on multiple bodies that are constantly shifting and incomplete, through the application of the metaphor of the grotesque body of the carnivalesque. I create five assemblages to serve this purpose. Describe your understanding of the notion of assemblage, and explain how this approach to re-thinking about home economics teachers can be useful.

In home economics fat, groovy, outdoors, playful and touching bodies are seen as freakish bodies. Explain why these bodies provoke surprise and horror for home economics as a field of study. Is there substance in this argument?

What does this postmodernist reading of atypical home economics teachers mean for the culture of home economics teaching as a whole?

A Shift From the Familiar to the Unfamiliar — Re-Thinking Home Economics

As explained at the outset, the thinking underpinning this book intentionally makes a departure from traditional and orthodox ways of thinking about home economics, shifting from the *familiar to the unfamiliar*. The ways in which this departure is realized is with respect to three main areas. These are:

- a challenge to the ardent acceptance and use of mainstream research and associated epistemologies as appropriate methodology. This challenge has been mounted because, for home economics research, limiting thinking which emerges from modernist approaches ensures certain outcomes and certain ways of thinking about the field which guarantees that it is *inevitably* stifled by master narratives. Home economics research which is restricted to *only* modernist techniques and thinking will always lead to an interpretation of the field as marginalised and disempowered. Thus, this work insists on utilizing postmodernist ways of re-looking and re-thinking about the field;

- the analysis of teachers in terms of a shift from the mind/body duality which comes with typical modernist research, to that of the body, where the pedagogical performance is not ignored. In so doing, the home economics teacher escapes the disembodied analyses that are constructed out of modernist ways of looking, which focus on the 'mind', rediscovering themselves as embodied pedagogical performers. Hence, the home economics teachers are attributed not just with a teaching mind, but also a teaching body that is engaged in a teacher-student relationship. The notion of performativity is central to this shift; and

↶• an understanding of teacher professionalism that emerges out of this research which refuses the binaries of professional/unprofessional and typical/atypical. Such binaries are products of orthodox thinking, providing neat ways of labeling individuals and attaching to them certain expectations and assumptions. These binaries are inadequate to represent all home economics teachers. The category 'atypical' has been shown to be insufficient to describe the conditions in which home economics teachers perform their work. Hence, the binary typical/atypical is dissolved. Similarly, the binary of professional/unprofessional has been revealed as an inadequate means of categorizing home economics teachers. Any future research should be cautioned by this project not to accept these categories. Instead, 'other' categories which focus on pedagogical performance rather than teacher perception allows new categories to emerge.

The re-thinking about home economics presented in this book may lead to a recognition by individual home economics teachers, and the profession as a collective, of the possibilities for new ways of making inquiries into the field. Informing professional organizations for home economics teachers and challenging mainstream advocacy practices (challenging heterosexual normativity of home economics practice) is one means of re-thinking the thinking that has dominated the decisions and direction of the field.

The final chapter of this book takes the reader through the shift from *the familiar to the unfamiliar*, attending to the three shifts (listed above), which have been fundamental to the work of this book.

The Familiar Tale of Home Economics

The familiar tale of home economics has been told in some of the pages of this book. I have documented the literature that contributes towards the cultural production of home economics teachers and home economics as a field of study, juxtaposing the work of Marjorie Brown (1993) as a prominent international theorist in home economics with the eight themes I identified in the literature which are particularly relevant for home economics in Queensland and Australia.

Brown (1993) identified what she described as the dissatisfactions and misunderstandings of the profession of home economics.

She suggested that these concerns are felt world wide as grievances among home economists. When I juxtaposed these
grievances with themes I identified as central to the field of home
economics, what emerged was a familiar story about home economics. This story has familiar scenes such as: the splintering
of specializations and of knowledge in the profession; research
as a small and piecemeal body of work; a reliance on off-shore
developments which are adopted without question; the loss
of common professional purpose; anti-intellectualism; a reluctance on the part of many professionals to be self-reflective about
their own concepts and beliefs and what is to be learned; a lack
of respect in the academic world and in public opinion; continuous struggles in attempts to gaining legitimacy; the apolitical orientation of members of the profession; social justice agendas for
home economics; and the difficult relationship between feminism
and home economics. Taken together, these themes tell the story
of a field of study and its practice that appears to be constantly
struggling for, and grieving the failure of attempts to establish
a legitimate identity.

Such familiar tales can be comforting for those in the field.
They encourage compliance. There can be a strong sense of cama-
raderie that comes from constantly fighting battles together, even
if those are *inevitably* losing battles. Home economists: *know* the
field of study is marginalised; *know* the field is devalued; *know*
this positioning is the result of the history and origins of the field;
know that it is recognized as 'women's work'; *know* that home
economics will always struggle for legitimation in a world of narratives which favor certain structures. Home economics teachers
know they will be called upon to cater for school functions; *know*
they will be seen as the 'cookers and sewers'; and *know* that they
will continually struggle for it to be otherwise. This is the familiar tale of home economics.

In Study One and Study Two that form some of the work
of this book, an examination was conducted of the cultural production of home economics teachers within this familiar landscape. The orthodox tools of surveys followed by orthodox readings of the data using orthodox statistical analysis provided a predictable reading. That is, that the familiar exists, at least in the
perception of many home economics teachers. The studies parallel others that reveal that typical home economics teachers can be
produced as *skilled* and *suffering*. These individuals work together to produce the normalized home economics teacher. To be normal, 'proper' home economics teachers is to possess what I have
termed the 'ideal body' (professional, organized ...) and the 'real

body' (stooped shoulders, exhausted ...). The 'ideal' home economics teacher is a gendered and disciplined body — a member
of a profession who is also organized, hardworking, caring, multi-
skilled, resourceful and creative. She is assumed to be a positive
role model, with the 'right' weight, willing to perform as the
redemptive savior, to produce quality products, and so on.
The 'real' is the ruined body — with dishpan hands, who is: cleaner; cook; and martyr. She has black rings under her eyes, is starving, stressed, and in poor health, exhausted and wrecked from
home economics work. These two bodies of home economics are
in some senses both symbolic and irreconcilable, as dualisms
always are. The real, ruined body of the home economics teacher
is the physical effect of 'normalizing' — the *sight* of the 'good'
home economics teacher at work.

These real and ideal bodies are the disciplined bodies of home
economics that are produced (and reproduced) out of the textual
data from Study One and Study Two. The ideal I have described
as a *skilled* body and the real as the *suffering* body. The social
production of the two bodies of home economics derives from
and adds to myths and folkloric value, and this is part of the normalizing tradition of home economics teaching, where seemingly irreconcilable parts remain in tension in the enactment
of pedagogical events.

It is not surprising that these studies, utilizing familiar, orthodox and rigorous frameworks would produce such a predictable
outcome. Thinking about home economics teaching is overwhelmingly dualistic, as I indicated earlier in this book, and this
condition is seen as 'normal'. It would have been easy to simply
conclude my thinking having conducted these studies, and
endorsing this picture. I would have reaffirmed familiar stories
and covered familiar terrain as the modernist studies and ways
of understanding about home economics that have preceded me.
However, this dualistic thinking (real/ideal, suffering/skilled, typ-
ical/atypical) is a limited way of understanding the nature
of home economics teachers. It is precisely this reductionist way
of thinking about home economics that stimulated me to push
further in the task of writing this book. For me, this 'known'
position of 'truth' became a starting point for engaging in new
ways of thinking about home economics teaching (Davis, 1997).

Beyond the Familiar Tale of Home Economics

Brown (1993) has urged researchers to recognize the need for a *re-thinking of the thinking* that has been done about home economics, arguing there is a need to disrupt these familiar tales about home economics. I have taken this challenge seriously, with all the theoretical and epistemological difficulties this entails.

In this book, this was undertaken by a shift to unorthodox tools that seek to dismantle the familiar. That is, a shift to posthumanist body theory. My argument is that thinking reliant upon orthodox frameworks is complicit in the relegation of home economics and home economists to the margins in the pedagogical culture of schools. In modernist research projects, no matter how much they might advocate otherwise, home economics continues to be located in the margins. Thus, its positioning "continually defeats us, pulling us back to [what] ... we wish to imagine beyond" (Davies, 1989, p. 12). The research methods and epistemology selected for this project are fundamental to this new imagining, allowing me as a researcher and home economist to 'stop thinking straight'. This is possible because postmodernist projects understand 'truths' differently. Games of truth and error are discursively constructed and performed through bodily and textual enactments. Postmodernist projects also reject 'binary dualities' which typify modernist work (Weiner, 1993), such as the studies in the early parts of this book. Here, some of the binaries such as professional/unprofessional and typical/atypical emerged. Hence, the first challenge is to look beyond the dominant assumptions in the field, and in so doing, to exploit rather than cover or conceal discrepancies or discontinuities in cultural practices. My argument is that there is more to be gained by seeking out the aberrant narratives and points of departure than by reaffirming familiar narratives.

Necessarily then, this work is 'post' in theoretical and methodological approach, inviting the reader to 'imagine beyond' modernity and thus beyond the two categories of binary pairs, and the theories which are central to such logic. As a poststructuralist, posthumanist and perhaps even postfeminist project, the inquiry departs from the epistemological assumptions that underpin structuralist research. The poststructuralist proposition at work here is that no culture is *condemned* to marginality; the field is open to contestation and change. One aspect of this conceptualization underpinning this project is a refusal to conform to the mind/body duality upon which modernist work is dependent. Instead, I privileged the body as a site/sight of pedagogical practice.

In this embodied analysis, home economics teachers and teaching can be seen as textual/material subjects in pedagogical work, continually shaped by and shaping the site of their pedagogy.

The Unfamiliar Tale of Home Economics

The task I set for this book then was to *reconfigure how to think* about home economics as a field of study and home economics teaching as a cultural practice. To achieve this, I explored how the culture of home economics is *contested from within,* by looking to four 'atypical' home economics teachers, arguing that their embodied pedagogical performances constitute the site/sight of pedagogical practice. In taking this approach, my argument is that the culture of home economics is constantly being challenged from within by home economics teachers performing as body subjects, always engaged in a labor of reinscription of themselves and others, and thus home economics pedagogy is never stable but is constantly being produced through such labor. To assert this is to challenge rational accounts of the inevitable marginalization of the field.

The four atypical home economics teachers and their practices were interrogated through interviews and the collection of materials such as photographs, journals and videos provided by the teachers themselves, that are relevant to their embodied classroom practice. My reading of these practices in terms of their radical possibilities was undertaken by documenting and describing their pedagogical performances then considering how the existence of such practices unsettles the idea of home economics as a monolithic culture. This was achieved by juxtaposing the 'disciplined body' of home economics teachers (produced out of Study One and Study Two) against the atypical teachers corporeal performances. I attempted to unsettle the mainstream culture of home economics research by blurring the distinctions between 'orthodox' and 'marginal' practices. To do so, I went on to investigate the atypical teachers as grotesque, carnivalesque performers, full of pleasure and even potential subversion, using the interpretive tools created by Bakhtin's (1968) carnival and Russo's (1994) grotesque body.

What the analysis of these pedagogical performances generated was the proposition that while the disciplined bodies of normal and proper (typical) home economics teachers could be produced as *skilled* and *suffering,* the atypical teachers were *skilled*, but did not appear to *suffer.* Rather, the atypical bodies were engaged in the giving and taking of *pleasure* and *fun*, rejecting the constraints on pedagogy imposed by the *suffering* typical of 'proper' home economics teachers. Parallels can be drawn here between this and 'achieving professionalism'. It could be assumed that in the binary professional/unprofessional which was set up in the early stages of this research, the 'professional' home economics teacher (also the typical home economics teacher) would be both *skilled* and *suffering*. If a teacher were not both *skilled* and *suffering*, they would be unprofessional, and atypical. However, on the contrary, there was no indication that these 'atypical' teachers who refused to *suffer* were unprofessional. Indeed, indications suggested otherwise, with students acting as strong advocates for these teachers, not only in terms of their pedagogical performances as teachers, but in terms of the students capacity to achieve meaningful academic outcomes.

In order to inquire into the transformation possibilities such marginal identities might offer to home economics pedagogy, a re-application of Foucault's (1985) categories emerging out of his analysis of the ethical individual in ancient Greek society was utilized. Foucault's analysis of how ancient Greek society recognized the struggles involved in the production of the ethical individual — and the way pleasure is derived — was developed by him after noting the use of terminology in certain texts. This terminology resulted in Foucault establishing categories of individuals who could be distinguished as being 'moderate' or 'immoderate', and for those 'immoderate' individuals, of being either 'continent' or 'incontinent'. The *immoderate* bodies of atypical home economics teachers worked hard to remain *continent*, fighting to maintain the bounds of the ethical individual. For these atypical home economics teachers, their desire is reined in by the norms and rules which govern typical home economics teachers to the extent that they are *moderate* and *suffering*. Regardless of their immoderate ethics, the atypical teachers were perhaps transgressive of typical home economics culture, but were not subversive nor radical.

Re-Thinking Home Economics

Until now, home economics as a lived culture has failed to recognize possibilities for reconstructing its own field beyond the confines of modernity. This research works to present home economics teachers and the profession as a reconfigured cultural practice, as an instance of the 'otherness' of the Other, and a refusal to collapse difference into the familiar. This is a space for re-thinking about home economics other than as a monolithic culture. Hence, this book has 'fleshed out' home economics beyond the usual boundaries of modernist theorizing by 'getting under the skin' to trouble orthodoxy, and in so doing, it has stepped beyond the usual comfort zone of the research epistemologies utilized in the field. As a *re-description* (Rorty, 1989) of the field, it shows how home economics works as a site/sight of culture which is open to contestation and change. This thinking captures moments of transgression that suggest that new possibilities are *already* being performed in the pedagogical practices of home economics teachers. The cultural practices of home economics as inevitably marginalised *are* being contested from within by those who adopt a within/against positioning of themselves (Lather, 1991).

This thinking does not solve the 'problems' of the field, such as those outlined in detail throughout the book. That is not the purpose. Instead, it argues that these 'problems' are symptomatic of understandings of home economics that are not simply a product of a gendered hierarchy of knowledge but are also a product of the very research that seeks to change this state of affairs. It is in this way that my project seeks to raise new issues for the field and for the theorists engaged with it.

There are many questions that emerge out of this postmodernist reading of home economics as a body of knowledge. These questions serve as pointers to remind us of the ongoing need to *re-think the thinking* that has already been done.

Some of the questions that the re-thinking in this book raises for future research about home economics teaching as a profession, relate to the epistemology of future analyses. These include:

- *What is a home economics teacher?* The thinking in this book reveals that it is not a simple matter of looking to binaries such as typical/atypical or professional/ unprofessional as a means of producing home economics teachers. Categories such as age, gender, clothing style and domestic boundaries have all been exploded in this research as inadequate for describing home economics teachers. Traditional conjecture about what a home economics teacher is, has been revealed to be deficient and misleading and has, in the past, led to compliance and *suffering*.

- *What further research work could be done?* The importance of the need for a shift in thinking from conspiracy theories of modernism to postmodernist conceptions of understanding and epistemology and hence of re-membering home economics have been articulated in order to inform future research in the field of study. Home economics researchers should be encouraged to look to their practitioners, and particularly to those 'atypical' practitioners as the *sight/site* of home economics, to re-think the thinking in the field.

‿• *How does this research inform the work of professional associations?* It encourages a challenge to mainstream advocacy practices that have dominated the approach taken thus far. Home economics professional bodies and the tertiary and secondary contexts which are the *site* of home economics education, can benefit from utilizing postmodernist approaches and challenging heterosexual normativity of home economics practice for transformative possibilities, rather than being stifled by their current goals of 'seeking legitimation' within grand narratives which drive current agendas.

Another interesting aspect to consider is the impact of the *skilled* and *suffering* construction of stereotypical home economics teachers on the status – real and perceived, of home economics teachers.

In a keynote address I presented at a national home economics conference, I explored questions about status issues of home economics teachers, and the teaching profession more generally (Pendergast, 2001). It is interesting to note that there are currently 57 million teachers in the world's formal education systems, compared to 16 million thirty years ago and in a majority of countries, school teachers are the largest single category of public sector employees (UNESCO, 1998). Yet, a series of reports on teacher supply and demand predict that the worst Australian teacher shortage crisis is looming (Preston, 1998; SEETR, 1998; Pendergast, Reynolds & Crane, 2000; Ramsey, 2000; AEU, 2001). This is not a local phenomenon, but is being repeated around the world, with for example the United Kingdom presently in the grip of a severe teacher shortage. Many Australian teachers are being enticed to other parts of the world including the United Kingdom to fill these gaps, adding to the shortage problems in Australia. Some of the major factors in the projected shortfalls of the general supply of teachers include:

‿• Insufficient supply of graduates;

‿• Aging of the teaching workforce;

‿• Projected increases in school student enrolments;

﹀· Loss of 'pools' of reserves of teachers seeking re-entry, some
due to changing professions (Preston, 1998).

There is an expectation that teachers are and will be transformers
of society as they prepare young people to deal with an ever-
changing world, yet, while this role has never been greater, the
status and respect once enjoyed by teachers has declined over the
past 30 years internationally (Maclean, 1999). In the report
A Class Act (1998), the two biggest problems facing the teaching
profession were identified as the expected shortage of teachers
coupled with the low status of the teaching profession, in the
words of the report "there is a widespread crisis of morale" and
"the status of the profession is disturbingly low" (p. 1). It is confirmed across all teaching disciplines that one of the most profound reasons for the factors identified by Preston (1998) leading
to a shortfall of teachers is the shift away from teaching as a desirable job with status, creating the challenge today and in the future
for teachers to be acknowledged as professionals (Hargreaves,
1999; Ramsey, 2000).

The status problem is an imbalance between what the community perceive teaching to be, and what it in fact is. That is,
teaching is seen publicly as not particularly complex or challenging. For example, *A Class Act* (1998) noted the stereotypical
view of teachers as working short hours, having long holidays,
and generally enjoying an easy life, yet, in reality "teaching
is becoming more demonstrably complex than it has ever been"
(Education Queensland 2000, p. 1). The *Queensland State Education
2010: New Basics* (Education Queensland, 2000) report identifies
the educational context, that is the *'new times'* that students must
be prepared for as being characterized by: new student identities;
new economies; new workplaces; new technology; diverse communities; and complex cultures. These new times, new students
and new technologies add to the complexity of teaching-learning
relationships – relationships of teachers to students and to new
forms of knowledge and forms of production and consumption
in society. This increasing complexity has had the effect that
"[M]any teachers are fatigued by waves of reform" (Education
Queensland 2000, p. 5), with teachers working in a constant
climate of change fatigue. This has taken a severe toll on the
appeal of teaching as a potential or continuing career, and has
contributed to the loss of job status and professionalism (Ramsey,
2000). It is no longer perceived to be 'fun', 'attractive' or 'pleasurable' to be a teacher, but rather a stressful role that can lead
to fatigue of the mind and body. All this while the community

maintains the stereotypical view that it is a, 'soft', non-professional job option.

Recent announcements of additional places in universities for teacher preparation have become common election promises, but the provision of places does not ensure that these quotas will be filled. Firstly, work needs to be done to address professionalism and status issues and this is being attended to by initiatives such as the *Review of Teacher Education in New South Wales* (Ramsey, 2000), which urges the New South Wales government to focus on professionalizing teaching. A national discussion paper *Standards of Professional Practice for Accomplished Teaching in Australian Classrooms* (2000) developed collaboratively by Australian College of Education, the Australian Curriculum Studies Association and the Australian Association for Research in Education, affords the opportunity for input into the development of professional standards in the teaching profession. Nevertheless, an aspect that is not addressed in these initiatives is that of the teacher engaged in embodied pedagogical practice, indeed most studies of this type ignore the material bodies of teacher and student unless in the frame of 'behaviors' (McWilliam, 1997).

This book demonstrates a refusal to ignore the embodied nature of teachers work, challenging assumptions about home economics teachers and embodied pedagogy. By extension, it makes a challenge to research about teachers generally, which has typically ignored the material body of teachers and led to stereotypes that have negatively impacted on the teaching profession.

In the concluding sentences in my masters thesis submitted in 1991, I argued that home economics was "a site ready for contestation and challenge". I was convinced that "home economics holds the key to its own escape from [the] bondage of modernist thought" (Pendergast, 1991, p. 276). What the thinking underpinning this book does is make an attempt to try out a key for size, to re-think home economics as not simply trapped by modernist epistemologies and frameworks of understanding. In doing so, it reveals that some home economists are challenging the taken-for-granted assumptions about home economics through their aberrant performances of pedagogy. They are rejecting their marginalised status and they refuse to suffer, instead engaging in embodied pedagogical practices that gives pleasure to both themselves and their students.

Based on this thinking, home economists need only look within their field for signs of transformation, especially in escaping the traumas of *suffering* which typify the 'proper', 'typical' and 'normal' home economics teacher. Home economics as a field of study and home economists as practitioners, need not be *inevitably* marginalised, unless there is no recognition of new possibilities which might seem to be outside of traditional ways of conceptualizing thinking. This is about how such thinking can be done within the field as a site/sight of cultural practice, including research practice. As a result of such work, home economics teachers and students and home economics professional bodies, who are complicit in the positioning of home economics as devalued and marginalised, may well be encouraged to re-think their thinking, looking again to the culture and the transformative opportunities which contest the *inevitably* marginalised status which has dominated the field to date.

The thinking I am proposing in this book rejects the boundedness of traditional truth claims and modernist dualisms, and instead alludes to the possibility for enacting a politics of difference. It does not attempt to 'overthrow' orthodoxies, including the heterosexual normativity of mainstream home economics pedagogy, just as four atypical teachers will not 'overturn' it. This thinking neither expects to nor has it embarked on this as a mission. The effects, however, can be unsettling.

Further Thinking

What is a home economics teacher?

What further research work could be done?

How does this research inform the work of home economics professional associations?

What possibilities for a radical reconfiguring of the culture of home economics teaching does the re-thinking in this book have?

References & Further Reading

References
and Further Reading

Agassi, J. (1992). Deconstructing post-modernism: Gellner and Crocodile Dundee. In J. Hall & I. Jarvie (Eds.) *Transition to Modernity* (pp. 213–230). Cambridge: Cambridge University Press.

Althusser, L. (1971). Ideology and ideological state apparatuses. In *Lenin and Philosophy and Other Essays*. New York: Monthly Review Press.

American Home Economics Association. (1993). *The Scottsdale Meeting: Positioning the Profession for the 21st Century*. Arizona: American Home Economics Association.

Angel, M. (1994). Pedagogies of the obscene: The specular body and demonstration. In J.J. Matthews (Ed.) *The Teachers' Breasts: Proceedings of the Jane Gallop Seminar and Public Lecture*. Canberra: The Humanities Research Centre.

Apelt, L. (1989). Contemporary home economics — the important issues. *Queensland Association of Home Economics Teachers Newsletter, 8*(4), 4–5.

Appignanesi, R. & Garratt, C. (1995). *Postmodernism for Beginners*. Cambridge: Icon Books.

Attar, D. (1990). *Wasting Girls Time: The History and Politics of Home Economics*. London: Virago Press.

Australian Bureau of Statistics. (1993). *An Introduction to Sample Surveys*. Melbourne: Australian Bureau of Statistics.

Australian College of Education; Australian Curriculum Studies Association; Australian Association for Research (2000). *Standards of Professional Practice for Accomplished Teaching in Australian Classrooms: A national discussion paper*

Australian Education Union. (2001). *Teacher Supply and Demand in the States and Territories*. www.aeufederal.org.au/Publications/-TeacherSupplyDemand.pdf

Bacchi, C. (1998). *Policy as discourse: What does it mean? Where does it get us?* Paper presented at the Postmodernism in Practice Conference, Adelaide, University of Adelaide, February 25 – March 1.

Badir, D. (1990). The feminist home economist: Do we have a choice? *Journal of the Home Economics Association of Australia, 22*(4), 98–104.

Bailey, M. (1993). Foucauldian feminism: Contesting bodies, sexuality and identity. In C. Ramazanoglu (Ed.) *Up Against Foucault* (pp. 99–122). London: Routledge.

Bakhtin, M. (1968). *Rabelais and His World*. Translation by Helene Iswolsky. Cambridge: MIT Press.

Baldwin, E. (1989). *Toward autonomy in the 90's: Problems and possibilities for practice in home economics*. Paper presented at the 9th Triennial Conference of the Home Economics Association of Australia, Launceston, January.

Baldwin, E. (1990). Family empowerment as a focus for home economics education. *Journal of Vocational Home Economics Education, 8*(2), 1–12.

Baldwin, E. (1991). The home economics movement: A "new" integrative paradigm. *Journal of Home Economics*, Winter, 42–48.

Baldwin, E. (1995). Shaping the future: Home economics education and public policy formation. In *Shaping the Future — Home Economics in Public Policy, Conference Proceedings* (pp. 7–15). Perth: Home Economics Institute of Australia.

Banes, K. (1992). Preparing home economics leaders. *Journal of Home Economics, 84*(1), 38–43.

Barrett, M. (1991). *The Politics of Truth: From Marx to Foucault.* Cambridge: Polity Press.

Barthes, R. (1978). *A Lover's Discourse: Fragments.* (Transcription Richard Hurley). New York: Hill & Wang.

Becher, T. (1990). The counter-culture of specialisation. *European Journal of Education, 25*(3), 333–346.

Bell, J. (1993). *Doing Your Research Project.* Milton Keynes: Open University Press.

Bennison, A., Jungek, S., Kantor, K. & Marshall, D. (1989). Teachers' voices in curriculum inquiry: A conversation among teacher educators. *Journal of Curriculum and Teaching, 9*(1), 71–105.

Bielski, J. (1987). Pushing rocks uphill: Gender issues in educational administration. In J. Blackmore & J. Kenway (Eds.) *Gender Issues in the Theory and Practice of Educational Administration and Policy.* Victoria: Deakin University Press.

Board of Senior Secondary School Studies. (1989). *Review of the Senior Home Economics Syllabus: Papers 1–6.* Brisbane: Board of Senior Secondary School Studies.

Board of Senior Secondary School Studies. (1994). *Statistics Bulletin.* Brisbane: Board of Senior Secondary School Studies.

Board of Senior Secondary School Studies. (1997). *Report to the Curriculum Committee Board of Senior Secondary School Studies — Major revision of the Syllabus in Home Economics.* Unpublished internal monograph.

Board of Senior Secondary School Studies. (1998). *Statistics Bulletin.* Brisbane: Board of Senior Secondary School Studies.

Bobbitt, N. (1993). Human ecology — What is it? In *The Scottsdale Meeting: Positioning the Profession for the 21st Century* (pp. B62–73). Arizona: American Home Economics Association.

Bordo, S. (1992). Postmodern subjects, postmodern bodies. *Feminist Studies, 18*(1), 159–175.

Bordo, S. (1993). Feminism, Foucault and the politics of the body. In C. Ramazanoglu (Ed.) *Up Against Foucault.* (pp. 179–202) London: Routledge.

Bradley, H. (1996). *Fractured Identities: Changing Patterns of Inequality.* Cambridge: Polity Press.

Brodribb, S. (1992). *Nothing Mat(t)ers.* Melbourne: Spinifex Press.

Brown, M. (1980). *What is Home Economics Education?* Minneapolis: University of Minneapolis.

Brown, M. (1981). Our intellectual ecology: Recitation of a definition — a case in point. *Journal of Home Economics, 73,* 14–18.

Brown, M. (1984). *Home economics: Proud past — promising future.* Paper presented at the American Home Economics Association Meeting, California, 26 June.

Brown, M. (1988a). *The purpose of home economics: Conceptual and political implications of critical theory.* Paper presented at the Postgraduate Summer School in Home Economics, Melbourne, January – February.

Brown, M. (1988b). *Appearance and reality in understanding society: Implications for home economics.* Paper presented to the Biennial Conference of the Western Region College and University Professors of Home Economics Education, Oregon State University.

Brown, M. (1993). *Philosophical Studies in Home Economics in the United States: Basic Ideas by Which Home Economists Understand Themselves.* Michigan: Michigan State University.

Brown, M. & Baldwin, E. (1995). *The Concept of Theory in Home Economics — A Philosophical Dialogue.* Michigan: Kappa Omicron Nu Honor Society.

Brunner, D. (1996). Silent bodies: Miming those killing norms of gender. *Journal of Curriculum and Teaching, 12*(1), 9–15.

Bulmer, M. (1984). *Sociological Research Methods, An Introduction.* Second edition. London: Macmillan.

Bunton, R. & Petersen, A. (1997). Foucault's medicine. In A. Petersen & R. Bunton (Eds.) *Foucault, Health and Medicine* (pp. 1–11). London: Routledge.

Burke, C. & Pendergast, D. (1996). Home economics in Queensland, Australia: its currency and future directions. *Journal of Family and Consumer Sciences, 88*(2), 15–25.

Butler, J. (1993). *Bodies That Matter.* New York: Routledge.

Calinescu, M. (1985). Introductory remarks. In M. Calinescu & D. Fokkema (Eds.) *Exploring Postmodernism.* Amsterdam: John Benjamins Publishing Company.

Callahan, K. (1993). A predictive model for the marketing of home economics. *Home Economics Research Journal, 21*(4), 422–439.

Callan, V. & Gallois, C. (1983). Ethnic stereotypes: Australian and Southern European youth. *Journal of Social Psychology, 119*, 288–288.

Carrion, M. (1996). The Queen's too bawdies. L. Fradenburg & C. Freccero (Eds.) *Premodern Sexualities* (pp. 45–69). New York: Routledge.

Carver, M. (1979). *Home Economics as an Academic Discipline.* Unpublished dissertation, Centre for the Study of Higher Education, College of Education, University of Arizona.

Cherryholmes, C. (1988). *Power and Criticism.* New York: Teachers College Press.

Cohen, L. & Manion, L. (1985). *Research Methods in Education,* 2nd edition. London: Groom Helm.

Connor, S. (1989). *Postmodernist Culture: An Introduction to Theories of the Contemporary.* Oxford: Basil Blackwell.

Corrigan, P. (1989). In/forming School. In D. Livingstone et al (Eds.) *Critical Pedagogy and Cultural Power.* London: Macmillan.

Cosic, M. (1999). Millenium women. *The Australian Magazine.* 18–19 December, 19–29.

Cranny-Francis, A. (1995). *The Body in the Text.* Melbourne: Melbourne University Press.

Creekmore, A. (1968). The concept basic to home economics. *Journal of Home Economics, 60*(2), 93–102.

Cunningham, R. (1992). *Curriculum Orientations of Home Economics Teachers.* Paper presented at the American Vocational Association Convention, St Louis.

Curriculum Corporation. (1996). *Home Economics in Secondary Schools.* Melbourne: Curriculum Corporation.

Davies, B. (1989). Education for sexism: A theoretical analysis of the sex/gender bias in education. *Educational Philosophy and Theory, 21*(1), 1–19.

Davis, K. (1997). Embody-ing theory: Beyond modernist and postmodernist readings of the body. In Davis, K. (Ed.) *Embodied Practices* (pp. 1–26). London: Sage Publications.

Den Hartog, D. & Alomes, S. (1991). Introduction: From popular culture to cultural studies — and beyond. In D. Den Hartog. & S. Alomes (Eds.) *Post Pop: Popular Culture, Nationalism and Postmodernism*, (pp. 1–26). Victoria University of Technology: Footprints.

Department of Employment, Education and Training (1990). Home economics: Does it have a future? *The Gen: Newsletter of the Gender Equity Network*, August, 1–3.

Deutscher, P. (1994). Eating the words of the other — ethics, erotics and cannibalism. In J.J. Matthews (Ed.) *The Teachers' Breasts: Proceedings of the Jane Gallop Seminar and Public Lecture*. Canberra: The Humanities Research Centre. (pp. 31–46).

Derkley, K. (1997). Going off the menu. *The Age*, Tuesday 16 September, 3–4.

Doll, W. (1993). *A Post-modern Perspective on Curriculum*. New York: Teachers College Press.

Draper, M. (1989). Women in the home. In D. Ironmonger (Ed.) *Households Work* (pp. 85–96). Sydney: Allen & Unwin.

Dykman, A. (1993). Out of the frying pan … and into the 90s. Home economics in transition as teachers update programs. *Vocational Education Journal*, *68*(3), 24–27.

Eagleton, T. (1990). *The Ideology of the Aesthetic*. Cambridge: Basil Blackwell.

Eckermann, L. (1997) Foucault, embodiment and gendered subjectivities. The case of voluntary self-starvation. In A. Petersen & R. Bunton (Eds.) *Foucault, Health and Medicine* (pp. 151–172). London: Routledge.

Education Queensland. (1999). *Queensland State Education 2010*. http://education.qld.gov.au/corporate/qse2010

Ehrenreich, B. & English, D. (1978). *For Her Own Good*. New York: Doubleday.

Eiby, P. (1989). *Student Perceptions Regarding Outcomes of Home Economics Education*. Unpublished Master in Education thesis, Canberra College of Advanced Education.

Eyre, L. (1989). Gender equity and home economics curriculum. *Illinois Teacher*, *33*(1), 22–25.

Eyre, L. (1991). Curriculum and pedagogy for gender equity. In *Proceedings of a Canadian Symposium: Issues and Direction of Home Economics/Family Studies Education* (pp. 98–108). Ottawa: Canadian Home Economics Association.

Felman, S. (1997). Psychoanalysis and education: Teaching terminable and interminable. In S. Todd (Ed.) *Learning Desire: Perspectives on Pedagogy, Culture, and the Unsaid* (pp. 17–43). New York: Routledge.

Ferguson, H. (1990). *The Science of Pleasure*. London: Routledge.

Finkelstein, J. (1997). Chic outrage and body politics. In. K. Davis (Ed.) *Embodied Practices: Feminist Perspectives on the Body*. (pp. 150–167). London: Sage Publications.

Flax, J. (1990). Postmodernism and gender relations in feminist theory. In L.J. Nicholson (Ed.) *Feminism/Postmodernism* (pp. 39–62). New York: Routledge.

Flax, J. (1990a). *Thinking Fragments: Psychoanalysis, Feminism and Postmodernism in the Contemporary West*. Berkeley: University of California Press.

Foster, S. (1996). *Corporealities: Dancing, Knowledge, Culture and Power*. London: Routledge.

Foucault, M. (1972). *The Archeology of Knowledge*. London: Tavistock.

Foucault, M. (1980). *Power/Knowledge*. London: Harvester.

Foucault, M. (1982). Afterword: The subject and the power. In H. Dreyfus & P. Rabinow (Eds.) *Michel Foucault: Beyond Structuralism and Hermeneutics* (pp. 208–228). Brighton: Harvester Press.

Foucault, M. (1985). *The Use of Pleasure: The History of Sexuality, Volume 2.* London: Harvester.

Fox, N. (1997). Is there life after Foucault? In A. Petersen & R. Bunton (Eds.) *Foucault, Health and Medicine* (pp. 31–50). London: Routledge.

Frank, M. (1992) On Foucault's concept of discourse. In T. Armstrong (trans) *Michel Foucault Philosopher.* (pp. 99–116). New York: Routledge.

Fraser, N. & Nicholson, L. (1990). Social criticism without philosophy: An encounter between feminism and postmodernism. In L. Nicholson (Ed.) *Feminism/ Postmodernism* (pp. 19–38). New York: Routledge.

Fraser, N. (1992). The uses and abuses of French discourse theories for feminist politics. In M. Featherstone (Ed.) *Cultural Theory and Cultural Change* (pp. 51–72). London: Sage Publications.

Gallop, J. (1997). *Feminist Accused of Sexual Harassment.* Durham: Duke University Press.

Gastil, R. (1993). *Progress: Critical Thinking about Historical Change.* Westport: Praeger Publishers.

Gibson, R. (1984). *Structuralism and Education.* London: Hodder and Stoughton Educational.

Gottlieb, E. (1988). The discursive construction of knowledge: The case of radical education discourse. *Qualitative Studies in Education,* 2(2), 131–144.

Grace, D. (1996). *Gummy Worms and Butt Jokes Student Video Production as a Site of Pleasure and Resistance in the Elementary Classroom.* Unpublished Doctor of Education Dissertation, University of Hawaii.

Greene, M. (1994). Epistemology and educational research: The influence of recent approaches to knowledge. In L. Darling-Hammond (Ed.) *Review of Research in Education* (pp. 423–463). United States of America: American Educational Research Association.

Grosz, E. (1994). *Volatile Bodies — Toward a Corporeal Feminism.* Bloomington: Indiana University Press.

Grumet, M. (1988). *Bitter Milk: Women and Teaching.* Amherst: University of Massachusetts.

Grumet, M. (1995). Masks for meaning. In J. Gallop (Ed.) *Pedagogy: The Question of Impersonation* (pp. 36–45). Bloomington: Indiana University Press.

Grundy, S. & Henry, M. (1995). Which way home economics? An examination of the conceptual orientation of home economics curricula. *Journal of Curriculum Studies,* 27(3), 281–297.

Halberstam, J. & Livingston, I. (1995). *Posthuman Bodies.* Bloomington: Indiana University Press.

Hamilton, D. (1994). Traditions, preferences, and postures in applied qualitative research. In N. Denzin & Y. Lincoln (Eds.) *Handbook of Qualitative Research* (pp. 60–69). London: Sage Publications.

Hamilton, D. & McWilliam. E. (in press). Multiple voices that frame research on teaching. In *Handbook of Research and Teaching, Volume 4.*

Haraway, D. (1991). *Simians, Cyborgs, and Women: The Reinvention of Nature.* London: Free Association Books.

Harding, J. (1997). Bodies at risk. Sex, surveillance and hormone replacement therapy. In A. Petersen & R. Bunton (Eds.) *Foucault, Health and Medicine* (pp. 134–150). London: Routledge.

Hargreaves, A. (1999). *Reinventing professionalism: Teacher education and teacher development for a changing world.* International Conference on Teacher Education Conference Proceedings, Hong Kong Institute of Education. CD Rom.

Hatcher, C. (1993). *Gender and Technology in Organisational Contexts.* Unpublished Master of Arts (Hons) thesis, Charles Sturt University.

Henry, M. (1989). *Towards a Critical Theory of Home Economics: The Case for Family Studies.* Unpublished Masters of Curriculum Studies thesis, University of New England.

Henry, M. (1991). *Defining Well Being: The Focus of Home Economics.* Unpublished Doctor of Philosophy thesis proposal, University of New England.

Henry, M. (1995). *Well-being the Focus of Home Economics: An Australian Perspective.* Unpublished Doctor of Philosophy thesis, University of New England.

Henry, M. (1996). Socially critical approaches to home economics: an overview. *Journal of the Home Economics Institute of Australia, 3*(3), 2–7.

Home Economics Institute of Australia. (1997). The Home Economics Institute of Australia. *Journal of the Home Economics Institute of Australia, 4*(1), i.

Home Economics Institute of Australia. (1997). *Home Economics Institute of Australia Council Minutes.* April. Unpublished.

Home Economics Institute of Australia. (1999). The Home Economics Institute of Australia. *Journal of the Home Economics Institute of Australia, 6*(1), i.

Horn, M. (1993). Proposal for the restructuring of home economics. In *The Scottsdale Meeting: Positioning the Profession for the 21st Century — Conference Proceedings,* (pp. B90–99). Arizona: American Home Economics Association.

Horrocks, C. & Jevtic, Z. (1997) *Foucault for Beginners.* Cambridge: Icon.

Inglis, F. (1990). *Media Theory: An Introduction.* Oxford: Basil Blackwell.

Isaac, S. & Michael, W. (1981). *Handbook in Research and Evaluation.* San Diego: Edits Publishers.

Jax, J. (1985). Home economics: A perspective for the future. *Journal of Home Economics, 77–78*(4), 22–27.

Jenks, C. (1996). The postmodern child. In J. Brannen & M. O'Brien (Eds.) *Children in Families: Research and Policy* (pp. 13–25). London: Falmer Press.

Johnson, R. (1997). *Imperialism and cargo cults in early childhood education: Does Reggio Emilia really exist?* Paper presented at the Centre for Applied Studies in Early Childhood, Queensland University of Technology, Brisbane, 16 May.

Johnson-Eilola, J. (1997). *Nostalgic Angels: Rearticulating Hypertext Writing.* New Jersey: Ablex Publishing Company.

Jones, R. (1994). *The O'Malley Trust Project on the Status of Post-Primary Home Economics.* Melbourne: King and Amy O'Malley Trust.

Jones, R. (1995). Questions the O'Malley Report poses for the profession of home economics: The Price of Policies. In *King and Amy O'Malley Fremantle Workshop Proceedings* (pp. 13–20). Fremantle: Home Economics Institute of Australia.

Kamler, B. (1997). Text as body, body as text. *Discourse: Studies in the Cultural Politics of Education, 18*(3), 369–387.

Kane, M. & Snyder, E. (1989). Sporting typing: The social "containment" of women in sport. *Arena Review, 13*(2), 77–96.

Kennedy, B. (1996). Pedagogies of the screen: Cyberfeminist futures in film-noir — The jouissance in the cyborg, or why Romeo is still bleeding. In E. McWilliam & P. Taylor (Eds.) *Pedagogy, Technology and the Body* (pp. 137–148). New York: Peter Lang.

Kenway, J. (1993). The wind beneath girls' wings: Gender justice, social change and home economics. *Queensland Association of Home Economics Teachers Newsletter,* September.

Kidder, L. H. & Judd, C. M. (1986). *Research Methods in Social Relations.* Japan: CBS.

Kirk, D. (1997). *Schooling Bodies: School Practice and Public Discourse 1880–1940.* Manuscript submitted for publication.

Kiziltan, M., Bain, J. & Canizares, A. (1990). Post-modern conditions: Rethinking public education. *Educational Theory, 40*(3), 351–369.

Kress, G. & Hodge, R. (1979). *Language as Ideology.* London: Routledge & Kegan Paul.

Lather, P. (1991a). *Getting Smart: Feminist Research and Pedagogy With/in the Postmodern.* New York: Routledge.

Lather, P. (1991b). *Feminist Research in Education: Within/Against.* Geelong: Deakin University Press.

Lather, P. (1996). *Methodology as subversive repetition: Practices toward a feminist double science.* Paper presented at the American Education Research Association Conference, New York City.

Lather, P. & Smithies, C. (1997). *Troubling the Angels: Women Living With HIV/AIDS.* London: Westview Press.

Lindstrom, L. (1993). *Cargo Cult: Strange Stories of Desire from Melanesia and Beyond.* Washington, DC: Smithsonian Institution Press.

Logan, C. (1981). *A Centenary History of Home Economics Education in Queensland 1881–1981.* Brisbane: Queensland Department of Education.

Lorde, A. (1984). *Sister Outsider.* Trumansburg, New York: Crossing Press.

Lupton, D. (1992) Discourse analysis: A new methodology for understanding the ideologies of health and illness. *Australian Journal of Public Health, 16*(2),145–150.

Lupton, D. (1994) Analysing news covering. In S. Chapman (Ed.) *The Fight for Public Health: Principles and Practice in Media Advocacy.* (pp. 23–57) London: BMJ.

Lupton, D. (1994). *Medicine as Culture: Illness, Disease and the Body in Western Societies.* London: Sage.

Lupton, D. (1996). *Food, the Body and the Self.* London: Sage.

Lyotard, J. (1984). *The Postmodern Condition.* Minneapolis: University of Minnesota Press.

Lyotard, J. (1993). Defining the postmodern. In S. During (Ed.) *The Cultural Studies Reader* (pp. 170–176). London: Routlege.

Maclean, R. (1999). *Developments in teacher education in Asia and the Pacific: Issues and prospects towards the twenty-first century.* International Conference on Teacher Education Conference Proceedings, Hong Kong Institute of Education. CD Rom.

Maidment, B. (1990). *Positioning yourself in the academic community.* Address to the Home Economics Association of Western Australia, Perth, 15–16 June.

Mander, E. (1987). A social-historical perspective on the development of home economics — human development and society. *Journal of the Home Economics Association of Australia, 14*(1).

Marcus, G. & Fischer, R. (1986). *Anthropology as Cultural Critique*. Chicago: University of Chicago Press.

McCullers, J. (1988). A commentary on the quest for a single theoretical framework for home economics. *Home Economics FORUM, 2*(2), 20–21.

McDowell, L. (1995). Body work. Heterosexual body performances in city workplaces. In D. Bell & G. Valentine (Eds.) *Mapping Desire — Geographies of Sexualities* (pp. 75–95). London: Routledge.

McWilliam, E. (1993). 'Post' haste: plodding research and galloping theory. *British Journal of Sociology of Education, 14*(2), 199–205.

McWilliam, E. (1996a). Pedagogies, technologies, bodies. In E. McWilliam & P. Taylor (Eds.) *Pedagogy, Technology and the Body* (pp. 1–22). New York: Peter Lang.

McWilliam, E. (1996b). (S)education: A risky inquiry into pleasurable teaching. *Education and Society, 14*(1), 15–24.

McWilliam, E. (1996c). Seductress or schoolmarm: On the improbability of the great female teacher. *Interchange, 27*(1), 1–11.

McWilliam, E. (1996d). Admitting impediments: Or things to do with bodies in the classroom. *Cambridge Journal of Education, 26*(3), 367–378.

McWilliam, E. (1997). No body to teach (with)?: The technological make over of the university teacher. *Australian Journal of Communication, 24*(1), 1–8.

McWilliam, E. (1997b). Beyond the missionary position: Teacher desire and radical pedagogy. In S. Todd (Ed.) *Learning Desire: Perspectives on Pedagogy, Culture and the Unsaid* (pp. 217–235). New York: Routledge.

McWilliam, E. (in press). *Pedagogical Pleasures*. New York: Peter Lang.

McWilliam, E. & Jones, A. (1996). Eros and pedagogical bodies: The state of (non)affairs. In E. McWilliam & P. Taylor (Eds.) *Pedagogy, Technology and the Body* (pp. 127–136). New York: Peter Lang.

McWilliam, E., Lather, P. & Morgan, W. (1997*). Headwork, Fieldwork, Textwork: A Textshop in New Feminist Research*. Brisbane: Queensland University of Technology.

McWilliam, E. & O'Donnell, S. (1997). Probing protocols: The genital examination as a pedagogical event. Unpublished paper. School of Cultural and Policy Studies: QUT.

McWilliam, E. & Palmer, P. (1995). Teaching tech(no)bodies: An open learning and postgraduate pedagogy. *Australian Universities Review, 2*, 32–34.

McWilliam, E. & Palmer, P. (1996). Pedagogues, tech(no)bods: Re-inventing postgraduate pedagogy. In E. McWilliam & P. Taylor (Eds.) *Pedagogy, Technology and the Body* (pp. 163–170). New York: Peter Lang.

Meighan, R. (1981). *A Sociology of Educating*. London: Holt, Rinehart & Winston.

Mellor, P. & Shilling, C. (1997). *Re-forming the Body*. London: Sage.

Mestrovic, T. (1993). *The Barbarian Temperament*. London: Routledge.

Midgley, M. (1989). *Wisdom, Information and Wonder*. London: Routledge.

Miller, B. (1991). *Dissatisfaction factors of Indiana home economics teachers*. Paper presented at the American Vocational Association Convention, Los Angeles, 6 December.

Moe, C. (1991). Descriptions of home economists from three perspectives. *Home Economics Research Journal, 20*(1), 6–15.

Mishler, E. (1990). Validation in inquiry-guided research: The role of exemplars in narrative studies. *Harvard Educational Review,* *60*(4), 415–442.

Mortvedt, M. (1984). Home economics at risk. *Illinois Teacher, 28*(4), 49–50.

National Council for the International Year of the Family. (1994*).* *The Heart of the Matter: Families at the Centre of Public Policy.* Canberra: Australian Government Publishing Service.

Newell, W. & Green, W. (1982). Defining and teaching interdisciplinary studies. *Improving College and University Teaching, 30*(1), 23–30.

Offen, K. (1988). Defining feminism: A comparative historical approach. *Signs, 14*(1), 119–157.

Osgood, C., Suci, G. & Tannebaum, P. (1957). *The Measurement of Meaning.* Urbana: University of Illinois Press.

Pendergast, D. (1991). *Feminist Poststructural Theory Applied to the Case of Home Economics Education in Queensland,* Unpublished Master of Education thesis, University of New England.

Pendergast, D. (1992). Feminist post-structural theory and home economics. In *Home Economics, Diverse and Enduring: Conference Proceedings* (pp. 47–51). Brisbane: Home Economics Institute of Australia.

Pendergast, D. (1995a). Gender and the home economics classroom: Boys in home economics — Is there a difference?. In *Shaping the Future - Home Economics in Public Policy, Conference Proceedings* (pp. 149–155). Perth: Home Economics Institute of Australia.

Pendergast, D. (1995b). Marginalisation in action: Home economics in Queensland. In L. Rowan & J. McNamee (Eds.) *Voices of a Margin* (pp. 149–159). Rockhampton: Central Queensland University Press.

Pendergast, D. (1996a). Research in home economics: The need for interdisciplinary research in an interdisciplinary subject. *Journal of the Home Economics Institute of Australia, 3*(1), 31–41.

Pendergast, D. (1996b). Home economics, poststructural theory, and the politics of feminism. *Journal of the Home Economics Institute of Australia, 3*(3), 13–16.

Pendergast, D. (1999). *Re-thinking Home Economics: From Modern to Postmodern Accounts of Pedagogical Bodies.* Unpublished Doctoral thesis, Queensland University of Technology.

Pendergast, D. (1999b). Marginal subjects: Towards a site of possibility in the teaching of home economics. In: *The International Conference on Teacher Education Conference Proceedings CD Rom.* Hong Kong: Hong Kong Institute of Education.

Pendergast, D. & McWilliam, E. (1999). Marginal pleasures: Teachers, transgression and transformation. *Australian Association for Research in Education Website.* http://www.swin.edu.au/aare/99p0ap/abs99.htm

Pendergast, D., Reynolds, J. & Crane, J. (2000). Home economics teacher supply and demand to 2003 – projections, implications and issues. *Journal of the Home Economics Institute of Australia, 7*(3), 1–41.

Pendergast, D. (2001). Placid beginnings/Turbulent times: Re-thinking home economics for the 21st century. *Journal of the Home Economics Institute of Australia, 8*(1), 2–13.

Pendergast, D. (in press). *Constructing a professional identity: A view from within.*

Peterat, L. (1990). The promise of feminist research practices. *Canadian Home Economics Journal, 40*(1), 33–36.

Peterat, L. (1993). *Implementing a global home economics education.* Unpublished manuscript, University of British Colombia, Canada.

Peterat, L. & Khamasi, J. (1995). *Disarray in home economics curricula in Canadian provinces in the 90's.* Paper presented at American Education Research Association Annual Meeting, San Francisco, California, April.

Petersen, A. & Lupton, D. (1996). *The New Public Health: Health and the Self in the Age of Risk.* Sydney: Allen & Unwin.

Pillow, W. (1996). *Pissed off in the master's house: An embodied analysis of policy theory and teen pregnancy.* Paper presented at American Education Research Association, New York City, April.

Pixley, J. (1984). Home economists: Forgotten but not gone. In *Fourth Women and Labour Conference Proceedings* (pp. 413–429). Brisbane: Women and Labour.

Popkewitz, T. (1997). Educational sciences and the normalisations of the teacher and the child: Some historical notes on current United States of America pedagogical reforms. In: I. Nilsson & L. Lundahl (Eds.) *Teachers, Curriculum and Policy: Critical Perspectives in Educational Research* (pp. 91–114). United States of America: Umea University.

Popkewitz, T. (1997b). A changing terrain of knowledge and power: A social epistemology of educational research. *Educational Researcher*, 26 (9), 18–29.

Preston, B. (1998) *Teacher Supply and Demand to 2004: Projections, Implications and Issues, 1998 Update Projections.* Canberra: Australian Council of Deans of Education.

Rabinowitz, P. (1995). Soft fiction and intimate documents: Can feminism be posthuman? In J. Halberstam & I. Livingston (Eds.) *Posthuman Bodies* (pp. 97–112). Bloomington: Indiana University Press.

Ramsey, G. (2000). *Quality Matters: Revitalising teaching: Critical times, critical choices. Report to the Review of Teacher Education, New South Wales.* www.det.nsw.edu.au/teachrev/reports/index.htm

Reiger, K. (1990). *Feminism and the future: Past lessons and present possibilities.* Unpublished address to the Queensland Association of Home Economics Teachers, Brisbane.

Richardson, L. (1990). Narrative and sociology. *Journal of Contemporary Ethnography*, 19(1), 116–135.

Rorty, R. (1989). *Irony, Contingency and Solidarity.* New York: Cambridge University Press.

Russo, M. (1994). *The Female Grotesque.* New York: Routledge.

Scott, J. (1990). Deconstructing equality — versus — difference: Or, the uses of poststructural theory for feminism. In M. Hirsch & E. Keller (Eds.) *Conflict in Feminism.* New York: Routledge Press.

Senate Employment, Education and Training References Committee (1998). *A Class Act: Inquiry into the Status of the Profession.* Canberra: Commonwealth of Australia. www.aph.gov.au/senate/committee/EETCTTE/classact/

Shapiro, S. (1994). Re-membering the body in critical pedagogy. *Education and Society*, 12(1), 61–79.

Shilling, C. (1993). *The Body and Social Theory.* London: Sage.

Shipley, F. (1989). Home economics name study. *Home Economics FORUM*, 4(1), 22–23.

Siedle, R. (1993). *A Strategic Plan to Strengthen and Promote the Home Economics Profession in Australia.* Victoria: Home Economics Association of Australia.

Simon, R. (1988). For a pedagogy of possibility. *Critical Pedagogy Networker, 1*(1), 1–4.

Slattery, P. (1995). *Curriculum Development in the Postmodern Era.* New York: Garland.

Smit, L. (1991). *Private Lives and Public Domains.* Canberra: Department of Employment, Education and Training.

Smith, R., Weinstein, E. & Tanur, J. (1991). Women, karate, and gender typing. *Sociological Inquiry, 51*(2), 113–120.

Smith, G. (1993). Reconceptualising for relevancy: Global home economics education. In *Issues and Directions for Home Economics/Family Studies Education: Proceedings of a Canadian Symposium* (pp. 71–79). Ottawa: Canadian Home Economics Association.

Smith, G. (1993). A conception of global education: A home economics education imperative. *Canadian Home Economics Journal, 43*(1), 21–26.

Smith, G. (1995). *Partners in education: Globalising home economics curricula in Canada.* Paper presented at the Special Interest Group for Home Economics Research, American Educational Research Association Annual Meeting, San Francisco, 19 April.

Smithsonian National Museum of American History. (1997). From Parlour to Politics and Beyond, Exhibition. Washington.

Snyder, I. (1996). *Hypertext: The Electronic Labyrinth.* Melbourne: Melbourne University Press.

Spitzack, C. (1987). Confession and signification: the systematic inscription of body consciousness. *Journal of Medicine and Philosophy, 12*(4), 357–369.

Squier, S. (1995). Reproducing the posthuman body: Ectogenic fetus, surrogate mother, pregnant man. In J. Halberstam & I. Livingston. (Eds.) *Posthuman Bodies* (pp. 113–132). Bloomington: Indiana University Press.

Synott, J. & Symes, C. (1995). The genealogy of the school: An iconography of badges and mottoes. *British Journal of Sociology of Education, 16*(2), 139–152.

Sztompka, P. (1993). *The Sociology of Social Change.* Oxford: Blackwell.

Thompson, P. (1986). *The public, the personal, and the patriarchal: The potential of hestian theory for family study.* Paper presented at the Theory and Methodology pre-conference workshop, National Council for Family Relations, New Orleans, 3 November.

Thompson, P. (1988). *Home Economics and Feminism: The Hestian Synthesis.* Charlottetown: Home Economics Publishing Collective.

Thompson, P. (1990). *Willystine Goodsell: The hestian educator and the discourse of domesticity.* Paper presented at the Annual Meeting of the American Educational Research Association, Boston, April.

Thompson, P. (1991). Toward a proactive theory of home economics: The hestian/hermian paradigm. *Themis: Journal of Theory in Home Economics, 1*(1), 15–34.

Thompson, P. (1992a). *Hestia, Heraclitus, and Heidegger: On being in home economics.* Paper presented at the International Federation of Home Economics Conference, Hannover, Germany, July.

Thompson, P. (1992b). *Implications of hestian feminist theory for an integrative discipline of everyday life.* Paper presented at the pre-conference workshop 'Home Economics and Feminism', International Federation of Home Economics, Wurzburg, Germany, 19 July.

Thompson, P. (1993a). *The place of theory, the theory of place: The hestian/hermian paradigm as explanatory theory.* Paper presented at the pre-conference workshop 'Theorising in Home Economics: Source, Method, Purpose', Annual Meeting of the American Home Economics Association, Orlando, Florida, 25 June.

Thompson, P. (1993b). Daily household life as a reflection of the domestic and the political economy from the hestian and hermian systems perspective. In I. Richarz (Ed.) *Household Management in the Past and Present* (pp. 153–163) Germany: Vandenhoeck & Ruprecht.

Thompson, P. (1995a). *Home economics: Crying need or crying shame in national and international women's studies.* Paper presented at the Annual Meeting of the Home Economics Special Interest Group, Annual Meeting of the American Educational Research Association, San Francisco, 19 April.

Thompson, P. (1995b). Reconceptualising the private/public spheres: A basis for home economics theory. *Canadian Home Economics Journal, 45*(1), 53–57.

Thompson, P. (1997). The reflective researcher: Reflexivity and praxis in home economics. Unpublished manuscript.

Thorne, (1980). The sociology of home economics: With particular reference to the economic status of women. *Home Economics. 26*(5), 5–18.

Turner, B. (1997). From governmentality to risk. Some reflections on Foucault's contribution to medical sociology. In A. Petersen & R. Bunton (Eds.) *Foucault, Health and Medicine* (pp. 9–21). London: Routledge.

Turney, (1981). *Anatomy of Teaching.* Sydney: Novak.

Ungar, S. (1982). The professor of desire. In the pedagogical imperative: teaching as a literary genre. *Yale French Studies, 63,* 81–97.

Valverde, M. (1991). As if subjects exist: Analysing social discourses. *Canadian Review of Anthropology and Sociology, 28*(2), 173–187.

Vaideanu, G. (1987). Interdisciplinarity in education: A tentative synthesis. *Prospects* XVII, *4,* 489–501.

Vick, M. (1996). Fixing the body: Prescriptions for pedagogy, 1850-1950. In E. McWilliam & P. Taylor (Eds) *Pedagogy, Technology and the Body* (pp. 113–126). New York: Peter Lang.

Vincent, A. (1994). What are the ideas by which home economists understand themselves? Toward a review of Brown's third volume. *Journal of the Home Economics Institute of Australia, 1*(1), 32–36.

Vincenti, V. (1990). Home economics in higher education: Communities of convenience or purpose? *Home Economics Research Journal, 19*(2), 184–193.

Viswasnaran, K. (1994). *Fictions of Feminist Ethnography.* Minneapolis: University of Minneapolis Press.

Walkerdine, V. & Lucey, H. (1989). *Democracy in the Kitchen: Regulating Mothers and Socialising Daughters.* London: Virago Press.

Warwick, D. P. & Lininger, C. A. (1975). *The Sample Survey: Theory and Practice.* United States of America: McGraw-Hill.

Waugh, P. (1992). *Practising Postmodernism Reading Modernism.* London: Edward Arnold.

Wearing, B. (1984). *The Ideology of Motherhood: A Study of Sydney Suburban Mothers.* Sydney: Allen & Unwin.

Weber, S. & Mitchell, C. (1995). *That's Funny, You Don't Look Like a Teacher.* London: Falmer Press.

Weedon, C. (1987). *Feminist Practice and Poststructuralist Theory.* New York: Basil Blackwell.

Weiler, K. (1991). Freire and a feminist pedagogy of difference. *Harvard Educational Review, 61*(4), 449–474.

Weiner, G. (1993). *The gendered curriculum - Producing the text: Developing a poststructural feminist analysis.* Paper presented at the Annual Conference of the Australian Association for Research in Education, Perth, December.

Wilkinson, S. (1988). The role of reflexivity in feminist psychology. *Women's Studies International Forum, 11*(5), 493–502.

Wilks, J. (1993). The social stereotype of Australian scuba divers. *Australian Journal of Science and Medicine in Sport*, June, 66–69.

Wilks, J. & Austin, D. (1991). An evaluation of a strategy for changing group stereotypes of the heroin user. *Drug and Alcohol Review, 10*, 107–113.

index

Index